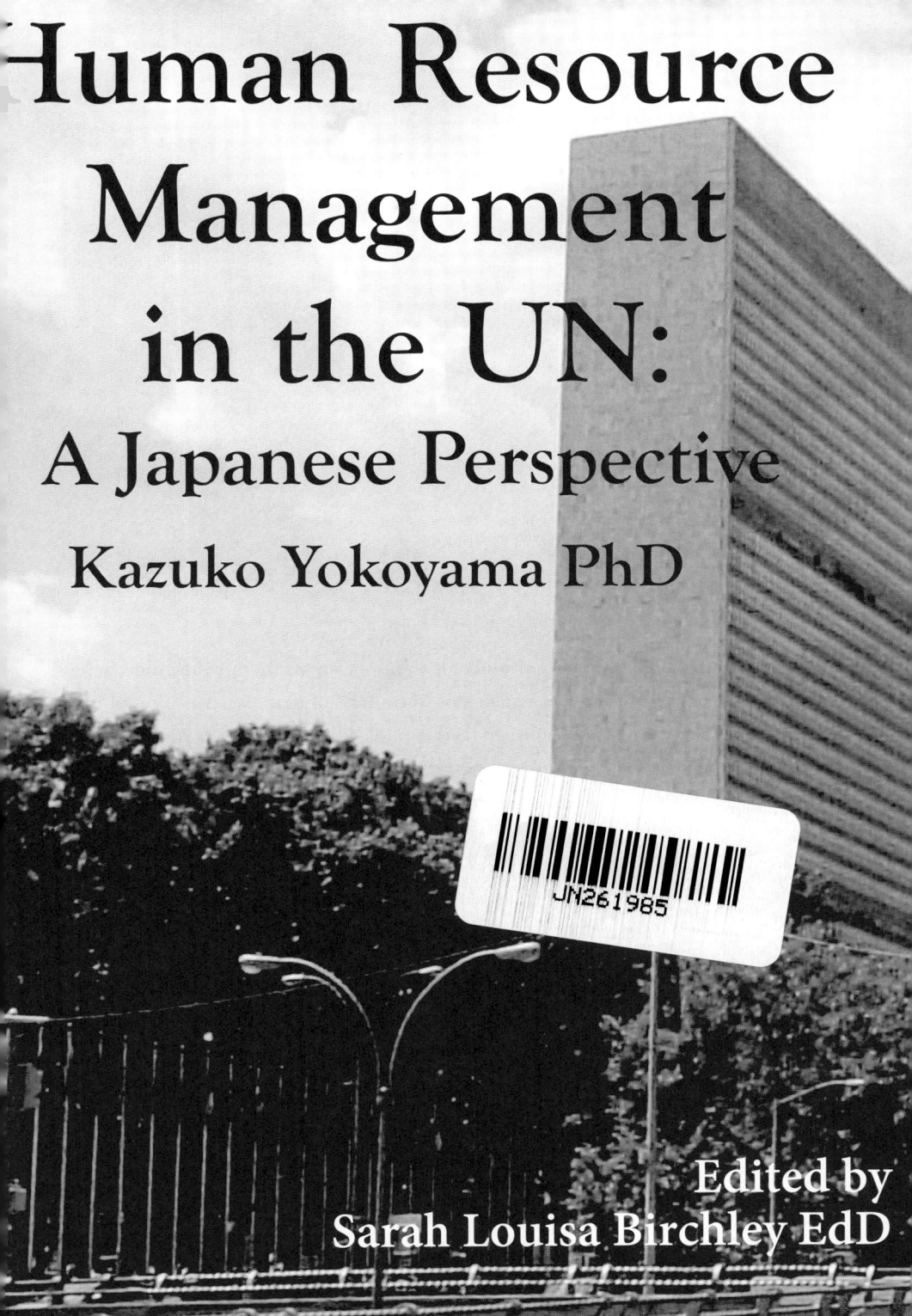

Human Resource Management in the UN:
A Japanese Perspective

Kazuko Yokoyama PhD

Edited by
Sarah Louisa Birchley EdD

HUMAN RESOURCE MANAGEMENT IN THE UN:
A JAPANESE PERSPECTIVE

ISBN 978-4-561-25627-4

Published by Hakuto-Shobo Publishing Company, Japan
5-1-15, Sotokanda, Chiyoda-ku, Tokyo, Japan
Zip 101-0021
www.hakutou.co.jp

First Published in 2014

© Kazuko Yokoyama, 2014
Cover Photo © 2014 Kazuko Yokoyama
All rights reserved
Printed in Japan

No part of this book may be reproduced, scanned, stored in, or distributed in any printed, electronic form or by any means without prior written permission of both copyright owner and the publisher of this book. Please do not participate in or encourage piracy of copyrighted materials in violation of the author's rights. Purchase only authorized editions.

The greatest care has been taken in compiling this book. However, no responsibility can be accepted by the publishers or compilers for the accuracy of the information presented.

Preface

For the past 10 years I have been teaching International Career Development to masters students and PhD candidates in Japan. My students, particularly those students from developing countries, often ask whether or not they have the skills and abilities needed to become international civil servants. I wondered what materials were available to guide them and answer their questions.

After an extensive search, I found that there was no such book providing a comprehensive guide to successfully working in the UN Common System. As a former international civil servant myself and currently as a university professor of HRM, I could see this gap in the research and the enormous difference between the performance-oriented HRM practices which are popular around the world, including the UN Common System, and the unique nature of Japanese HRM practices. As such, I was and remain convinced that in order for Japanese enterprises to become more globalized, Japanese HRM practices need to change to reflect more performance-based HRM practices, such as those employed in the UN Common System.

With these two points in mind, I decided to focus my research in this area and write a book to meet the demands of various stakeholders.

This book is primarily aimed at those who have suitable qualifications to work for UN organizations in the UN Common System and who have a strong desire to work for such international organizations.

Secondly, the book is for management scholars concerned with cross-cultural management and issues in comparative HRM, particularly those interested in Japanese HRM practices.

Thirdly, this book provides advice to Japanese enterprises, which need to change their HRM practices in order to expand their business to a global market, utilizing talented human resources overseas.

This book is based on the *Career Design of International Civil Servants*, which was written in Japanese and published in 2011. This English version has been redesigned and updated with digital content to provide a more comprehensive guide to working as an international civil servant and can be downloaded in digital form from Amazon.

It has been 10 years since I initially decided to write this book. During that time two surveys were conducted via email, one targeted just Japanese staff members employed by the UN Common System and one at both non-Japanese and Japanese staff. Interviews with international civil servants took place in New York, Geneva and Rome.

The structure of this book is as follows: Chapter 1 provides an overview of globalization and its impact on this field. Chapter 2 briefly illustrates HRM management practices in the UN Common System, comparing them with those in Japan. Chapter 3 introduces the first survey of Japanese staff members employed in the UN Common System and Chapter 4 focuses on analyzing their characteristics using statistical methods. Extending the target group to non-Japanese staff members, Chapter 5 introduces the characteristics of these employees, and compares the two groups. Chapter 6 is a complementary qualitative review of the satisfaction of the interview collaborators by occupational group. Finally, Chapter 7 provides reflections and recommendations for the successful career development of staff members in the UN Common System and recommendations for the globalization of Japanese enterprises.

I would like to extend my sincere thanks to the interview collaborators who approved to include their interview records in this book, spending their time to review the draft interview records and to modify them. Also, I wish to say special thanks to Pranvera Zhaka PhD who advised and encouraged me to publish an English version of *the Career Design of International Civil Servants* and to Ms. Motoko Tsuchiya who took part in translation, pushing me to review and going forward. Besides, I would like to say many thanks to Dr. Sarah L. Birchley who reviewed and edited the whole text from a native's standpoint. I thoroughly enjoyed discussions with her in the course of making this book. I also appreciate support from Toyo Gakuen University. I have to say without the support of these people, this book will never be published.

I hope that through reading this book you will be able to successfully design your own career as an international civil servant while also learning more about the intriguing field of HRM.

Kazuko Yokoyama
Tokyo, December 2013

Human Resource Management in the UN: A Japanese Perspective

Key words: *HRM, UN Common System, Global HR, Career, Japanese, International Career, Qualitative Interviews, Quantitative Survey, Case Studies*

Contents

List of Abbreviations
List of Figures
List of Tables

Chapter 1   Introduction ─────────────────────────── *1*

    The Age of Globalization   *1*
    The Move Towards Utilizing More International Human Resources   *1*
    Growing Interest in Social and International Contribution   *2*
    Diversity Management   *3*
    Literature Review   *3*
    Studies in the Field of International Management   *3*
    Studies in Career Development   *5*
    Purpose and Hypothesis   *7*
    Purpose   *7*
    Research Questions   *7*
    Hypotheses   *8*
    Research Methods   *8*
    Outline of the Book   *8*

Chapter 2   Human Resource Management (HRM) Practices in the UN Common System — A Comparison with Japanese HRM ─ *11*

    The Human Resource Management Practices in the UN Common System: Overview   *11*
    Target Group of Staff Members   *13*
    Grade   *15*

Nationality of Staff Members   16
Duty Station   17
Languages   18
Salary   19
Fringe Benefits   21
Working Hours   22
Annual Paid Leave   22
Maternity Leave   22
Home Leave   23
Diversity Management Strategies   23
The General Recruitment Policies in the International Organizations of the
    UN Common System   28
Methods of Recruitment to the UN Common System   31
Promotion and the Assignment of Staff Members   32
The Recruitment Policies of the Major International Organizations in the
    UN Common System by Organizational Characteristics   34
The Recruitment Policy of the UN Secretariat   34
The Recruitment Policy of the UNDP   35
The Recruitment Policy of Humanitarian Assistance Organizations   35
The Recruitment Policy of Specialized Organizations   35
Discussion   36
Main Findings and Recommendations   37

Chapter 3   The First Survey Conducted on the Careers of Japanese International Civil Servants —————————— 41

Introduction   41
Data Collection   41
Findings   43
Overview   43
Cross Tabulation and Results   45
Educational Background   45
Occupational Field   46
Grade   48
Preparation   48
Motivations for Working in the UN Common System   49
Age   50
Prior Work Experience   51

Entry Method   52
Important Factors to Consider When Working for the UN Common System   53
Job Satisfaction   54
Working Hours   55
Salary   56
Fringe Benefits   57
Satisfaction at Duty Station   57
Overall Satisfaction   57
Future Increase of Japanese International Civil Servants   59
Difficulties at Duty Stations   60
Continuing to Work at the UN Common System until the Mandatory Retirement Age   61
Finding a Job in Japan   62
Current Concerns   62
Discussion   63
Main Findings and Recommendations   65

Chapter 4   A Statistical Analysis of the First Survey - Characteristics of Japanese Formal Staff Members —— 69

t-test   69
Factor Analysis   73
Factor Analysis by Gender   76
Multiple Regression Analysis   78
Discussion   80
Main Findings and Recommendations   83

Chapter 5   The Second Survey Conducted on the Career of International Civil Servants — Comparative Analysis between Japanese Formal Staff Members and Non-Japanese Staff Members —————— 85

Target Group and Data Collection   85
The Relationship between the First Survey and the Second Survey   87
Problems Encountered during Data Collection   87

Overview — Comparison between Japanese Formal Staff Members and Non-Japanese Staff Members   88
Age   89
Nationality   89
Country of Duty Stations   89
Number of Countries of their Duty Stations   89
Years of Service   90
Academic Qualifications   90
Specialized Field of Study at the Last Degree Held   90
Organizations   91
Grade   91
Salary   91
Subordinates   92
Field of Specialization and Occupational Field   92
Organization Prior to Recruitment in the UN Common System   92
Age on Becoming a Formal Staff Member   93
Entry Routes   93
Motivations for Working in the UN Common System   94
Preparation   94
Utilization of Professional Skills   95
Professional Development   95
Working Hours   96
Fringe Benefits   96
Overall Satisfaction   96
Important Factors to Consider When Working for the UN Common System   97
Difficulties at Duty Station   97
Current Concerns: Job-related and Outside the Workplace   97
Continuing to Work in the UN Common System until the Mandatory Retirement Age   99
Finding a Job Outside the UN Common System   99
Discussion   99
Main Findings and Recommendations   102

Chapter 6 Job Satisfaction by Occupational Field — Results from Interviews with Japanese Formal Staff Members Employed by the UN Common System ——————— 105

Purpose of Interviews and Methods   *106*
Overview of Interview Respondents and Summary of Interviews   *108*
Study Abroad Experience   *116*
Job Satisfaction by Occupational Field   *118*
Specialist Group   *119*
Finance Specialist Group   *119*
The Program Management Coordination Group   *120*
Administration and HR Group   *120*
Assistance to Developing Countries Group   *121*
Changing of Specialized Field and Transferring to other Occupational Groups   *122*
Career Anchor   *125*
Main Findings and Recommendations   *126*

Chapter 7   Final Reflections and Recommendations ──── *129*

Overview of Survey Results   *129*
Tests of the Hypotheses   *131*
Characteristics of International Civil Servants   *134*
Reflections on Methods   *136*
Value of Interview Records   *137*
Final Recommendations for the Career Development of International Civil Servants   *137*
Final Recommendations for the Globalization of Japanese Enterprises   *139*
Recommendations for Future Research   *141*
Future Prospects   *142*

Appendix 1   The 23 Interviews from International Civil Servants and a Description of their Career Paths   *143*
Appendix 2   Results of the First Survey Conducted on Japanese Formal Staff Members Employed in the UN Common System   *247*
Appendix 3   Results of the Second Survey Conducted on Japanese and Non-Japanese Staff Members Employed in the UN Common System   *261*
Recommended Links   *271*
Postscript   *273*
Bibliography   *274*

Index *282*
About the Author *288*

List of Abbreviations

Abbreviation	Definition
AE	Associate Expert
CEB	Chief Executive Board of Coordination
CPA	Certified Public Accountant
D	Director
FAO	Food and Agriculture Organization of the United Nations
G/S	General Service Category and distributes from G-1 to G-7
IAEA	International Atomic Energy Agency
IBRD	the International Bank for Reconstruction and Development
ICAO	International Civil Aviation Organization
ICATILO	International Training Centre of the ILO
ICJ	International Court of Justice
ICSC	International Civil Service Commission
IFAD	International Fund for Agricultural Development
ILO	International Labour Organization
IMO	International Maritime Organization
ITC	International Trade Centre
ITU	International Telecommunication Union
JPO	Junior Professional Officer
L	Field Service Level
MBA	Master of Business Administration
ODA	Official Development Assistance
P	Professional Category and distributes from P-1 to P-5. There is P-6 only at WHO.
PAHO	Pan American Health Organization
SG	The Secretary General
Step	Increment of salary within the same grade. One step is normally added after one year of employment
UN	United Nations, is often called as the UN Secretariat.
UNAID	Joint United Nations Programme on HIV/AIDS
UNCTAD	United Nations Conference on Trade and Development
UNDP	United Nations Development Programme
UNESCO	United Nations Educational, Scientific and Cultural Organization
UNFPA	United Nations Population Fund

UN-HABITAT	United Nations Human Settlements Programme
UNHCR	Office of the United Nations High Commissioner for Refugees
UNIDO	United Nations Industrial Development Organization
UNITAR	United Nations Institute for Training and Research
UNJSPF	United Nations Joint Staff Pension Fund
UNOPS	United Nations Office for Project Service
UNRWA	United Nations Relief and Works Agency for Palestine Refugees in the Near East
UNU	United Nations University
UNWTO	World Tourism Organization
UPU	Universal Postal Union
WFP	World Food Programme
WHO	World Health Organization
WIPO	World Intellectual Property Organization
WMO	World Meteorological Organization
YPP	Young Professional Program. This is the independent program for Junior Experts. YPP exam is an examination implemented at the UN Secretariat and this exam is different from YPP program.

List of Figures

Chapter 3
Figure 1: Specialized field of study related to the last degree held
Figure 2: Grade distribution of female and male staff members

Chapter 6
Figure 1: Change of specialized field and transferring to another occupational group

Chapter 7
Figure 1: Career Behavior in the UN Common System

List of Tables

Chapter 2

Table 1:	Thirty-five organizations in the UN Common System
Table 2:	The number of staff members in the professional and higher categories employed in the UN Common System
Table 3:	Grade Distribution of staff members employed in the UN Common System
Table 4:	The number of staff members by their nationality and the percentage in the professional and higher categories
Table 5:	Calculation of monthly post adjustment in New York
Table 6:	Salary scale for the professional and higher categories
Table 7:	The number of female staff members in the professional and higher categories
Table 8:	Historical trend of female staff members employed in the UN Common System since 1974
Table 9:	The number and percentage of staff members by sex, educational level and managerial level where the size of the organization is 100 or more
Table 10:	Selection of candidates in the UN Common System
Table 11:	Comparison of HRM between the UN Common System and traditional Japanese companies

Chapter 3

Table 1:	170 Japanese respondents in the UN Common System
Table 2:	Respondents by Gender and Organizational Category
Table 3:	Current occupational field(s)
Table 4:	Change of occupational field upon recruitment by the UN Common System
Table 5:	Time when first considered working for the UN Common System
Table 6:	Motions for applying for a UN Common System post
Table 7:	Age when became a formal staff member in the UN Common System
Table 8:	Prior work experience in Japan

Table 9:	Entry method by gender
Table 10:	Summary of entry method by gender
Table 11:	The most important factors when working in the UN Common System
Table 12:	Job satisfaction at the UN Common System
Table 13:	The reasons for job satisfaction
Table 14:	Comparison of working hours with those in Japan
Table 15:	Evaluation of salary in the UN Common System
Table 16:	Comparison of the present salary with that received in Japan
Table 17:	Fringe benefits in the UN Common System
Table 18:	Satisfaction at duty station
Table 19:	Overall satisfaction
Table 20:	Evaluation of overall satisfaction
Table 21:	Opinions on the increase of Japanese staff members in the UN Common System in the future
Table 22:	Reasons for the answers given in Table 21
Table 23:	Reasons for the answers in Table 21
Table 24:	Adjustment difficulties when assigned to a new duty station
Table 25:	Desire to work for the UN Common System until the mandatory retirement age
Table 26:	Staff members who have given serious consideration to resigning and to finding a job in Japan
Table 27:	The most pressing concerns of respondents

Chapter 4

Table 1:	t-test for the means of male and female formal staff members
Table 2:	Descriptive statistics of key variables
Table 3:	Total variance explained
Table 4:	Factor analysis with Promax rotation of the staff members
Table 5:	Correlation matrix among variables in the study
Table 6:	Major characteristics of formal staff members extracted via factor analysis
Table 7:	Factor analysis with Promax rotation of male formal staff members
Table 8:	Factor analysis with Promax rotation of female staff members
Table 9:	Multiple regression analysis for overall satisfaction

Table 10: Model summary
Table 11: Satisfaction determinants by gender
Table 12: The relationship between career satisfaction and treatment satisfaction

Chapter 5

Table 1: Responses to the second survey
Table 2: Country of Duty Stations
Table 3: Specialized field of study of last degree held
Table 4: Number of subordinates in professional category and general service category
Table 5: Organizations prior to recruitment in the UN
Table 6: Entry routes to the UN Common System
Table 7: Motivations for working in the UN Common System
Table 8: Preparation for working in the UN Common System
Table 9: Degree of using specialized skills in the workplace
Table 10: Satisfaction of working hours
Table 11: Overall satisfaction
Table 12: Most pressing job related concerns
Table 13: Most pressing concerns outside the workplace
Table 14: Respondents' thoughts on resigning and finding a job outside the UN Common System

Chapter 6

Table 1: Summary of respondents
Table 2: Summary of interview respondents
Table 3: Entry routes to the UN Common System
Table 4: Entry method
Table 5: Where staff members were educated
Table 6: Work experience in Japan
Table 7: Type of organization worked for in Japan
Table 8: Evaluation of work experience in Japan prior to recruitment in the UN Common System
Table 9: Mentor(s)
Table 10: Desire to work for the UN Common System until the mandatory

	retirement age
Table 11:	Importance of salary
Table 12:	Japanese Interview respondents and non-Japanese respondents during the second survey
Table 13:	Sources of education overseas
Table 14:	Interview respondents by occupational group
Table 15:	Interview respondent's field of specialization at their last academic degree and their present occupational post
Table 16:	Career Anchors of the Japanese staff members

Chapter 7

Table 1:	Relationship between satisfaction and gender
Table 2:	Relationship between satisfaction by group and gender
Table 3:	Satisfaction and occupational group

Chapter 1

Introduction

Our life is no longer constrained by borders; in our borderless world we are able to exchange information, goods and services via the Internet and we can work alongside others from different parts of the world. Local companies have grown to become global companies and the time has also come for Japanese employees to engage in work outside Japan. The purpose of this book is to explore the characteristics and the attitudes towards work of Japanese employees working in International Organizations. Since half of such international civil servants have previously worked for Japanese companies, studying these employees in the context of an International Organization can provide Japanese companies with valuable HRM knowledge that will help them to further enhance their career development programs.

In the first section of this chapter, the characteristics of such a globalized world are discussed. This is followed by a literature review of the fields of international business management and career studies. In the third section, the objectives and hypotheses of this study are presented. In the fourth section, the research methods employed in this study are explained and in the final section, the structure of the entire book is laid out.

The Age of Globalization
The Move Towards Utilizing More International Human Resources

In order to survive in the new global era, pioneering enterprises in Japan have started utilizing international human resources more positively. First Retailing[1] (owners of the now global brand UNIQLO) announced that in order to promote their policy to internationalize their operations, they have increased the percentage of newly recruited non-Japanese employees. Panasonic[2] Co. also announced that in the future they are planning to recruit more highly qualified non-Japanese employees than they have in previous years. One of the key manufacturers in Japan, Hitachi[3], Ltd. announced that out of the new graduate employees in 2012, all of the *Bunkei* candidates (students who graduate with a background in humanities and social science) and a half of the *Rikei* candidates (students who graduate with a background in science and engineering) are, as a prerequisite, supposed to work outside Japan. In addition, Mitsui[4] & Co. Ltd. introduced a global personnel system to implement personnel evaluations based on a uniform world standard. They are also planning to transfer their non-Japanese employees who work in affiliated companies overseas to the head office in Japan. Furthermore, Rakuten, Inc., changed their official working language from Japanese to English in order to materialize their world business strategy. All of these companies are clearly aiming to become truly global corporations. By consolidating their internal systems, it is clear that Japanese enterprises are aiming to become global–scale enterprises.

Growing Interest in Social and International Contribution

Employees in Japan considered it a 'good life' to be employed by a distinguished company and to live a stable life in that company until their mandatory retirement age. Japanese companies guaranteed their formal employees long-term employment until their mandatory retirement age, (which is usually sixty-years old). The HR department transferred or promoted employees unilaterally according to the company's long-term organizational strategy. As a result, employees entrusted their working life to the company.

However, in recent years there are more Japanese who wish to take more control over their life or who wish to contribute something more directly to society. There are many who have left foreign capital companies that guarantee high salaries, to move to work in NGOs, developing countries or to an International Organization that contributes to the enhancement of society, through technical cooperation and other relevant activities.

Since, 1990, while teaching at university and after having worked in the UN Common System for nine years (which will be further discussed in Chapter 2) the author has been conducting career counseling[5] for those who wish to work for International Organizations. Many of her clients have a clear vision for their life and express that as long as they have a sufficient salary they would like to help people and societies in developing countries. In order to realize their dream, they are willing to invest their time and money in gaining a graduate degree outside of Japan. In addition, by working for a large company in Japan, the strong yen enables them to save money to go abroad and take such programs.

Diversity Management

Since the 1990's, in the United States, Diversity Management has been considered as a human resource strategy. Yet, it is only in recent years that the field has been given attention in Japan. Diversity Management is the idea that management utilizes diverse human resources regardless of race, nationality, gender and age.

When the activities of enterprises become global and society more complicated, many companies promote diversity. As an example, by utilizing the diversity of their human resources IBM created a stronger and more lucrative company.[6]

In the field of Diversity Management the most frequently argued point is that of equal employment opportunity, particularly the role and power of women in the workplace. The Japanese government is trying to achieve equal employment opportunity for men and women by enacting the *Equal Employment Opportunity Law*, as in Japan the contribution of women to working society is significantly lower than that of other developed countries (further discussion of this point can be found in Chapter 2). Women make up 40% of the employees working in International Organizations in the UN Common System. As such, diversity management practices can be widely found in most International Organizations, in the UN Common System.

Literature Review
Studies in the Field of International Management

When conceptualizing the purpose of this study, the author found answers in the concept of transnational management as advocated by Bartlett and Ghoshal (1989) and multinational corporation development theory developed by Perlmutter (1969). In their book, *Managing across borders: the transnational solution*, Bartlett and Ghoshal (1989) argued that the creation and sharing of innovation at various operation bases and the integration of knowledge among them is the key for the success of multinational corporations. Transnational management (TN-M) is a key concept for global corporations, allowing them to make full use of their potential by better networking their business operations all over the world. The concept of TN-M has been well integrated in the main strategic platforms of many global corporations. Twenty years before this concept was announced, Perlmutter (1969) defined three categories of multinational corporations: *Ethnocentric, Polycentric, and Geocentric*. This classification has been widely used as a basic concept for understanding international business.

Ethnocentric types of organizations rely on home-country nationals who are seen as more competent and trustworthy than host-country nationals who are seen as less motivated and not reliable. Many Japanese and American corporations belong to the *Ethnocentric* type of organization.

Polycentric types of organizations rely on host-country nationals who are thought to have better knowledge of their own country. As long as there is profit, headquarters will not intervene with the management of local operations. Many European corporations belong to this type of organization.

Geocentric types of organizations are considered the ultimate form of multinational corporations. This type of organization assigns their staff all over the world based on their talent, regardless of their nationality.

With regard to Japanese studies in this field, the most well known are those by Ishida (1985), Koike (1996; 2006), and Shiraki (1995; 2006). Ishida (1985) examined the characteristics of Japanese managers deemed successful in overseas operations. He also examined the transferability of Japanese-style management practices to overseas operations pointing out the problems that can occur with it with regard to the Japanese-style management practices. Koike (1996) compared the way Japanese blue-collar employees in Japan and blue-collar employees in the Japanese subsidiaries overseas work. He found that Japanese-style management practices could be transferred outside of Japan. Shiraki (1995) also examined human resource management practices in Japanese subsidiaries in South East Asia and China. He found that Japanese companies make greater use of Japanese expatriates compared to western multinational companies.

The subjects of this book are staff members who were employed in the UN Common System and who were recruited from different countries around the world. Their duty stations were also outside of their home country. There are 193 member countries in the UN. Staff members come from 191 different nationalities and they work in 180 duty stations across 612 cities and villages over the world[10]. According to Perlmutter's (1969) theory, the UN is the ultimate form of *Geocentric* organization. Further details will be discussed in Chapter 2.

Nowadays, in the age of globalization, the number of Japanese companies[11] aiming to globalize their operations is increasing; yet few companies exhibit global practices. In reality, Japan is suffering from a decline in population, and as such, it cannot expect a large increase in domestic markets. Taking this into consideration, Japanese enterprises are forced to become globalized. We can gain a greater understanding of global HRM practices by analyzing how International Civil Servants working overseas design their careers.

Studies in Career Development

The field of career studies began approximately a hundred years ago in the United States. The leading authority in the field, D. E. Super, defined a career as a series or combination of roles an individual person plays in his or her life (Super, 1980). Career is also considered to mean an occupation, work, post, area of responsibility, future route, or in a broader definition, an individual expresses their life and lifestyle (Schein, 1985). In this book, this broader definition of a career is adopted.

Reviewing the history of research in this field, the beginning was marked by the leading authority, F. Parsons (1909) who first advocated the *Three-Step Process* when choosing a career. The three-step process focuses on 1) better understanding oneself; 2) knowledge of the requirements of work and prospects for the future; and 3) the connection between step one and step two. Parsons advocated matching personality with job, which later became the basis of trait/factor theory in HRM research. At the beginning of the 20th century the *Trade Board of Boston* in the U.S.A. adopted his theory and started a vocational guidance. Following that, Williamson (1939) analyzed 'characteristic traits' and 'factors' such as the contents of work and job requirements, and put forward his *Theory of Characteristic Parameter*.

In the middle of the 20th century, Super (1986) designed the *Theory of Life Stages* in which life was divided into five development stages: growth, exploration, establishment, maintenance and decline. He established a comprehensive theory with the emphasis on the importance of self-concept and how it relates to career development and claimed that the development of an individual's career and their personal growth can mutually affect each other. This theory developed into his *Life-role Theory*.

Continuing the theme of transition, Schlossberg (1981) developed a *4-S Transition Model*. According to this model, life is a continuation of transitions and ones career is developed by the process of overcoming each transition.

Schein (1985) defined a career as the occupation throughout one's life, the way of living through one's life, and the way of expressing one's life. He developed the concept of a *Career Anchor*. A career anchor is a person's self-image of competence, their motivation, and their values. During the course of their working life, people develop an underlying anchor that will guide their life. Schein also explored the role and importance of the mentor.

A well-known Japanese study in career development is that of Ota (1999) who advocated the concept of *shigoto-jin*. According to his research, a *shigoto-jin* is an employee who acquires skills and abilities that will enable him/her to negotiate and carry out work on an equal basis with his/her employing organization. Another prominent Japanese researcher, Sato (2011) has worked extensively on work-life balance in Japanese society. Wakisaka (2008), who has been researching the effective utilization of females in the workplace for over 30 years, has also been an advocate of work-life balance as a management strategy.

The above review shows that despite the fact that career development studies have been prominent in the United States, in Japan, it is still a relatively new field. In

1995, The *Japan Business Federation* (*Nikkei-ren*[12]) recommended the introduction of performance-based management practices. Their recommendations suggested that Japanese corporations no longer needed to ensure job security and lifetime employment for all of their staff members. Since then, employees in Japanese corporations have felt the need to take responsibility for their own career development and can not entrust their working life to one company. As a consequence, both individuals and organizations in Japan are paying more attention to the field of career development.

Purpose and Hypothesis
Purpose

The purpose of this book is to study the characteristics and the attitudes toward work of Japanese employees employed in the UN Common System and to recommend changes to Japanese HRM practices. In addition, this book gives advice to individuals on how they can better design their own career path.

Research Questions

Private organizations are supported by the funds of the investors. On the contrary, organizations in the UN Common System are supported by the contributions of the member states, with the mandate of ensuring peace and security in the world, assisting developing countries, and promoting friendly relationships among member states. Staff members employed by International Organizations are called International Civil Servants. They work alongside colleagues of various nationalities. Despite some differences between International Organizations, HRM practices within International Organizations are performance based.

The author's interest in this topic began through her extensive experience working in UN organizations. Her research interests have always focused on examining whether work experience in Japan is useful for Japanese nationals when developing a career in the UN Common System. To date there are no such studies related to career development in the UN Common System from a Japanese perspective. As such, the results of this study are considered useful for not only for those who wish to work for the UN Common System, but also for those who wish to work for multinational companies that have HRM practices that are similar to those used in the UN Common System.

Hypotheses

Two hypotheses were developed:

Hypothesis 1: *Work experience in Japan is useful for career and professional development in International Organizations within the UN Common System.*

Hypothesis 2: *There are no differences between Japanese males and Japanese females with regard to their satisfaction in International Organizations within the UN Common System.*

Research Methods

An exploratory study was initiated in early 2000 and at this stage preliminary interviews were also conducted. Based on the results of these preliminary interviews, two further questionnaire surveys were conducted via email and follow-up interviews were conducted in New York, Geneva, Rome and Tokyo, Japan.

Outline of the Book

In Chapter 2, HRM practices in the UN Common System are explored and comparisons are made with Japanese-style management practices.

The results of a cross tabulation analysis (based on the data obtained from the first survey) are examined in Chapter 3. This includes information on the characteristics of formal Japanese staff members employed by the UN Common System.

Chapter 4 presents information on the characteristics of Japanese formal staff members, based on the use of various statistical tools, such as t-test, factor analysis, and regression analysis.

Chapter 5 presents the results of the second survey, comparing the characteristics of Japanese formal staff members with non-Japanese staff members employed by the UN Common System.

The relationship between employee job satisfaction and their occupational group is explored in Chapter 6.

Finally, a summary of findings, an explanation of limitations, and comments on the contribution of this study to the field of international HRM, are presented in Chapter 7.

The book concludes with an appendix, where the reader can find detailed accounts of the 23 case research interviews and diagrammatic representations of their career paths, along with full numerical survey results.

Notes:
1. Nippon Keizai Newspaper, May 12, 2010.
2. Nippon Keizai Newspaper, June 15, 2010.
3. Nippon Keizai Newspaper, September 9, 2010.
4. Nippon Keizai Newspaper, January 9th, 2011.
5. Sendagaya Open Campus of Tsuda College, Tokyo, Japan.
6. Mercer Japan Consulting (2008). The Individualized Diversity Strategy, First Press. pp.16.
7. Bartlett, C. and S. Ghoshal (1989). Managing Across Borders: The Transnational Solution, Harvard Business School Press.
8. Perlmutter, H.V., (1969). The Tortuous Evolution of the Multinational Corporation, The Colombia Journal of World Business, January-February, pp.9-18.
9. As of 13 October 2012.
10. Compiled from Personal Statistics Data as at 31 December 2011 (CEB/2012/HLCM/HR/16) United Nations system Chief Executives Board for Coordination.
11. In order to expand overseas operations some Japanese Companies such as UNIQLO have introduced staff career development where nationality of employees is not a consideration. According to Nippon Keizai Newspaper dated 2 September, 2009, UNIQLO established their staff career development centers in Japan, the USA and China for Japanese, non-Japanese and staff members recruited overseas.
12. Keidan-ren (2002) The Japan Business Federation was formerly called the Nihon Keisha Dantai Renmei when it was published in 1995.

Chapter 2

Human Resource Management (HRM) Practices in the UN Common System — A Comparison with Japanese HRM

This chapter introduces and discusses the organizational structure of International Organizations in the UN Common System from a Human Resource Management (HRM) perspective. Activities and programs executed by the United Nations such as the maintenance of peace and security, human rights, protecting the global environment, humanitarian activities etc. are well known by the general public around the world. However, in this chapter, the focus is on discussing the managerial structure of International Organizations in the UN Common System where they adopt a performance-based approach to management, which is different to the style that is used in Japan. By comparing the HRM practices in the UN Common System with those in private corporations in Japan, the author clarifies the issues for Japanese companies, when they try to adopt global management styles.

The first section of Chapter 2 provides an overview of the features of staff members and HRM practices employed by the UN Common System. The second section outlines Diversity Management strategies executed in the UN Common System. The third section focuses on general recruitment policies in the International Organizations of the UN Common System, including discussions of recruitment methods to the UN Common System and the promotion and assignment of staff members. The fourth section focuses on the recruitment policies of the major organizations by organizational characteristics. The fifth section includes further discussion and the sixth section provides major findings and recommendations.

The Human Resource Management Policies in the UN Common System: Overview

International Organizations are defined as organizations that are established to promote common interests among member countries of the UN. Those member countries contribute to their funds. As shown in Table 1, there are 35 organizations that are members of the UN Common System and the Chief Executive Board for Coordination (CEB) coordinates them.

With regard to job classification, appointment of staff members, salary and other working conditions, the International Organizations included in the UN Common System (Table 1) apply the same regulations. For example, if staff members hold similar duties at the same duty station, they receive the same level of salary and the same administrative treatment no matter which organization they work for. This system is generally referred to as the United Nations Common System.

Table 1: Thirty-five organizations in the UN Common System

1 United Nations		
a	**UN**	United Nations*
	ICJ	International Court of Justice
	ICSC	International Civil Service Commission
	UNJSPF	United Nations Joint Staff Pension Fund
b	**Subsidiary Organizations****	
	UNDP	United Nations Development Program
	UNFCCC	United Nations Framework Convention on Climate Change
	UNFPA	United Nations Population Fund
	UNOPS	United Nations Office for Project Service
	UNHCR	Office of the United Nations High Commissioner for Refugees
	UNICEF	United Nations Children's Fund
	UNRWA	United Nations Relief and Works Agency for Palestinian Refugees in the Near East
	UNU	United Nations University
	WFP	World Food Program
	UN Women	United Nations Entity for Gender Equality and the Empowerment of Women
c	**Joint Organizations with other Agencies**	
	UNAIDS	Joint United Nations Program on HIV/AIDS
	UNICC	United Nations International Computing Centre
	ITC	International Trade Center
2 Specialized Organizations		
	FAO	Food and Agriculture Organization of the United Nations
	ICAO	International Civil Aviation Organization

IFAD	International Fund for Agricultural Development
ILO	International Labour Organization
IMO	International Maritime Organization
ITU	International Telecommunication Union
UNESCO	United Nations Educational, Scientific and Cultural Organization
UNIDO	United Nations Industrial Development Organization
UPU	Universal Postal Union
WHO	World Health Organization
WIPO	World Intellectual Property Organization
WMO	World Meteorological Organization
UNWTO	World Tourism Organization
3 Other Agency/Organizations	
IAEA	International Atomic Energy Agency
ICATILO	International Training Center of the ILO
PAHO	Pan American Health Organization
UNITAR	United Nations Institute for Training and Research
UNSSC	United Nations System Staff College

* includes major organizations, Regional Commissions and other Commissions
** organizations which were established by the resolutions of the General Assembly of the United Nations
Source: Compiled from Personnel Statistics Data as of 31 December 2012 (CEB/2012/HLCM/HR/16) United Nations system Chief Executives Board for Coordination.

Over 30,000 professional staff members are employed in the 35 organizations within the UN Common System (as of December 2011) and these represent 191 different nationalities. As there are 193 Member States[1] in the United Nations, it can be concluded that the International Organizations in the UN Common System have recruited staff members from almost all the member states.

It is important to note that the World Bank Group[2] and the World Trade Organization (WTO) are not member organizations of the UN Common System and there are some differences in entitlements given to their staff members. Staff members in these two organizations were only included in the first survey of this research because it was difficult to forecast the number of replies from eligible staff members.

Target Group of Staff Members

Staff members employed by the Secretariat of the United Nations, Subsidiary Organizations of the United Nations and Specialized Organizations are classified as International Civil Servants in the UN Common System.

International Civil Servants are requested to work for the organization they were selected for and for the common interests of international society, not for the country where they were born or the interests of a specific country.

The target group under investigation in this research was formal staff members working for the International Organizations as shown in Table 1. Those formal staff members were deemed to be in professional and higher categories and the duration of their contract was one year or longer. As the purpose of this research was to explore the professional development of professional staff members and not the General Service Category staff members who assist staff in professional and higher categories, staff members in the General Category were not included. Table 2 shows the number of staff members whose contract is one year or longer, by organization and category.

Table 2: The number of staff members in the professional and higher categories employed in the UN Common System

Organization	Professional and higher categories	General Service	Total
UN	10,158	23,416	33,574
UNDP	2,582	3,932	6,514
UNICEF	2,845	5,220	8,065
WFP	1,441	2,813	4,254
FAO	1,681	1,828	3,509
WHO	2,175	3,680	5,855
UNESCO	932	996	1,928
ILO	1,035	1,354	2,389
Other 27 Organizations	8,148	10,118	18,266
Total	30,997	53,357	84,354

Data as of 31 December 2011
Source: compiled from CEB/2012/HLCM/HR/16

Junior Professional Officers (JPO) are provided with international work experience within the UN Common System at the expense of their governments or the governments in some developed countries, these officers were not included in the target group. It is important to acknowledge that many governments in developed countries have independent relationship agreements with various UN organizations. They send their young and qualified nationals as JPOs to the respective International Organizations in the UN Common System. The Japanese government had used the terminology, Associate Experts (AE) before it officially started using the terminology of JPO from March 2009. The term JPO is used throughout this book, yet when it is appropriate, the word AE is also used.

Grade

Staff members in the Professional category are distributed between grade P-1 to P-5 level, as P signifies they are at the Professional level. Managerial staff members are distributed from D-1 to the ungraded level, including the Assistant Secretary-General, the Under Secretary-General and the Secretary-General. D-1 refers to the Director level in many organizations; however, it also applies to the Deputy Director level in some organizations. Table 3 shows the grade distribution of staff members employed in the UN Common System.

Table 3: Grade Distribution of staff members employed in the UN Common System

Grade	Number	Percentage
UG (Un-graded)	255	1%
D-2 (Director)	582	2%
D-1 (Deputy-Director)	1,823	6%
P-5 (Division Chief)	5,857	19%
P-4 (Chief)	9,462	30%
P-3	8,701	29%
P-2	3,386	11%
P-1	117	1%
Total	30,187	100%

As of December 2011
Source: Compiled from CEB/2012/HLCM/HR/16

Some staff members are employed on a project basis, with a specific term of contract. These are mainly in the technical cooperation projects, peacekeeping missions, etc. Those assigned to these projects are called L level staff or staff in the field service category. The conditions for L level staff members are almost the same as that of formal staff members. Thus, L level staff members were included in the target group of this research, as long as their contract duration was longer than one year.

Nationality of Staff Members

Staff members are recruited and promoted by taking into account the contribution of the member state concerned in the UN Common System. This policy is called *Geographic Distribution* and is stipulated in article 101.3 of the UN Charter[3]. The aim of this policy is to avoid an imbalanced representation of particular countries in the composition of staff.

However, if one looks in detail, a different picture can be seen. Contributions from developed countries represent a high percentage of total contributions to International Organizations in the UN Common System. In fact, more than 50% of staff members are from developed countries, particularly from North American and European countries. As seen in Table 2, there are over 30,000 members of staff employed in the UN Common System throughout the world.

Table 4 shows the number of staff members employed in the UN Common System by nationality, in the order of the number of staff members. From this table we can see that U.S. nationals represent the highest percentage of staff (9.6%), French nationals make up 6.0%, while British nationals make up 5.1%. This means that staff members from the USA, France and the UK occupy over 20% of all formal staff members employed in the UN Common System.

There are 193 counties represented in the UN Common System. Fourteen countries (in Table 4) share approximately 48% of the UN Common System workforce. Within these 14 countries, only India (2.6%) and China (1.7%) are developing countries.

There are three reasons for the high percentage of staff members employed from the top three countries. Firstly, the working language at the UN is mainly English or French. The second reason is that these countries were successful during World War II and were the founding nations of the United Nations. Thirdly, it has been common practice in the UN Common System that high ranked posts have been filled by candidates from the former *League of Nations*.

Table 4: The number of staff members by their nationality and the percentage in the professional and higher categories*

Member State	Number of Staff Members	Percentage
USA	2,969	9.6%
France	1,856	6.0%
United Kingdom	1,577	5.1%
Italy	1,335	4.3%
Canada	1,239	4.0%
Germany	1,160	3.7%
Spain	836	2.7%
India	807	2.6%
Japan	806	2.6%
Netherlands	545	1.8%
China	531	1.7%
Belgium	479	1.5%
Sweden	344	1.1%
Denmark	332	1.1%
Total staff members from the above 14 Member States	14,816	47.8%
Total Staff Members from remaining Member States	16,181	52.2%
Grand Total	30,997	100%

* Staff Members whose grade is at P-1 to the Secretary General
Data as of 31 December 2011
Source: compiled from CEB/2012/HLCM/HR/16

Duty Station

One of the major responsibilities of International Organizations is to promote the social and economic development of developing countries. This requires a substantial portion of staff members to be stationed in developing countries. At present, staff members are scattered at duty stations over 180 countries, covering 612 cities and villages[4].

As will be discussed later in this chapter, some humanitarian assistance organizations such as the UNHCR, UNICEF, and the WFP have a rotation policy. In these organizations, most staff members not only work in capital cities in developing countries but also at sub-offices in a small city or village in developing countries.

Thus, their living conditions are often very tough. On the other hand, most staff members employed by specialized organizations tend to work in the headquarters of their organizations, which are often located in developed countries.

According to the statistics provided by the Ministry of Foreign Affairs[5], many Japanese employees dispatched by their Japanese companies are assigned to big cities in developed countries such as Los Angeles, the New York Metropolitan area, London, etc. Even when they are dispatched to developing countries, their duty stations are in cities such as Shanghai, Hong Kong, Sao Paulo, San Tiago, etc. On the contrary, staff members working for humanitarian assistance organizations are assigned not only to the capital city but also to a small sub-office or a village in developing countries. Therefore, the living conditions of staff members employed by the humanitarian assistance organizations in the UN Common System are considered tougher than for those Japanese dispatched overseas by Japanese private companies.

In principle, staff members are required to work outside their respective home country. Thus, staff members need to understand that they will likely work outside their home country until their mandatory retirement age. In some special cases, some staff members are assigned to their home country. But, these cases should be considered as an exception rather than the rule.

Languages

International Organizations assign their official languages and these languages independently are used at the international conferences within each organization. In the case of the United Nations, six languages: Arabic, Chinese, English, French, Russian, Spanish are authorized as the official languages.

At workplaces within the UN Common System, English has been widely used as the primary working language due to the fact that the language used in personal computers is often English and using a PC is as essential part of the daily work of a staff member around the world. Yet, in some duty stations, French or Spanish is also used alongside English. At the time of recruitment to the UN Common System and at the time of promotion, some organizations request candidates to be fluent in or pass a UN language exam in at least one official language in addition to English.

Salary

The salary in the professional and higher categories is calculated in US dollars and paid in the currency of the staff member's choice. The salary is composed of the basic salary, post adjustment and various allowances such as education grants and housing allowance. The total annual salary is divided into twelve and paid monthly to the staff member concerned. There are no bonuses or other special payments to staff members. The level of salaries for Professional staff is determined on the basis of the *Noblemaire Principle*[10] which states that the international civil servants should be able to recruit staff from its Member States, including the highest-paid. The UN salary structure was established in 1945 based on the one implemented for the Federal Civil Service in the United States. Through a periodic survey conducted by the International Civil Service Commission (ICSC), the federal civil service of the United States of America has to date, been taken as the highest paid national civil service.

In the UN Common System, salary scales for the Professional and Higher categories are based on five Professional grades (P-1 to P-5), two Director levels (D-1 and D-2) as well as the levels of Assistant Secretary-General and Under Secretary-General. The scales are expressed as gross and net (dependency and single) base salaries and applied uniformly, worldwide, by all organizations in the United Nations Common System. Net base salary is obtained by deducting staff assessment from gross base salary. Staff assessment is a form of internal tax administered by the organizations. Staff assessment rates are derived from income tax rates applicable at the eight headquarters cities of the organizations in the Common System (Geneva, London, Madrid, Montreal, New York, Paris, Rome, and Vienna). Most member states have granted United Nations staff exemption from national income taxation on their United Nations emoluments. However, a few member States do tax the emoluments of their nationals. In such cases, the organizations reimburse the income tax to the staff member.

Table 5: Calculation of monthly post adjustment in New York

Adjustment	Amount
Post adjustment multiplier for New York (1)	65.5
Annual net salary at P-4 Step 1 single rate (2) in Table 6	US$67,483.00
Annual post adjustment amount for P-4 Step 1 single rate (3)=[(1)/100]x (2) shown in Table 6	US$44,201.37
Monthly post adjustment (3)/12	US$3,683.45

The post adjustment is one of two main elements (base salary and post adjustment) comprising the salary of staff in the Professional and higher categories. The cost-of-living varies significantly between duty stations. The post adjustment is designed to compensate the differences in living costs, thereby providing the staff with the same purchasing power at all duty stations. Staff members in the Professional and Higher categories and in the Field Service category are entitled to receive the post adjustment.

Differences in living costs are measured through periodic place-to-place surveys conducted at all duty stations. The surveys measure the cost-of-living of a duty station relative to the cost-of-living at the base of the system (New York) and the results are reflected in a post adjustment index for each duty station. Duty stations with higher costs of living than New York have higher post adjustment indices. Post adjustment indices for duty stations are updated monthly on the basis of prevailing local conditions. These updated post adjustment indices provide the basis for establishing the post adjustment classifications, which specify the number of multiplier points of post adjustment, and one multiplier point is equal to 1 per cent of base salary. The calculation of the post adjustment, for example in New York, is shown in Table 5. Also, Table 6 shows the salary scale[11] for the professional and higher categories showing the annual gross salaries and net equivalents after the application of staff assessment (in US dollars). Please note that the term step refers to the increment of salary within the same grade and normally, one step is added for each year the staff member works for the organization.

Table 6: Salary scale for the Professional and higher categories showing annual gross salaries and net equivalents after application of staff assessment (in United States dollars) Effective 1 January 2012

Level		I	II	III	IV	V	VI	VII	VIII	IX	X	XI	XII	XIII	XIV	XV
							S	T E P	S							
USG	Gross	189,349														
	Net D	146,044														
	Net S	131,432														
ASG	Gross	172,071														
	Net D	133,950														
	Net S	121,297														
D-2	Gross	141,227	144,223*	147,221*	150,227*	153,351*	156,476*									
	Net D	112,096	114,283	116,471	118,659	120,846	123,033									
	Net S	102,981	104,827	106,666	108,500	110,329	112,147									
D-1	Gross	129,047	131,678	134,304	136,936*	139,568*	142,197*	144,830*	147,459*	150,093*						
	Net D	103,204	105,125	107,042	108,963	110,885	112,804	114,726	116,645	118,565						
	Net S	95,394	97,062	98,728	100,388	102,047	103,702	105,349	106,996	108,638						
P-5	Gross	106,718	108,955	111,195	113,430	115,670	117,905	120,147	122,384	124,622	126,860	129,099*	131,336*	133,575*		
	Net D	86,904	88,537	90,172	91,804	93,439	95,071	96,707	98,340	99,974	101,608	103,242	104,875	106,510		
	Net S	80,734	82,186	83,633	85,079	86,524	87,963	89,402	90,838	92,272	93,703	95,132	96,556	97,981		
P-4	Gross	87,933	89,929	91,924	93,919	95,916	97,910	99,908	102,059	104,219	106,377	108,540	110,696	112,856*	115,018*	117,178*
	Net D	72,467	74,044	75,620	77,196	78,774	80,349	81,927	83,503	85,080	86,655	88,234	89,808	91,385	92,963	94,540
	Net S	67,483	68,918	70,354	71,784	73,215	74,645	76,074	77,500	78,924	80,349	81,770	83,191	84,612	86,030	87,447
P-3	Gross	72,267	74,114	75,962	77,808	79,657	81,503	83,348	85,199	87,046	88,892	90,742	92,586	94,437	96,282*	98,128*
	Net D	60,091	61,550	63,010	64,468	65,929	67,387	68,845	70,307	71,766	73,225	74,686	76,143	77,605	79,063	80,521
	Net S	56,091	57,433	58,777	60,118	61,462	62,803	64,143	65,488	66,828	68,170	69,508	70,847	72,182	73,521	74,859
P-2	Gross	59,267	60,920	62,571	64,225	65,877	67,528	69,182	70,832	72,485	74,139	75,790	77,443*			
	Net D	49,821	51,127	52,431	53,738	55,043	56,347	57,654	58,957	60,263	61,570	62,874	64,180			
	Net S	46,730	47,915	49,096	50,279	51,461	52,645	53,847	55,046	56,251	57,452	58,650	59,854			
P-1	Gross	46,399	47,878	49,348	50,891	52,476	54,063	55,653	57,243	58,827	60,415					
	Net D	39,439	40,696	41,946	43,204	44,456	45,710	46,966	48,222	49,473	50,728					
	Net S	37,202	38,359	39,516	40,671	41,827	42,982	44,138	45,280	46,416	47,553					

D = Rate applicable to staff members with a dependent spouse or child.
S = Rate applicable to staff members with no dependent spouse or child.
* = The normal qualifying period for in-grade movement between consecutive steps is one year, except at those steps marked with an asterisk for which a two-year period at the preceding step is required.

Fringe Benefits

Staff members who were employed by International Organizations within the UN Common System for more than five years can receive pension from the UN at the age of 62, those who were recruited before 1989 can receive the pension at the age of 60. The United Nations Joint Staff Pension Funds (UNJSPF) is responsible for the investment of pension funds contributed by staff members. It is important to note that the contribution ratio to the pension funds between the UN organizations and staff members are two to one. This ratio is very favorable to staff members since the contribution ratio at most organizations around the world is one to one in the private and public sectors.

As for health insurance, the individual organization makes a contract with an insurance company and this covers 80% to 90% of medical expenses. The contribution ratio between the organization and a staff member is one to one yet staff members can receive medical treatment in any country they wish. In conclusion, there is a high level of fringe benefits for International Civil Servants.

Working Hours

Performance at the work place in the UN Common System is evaluated by the quality of work and not by the hours spent in work. It is the staff member's responsibility to plan and carry out the assigned work by the deadline set by the organization. This means that time management is up to the individual's own discretion. Staff members are not always considered to be competent just because they demonstrate their loyalty to their boss and to the organization by remaining late at the office. An individual office or a shared office with one or two colleagues is assigned to professional staff in the UN Common System. The individual office arrangement allows each staff member to better control his or her time. Many International Organizations introduce flextime and this is quite different from the working environment in Japan.

Annual Paid Leave

As a rule, staff members are given 2.5 days of paid leave per month, thus 30 days a year. In addition, each organization and the country of duty station assign approximately eight to ten days holidays. Therefore, if the holidays mentioned above and the weekends are added, staff members are guaranteed to enjoy holidays for more than one-third of a year. In Japan, employees are reluctant to take the paid leave and the rate of using the annual paid leave is 46.7%[12], less than 50%. However, in the UN Common System, the majority of staff members takes full paid leave as a matter of course and spend their full holiday entitlement every year.

Maternity Leave

All female staff members employed by International Organizations in the UN Common System are entitled to a total of 4 months (16 weeks) maternity leave before and after delivery. 100% pay is guaranteed during the whole period of maternity leave. As a rule, staff members are given 2.5 days of annual paid leave per month. Women on maternity leave also receive 2.5 days annual leave per month even though they are not working during the maternity leave. Most female staff members who have babies concentrate on bringing up their newborns for several months before they return to work with full pay, combining the paid maternity leave with the accumulated annual leave. In addition, it is a customary practice for the HR department to authorize the request for further leave without pay by female staff members who would like to continue to concentrate on childrearing.

Furthermore, as mentioned previously, the right to return to the previous post is fully guaranteed when maternity leave is over. Because maternity leave can have a negative influence on the possibilities of promotion, the staff regulations clearly state pregnancy is the right of female staff members. If a supervisor takes action against a female staff member because of pregnancy or maternity leave, the female staff member can make an appeal before the grievance committee within the organization to protect their rights. Statistics show that most plaintiffs win their cases.

Home Leave

As staff members are assigned outside their home country, they tend to have less contact with the people and culture of their homeland. In order to maintain their relationship with their home country, employees are granted Home Leave. This means that formal staff members and their family members are entitled to return to their home country every other year, or every year depending on their assigned duty station. All expenses incurred when visiting their hometown from their duty station are paid for by their employing organization. The home leave entitlement needs to come out of an employees' annual leave, meaning that employees spend at least two weeks in their home country from their annual leave entitlement.

Diversity Management Strategies

This section discusses how Diversity Management strategies have been implemented in the UN Common System. Affirmative Action Programs have been implemented in the UN Common System to promote the principle of equal rights between men and women and to increase the status of women to achieve diversity management aims.

There were a total of 12,677 female staff members in the professional and higher categories working in the UN Common System as of 31 December 2011 constituting 41% of the total workforce. Table 7 shows that the representation of female staff members is 41% throughout the UN Common System; 39% in the UN; 50% in UNICEF; 51% in UNESCO and 43% in UNHCR. In these organizations, a considerable number of female staff members play important roles not only at the professional level but also at the higher decision-making level. However, there are some organizations where female representation is still low; 35% in the FAO and 24% in the IAEA, possibly due to the characteristics of these organizations. Regarding the advancement of female staff members at the managerial level in the UN Common System, 30% are in the director or higher category and this percentage has been increasing every year.

In relation to the promotion of the status of women, *a Convention on the Elimination of All Forms of Discrimination against Women* was adopted at the UN General Assembly in 1979 and took effect in September 1981. The purpose of the convention was to eliminate any forms of discrimination against women. In order to convince the member states to implement the policies to improve the status of women in their own countries, the UN needed to demonstrate an increase in the number of female staff members at the UN itself as well as within the UN Common System. For example, in order to achieve parity between men and women, the UN Secretariat set up a policy to increase the percentage of female staff members to 50%. Although the female representation was 30% in 1994, it increased to 37% in 2003 and 38% in 2008. UNICEF also established a similar affirmative action program. Thanks to its organizational efforts, female representation in UNICEF increased to 38% in 1994, 41% in 2000, 49% in 2007 and finally met its goal of 50% in 2009.

Several measures have been taken to increase the number of female staff members in each organization. For example, many organizations state in their vacancy announcements that female candidates are welcome to apply for vacant posts, specifying that female candidates will be given priority if qualifications are similar or equal to those of their male counterparts.

Table 7: The number of female staff members in the professional and higher categories employed in the UN Common System and their percentage

Organization	Female Staff Members	Total Staff Members (Male and Female)	Percentage
UN	3,977	10,158	39%
UNDP	1,088	2,582	42%
UNICEF	1,418	2,845	50%
WHO	858	2,175	39%
UNHCR	663	1,544	43%
WFP	589	1,441	41%
UNESCO	479	932	51%
FAO	592	1,681	35%
ILO	464	1,035	45%
IAEA	284	1,160	24%
Remaining 25 Organizations	2,265	5,444	42%
Total	12,677	30,997	41%

Data as of 31 December 2011
Source: compiled from CEB/2012/HLCM/HR/16

The Chief Executive Board for Coordination (CEB), which is responsible for coordinating personnel related matters in the UN Common System, requests all the 35 organizations in the UN Common System to submit a yearly report that details the percentage of female staff in their respective organizations and their ongoing efforts to recruit females. The data is published in the annual report of the CEB. This encourages organizations to make serious efforts to recruit and promote female employees. In the case of the UN Secretariat, it requests every section, division and department to report the percentage of female staff and their recruitment efforts to the HR department. The compiled data on female staff members is reported to the UN General Assembly every year.

In addition, when maternity leave is over, the right for a woman to return to the previous post is fully guaranteed. Even if a substitute is deemed to have performed the role far better than the person on maternity leave, temporary staff must be removed from that post when the maternity leave is over. Besides, the staff regulations clearly state that pregnancy is a right of female staff members[6]. Thus, organizations are legally responsible for respecting equal employment opportunities between male and female staff members. Some organizations provide day-care centers within their building, providing facilities to enable women to continue working after their pregnancy. Thus, it can be concluded that top management within the organizations in the UN Common System took initiatives to increase the number of female staff members. Table 8 shows the historical trend of female staff members employed in the UN Common System for the past 40 years. This

Table 8: Historical trend of female staff members employed in the UN Common System since 1974*

Year	Percentage		
	Total	D-1 and Above	P-1 to P-5
1974	13	2	14
1976	13	2	15
1978	14	2	15
1979	14	2	15
1980	14	3	16
1981	15	3	16
1982	16	3	18
1983	16	3	18
1984	17	3	19
1985	18	4	20
1986	19	4	21
1987	20	4	22
1988	21	5	23
1989	22	5	24
1990	23	6	25
1991	24	6	26
1992	25	7	27
1993	27	9	29
1994	28	10	30
1995	28	12	30
1996	30	13	32
1997	31	15	33
2000	33	20	35
2003	36	22	38
2004	37	24	38
2005	37	25	39
2006	38	25	39
2007	38	26	39
2008	39	28	40
2009	40	28	41
2010	40	29	42
2011	41	30	42

* If the year is not indicated, the data was not published. The data was available from 1974 and the above table was prepared by either ICSC or CEB.
Source: author

table indicates that it takes a considerable amount of time to promote the status of female staff members.

If we compare this figure to that in Japan, we can clearly see how low the percentage is in Japan. *The Equal Employment Opportunity Law* that was passed in 1985 aimed to achieve a society where men and women participate in work on an equal basis. However, at companies with more than 100 employees, the percentage of female staff members at *kakaricho* (section chief level) and above in Japan is only 7.9%, as shown in Table 9. This is considered to be extremely low when compared with 40% across all grades in the UN Common System. Furthermore, when female representation at the managerial level is reviewed, the situation is also far from convincing. The number of female staff members at the *bucho* level (directors and above) is only 3.1% in Japan while it stands at 28% in the UN Common System. Although the number of female staff members has gradually increased, the representation of women at managerial levels is still very low in Japan.

A further survey by the Ministry of Health, Labour Labour and Welfare in Japan in 2008[7] found that the percentage of females recruited on career track (*sogo shoku*) paths was only 16.9% in the companies that had implemented the career-track employment management system.

Comparing the importance females play in roles at the workplace in the UN Common System and in Japanese private companies, it can be concluded that the UN Common System has made efforts to promote the status of women where male staff members and female staff members participate in work on an equal basis. The status of females is still very low is Japan. As was found in the first survey to be explored in the following chapters, around 50%, of Japanese staff members in the UN Common System, have previously worked in private companies in Japan. Therefore, it is important to highlight the issue of difference, although the HRM practices are different between the private and public sectors.

Table 9: The number and percentage of staff members by sex, educational level and managerial level where the size of the organization is 100 or more

	Managerial level				Non-managerial level	Total
	Sub-total	Director and above	Division Chief	Section Chief		
Female, graduated from university or graduate school	56,800 4.90%	8,260 3.10%	21,480 3.90%	27,060 7.90%	673,390 23.30%	754,650 16.90%
Male, graduated from University or graduate school	1,098,320 95.10%	260,680 96.90%	522,360 96.10%	315,280 92.10%	2,216,030 76.70%	3,718,750 83.10%
Total	1,155,120 100%	268,940 100%	543,840 100%	342,340 100%	2,889,420 100%	4,473,400 100%

Source: Basic Survey on Wage Structure conducted by the Ministry of Health, Labour and Welfare and published in 2007

The General Recruitment Policies in the International Organizations of the UN Common System

Regardless of the type organization, it is important to recruit the most competent and highly qualified candidates. However, the concept of recruitment and employment management are different between International Organizations in the UN Common System and the private and public organizations in Japan.

There are three basic recruitment policies in the UN Common System. The first is to recruit the most qualified candidates, the second is to recruit staff members from the Member Countries in accordance with the size of their financial contributions to the International Organizations, and the third is through affirmative action programs. It is not necessary to explain the contents for the first policy. The second and the third policy will be discussed later in this chapter.

In the UN Common System, whenever it is necessary to establish a new post or to fill a post upon resignation or retirement of staff, it is mandatory to advertise the vacancy announcements in all member states to select the most qualified candidate. In Japan, however, private and public organizations recruit a specified number of fresh university graduates based on the long-term strategy of each organization. Thus, those Japanese organizations allocate human resources to suitable positions under the direction of the HR department (*jinji-bu*) in accordance with their competence, characteristics, the long-term strategy of the organizations, etc.

In addition to the difference in recruitment between International Organizations and the private and public organizations in Japan, there are two special features in recruitment, that are only applicable to the UN Common System. The first feature is to recruit staff members from the Member Countries in accordance with the size of their financial contributions to the International Organizations. Each government is classified as *over-represented, equitably represented, under-represented or non-represented* based on the size of their financial contributions. If the qualifications of candidates are considered to be similar or equal, the candidates from *non-represented or under-represented countries* are given priority. The second feature is the affirmative action program. Many organizations state in their vacancy announcement that women are welcome to apply for vacant posts. Female candidates are given priority if their qualifications are similar or equal to their male counterparts in order to increase the number of female staff members at International Organizations in the UN Common System. The second policy reflects a fundamental principle of the United Nations to promote a parity of men and women at the workplace as mentioned in the previous section. The UN acts as a role model to other member countries.

There are 193 member countries and their staff members are employed from 191 member countries in the UN Common System. As an example, in relation to the first policy, if a candidate from the country of 0.001% contribution applied for a post and there are currently no staff members employed by that country, priority will be given to that candidate if other qualifications are similar. By applying this policy, the UN Secretariat employs staff members with 191 nationalities out of 193 member countries, employing at least one staff member from the UN member countries.

It may be interesting to learn that in the case of the UN Secretariat, a number of fixed posts are allocated under the Geographic Distribution system of posts. In this case, the number of posts available is based on a country's population, the contribution percentage to the UN, and membership status. Other International Organizations in the UN Common System use similar recruitment policies to determine the desirable number of staff members they need.

Table 10: Selection of candidates in the UN Common System

NR = Non Represented
UR = Under Represented
ER= Equitably Represented
OR= Over Represented

Candidate	A	B	C	D	E
Status of Geographic Distribution	UR	ER	UR	NR	OR
Highest Academic degree	MA	PhD	MA	MA	PhD
Gender	Male	Female	Female	Male	Female
Order of Selection	3	2	2	1	4

Table 10 shows the order of preference when selecting candidates for positions in the UN Common System. In order to achieve transparency in decision-making among member countries, this table shows that although Geographic Distributions are initially taken into account, difficulties can occur when evaluating the competencies of candidates from different nationalities. In these cases, consideration is often given to the candidates based on their level of education and gender. For example, as can be seen in Table 10, a candidate from a country that is not currently represented by an employee in the UN Common System (Country D) would be selected first. Secondly, consideration would then be given to a candidate from an under-represented country or equitably represented country, but if there were more than two candidates from that country, consideration would then be given to their gender and/or their academic qualifications. Additionally, regardless of the country where the qualification was obtained, an MA and/or PhD would be regarded in the same way.

Methods of Recruitment to the UN Common System

At any time during the year, people who have relevant work experience can be considered for recruitment in the UN Common System. International Organizations rarely recruit fresh graduates from universities or graduate schools on an academic calendar basis. For the purpose of this study, the author has identified two entry methods for working in International Organizations in the UN Common system: 1) the *early-career* entry method and 2) the *mid-career* entry method. The *early-career* entry method relates to people who are recruited to the UN Common System between their mid-20s to mid-30s and upon recruitment they climb the career ladder within the UN Common System. Under this scheme, there is the YPP exam (former UN staff member Competitive Exam), the JPO scheme and the YPP program.

As for the *mid-career* entry method, these candidates apply for vacancy announcements and/or take exams through what is called a recruitment mission, which will be discussed later in this section. The YPP exam gives an opportunity to nationals whose country contributions are *under-represented* or *non-represented* and the qualifying age is under 32 years old. Those who became formal staff members via this exam are guaranteed employment within the UN Secretariat until the mandatory retirement age.

Governments in some developed countries have implemented the JPO scheme in order to increase the number of younger staff members by providing necessary funds for their employment in an International Organization. These candidates can apply for a position up until the age of 32, but in Japan the age limit is 35 years old. These governments make a relationship agreement independently with various International Organizations in the UN Common System. In the case of Japanese JPOs, they work in this scheme for a two-year contract and approximately 30 people are selected for this exam per year. Depending on the organization, the transition ratio to move from a JPO position to a formal staff member is between 50-70%. The JPO scheme provides solid, professional work experience within International Organizations.

In order to qualify for the YPP program, one must have obtained an MA qualification and be under 30 years old. Organizations such as the World Bank, OECD, Asian Development Bank, UNIDO and UNICEF have their own YPP programs. The YPP exam and the YPP program, despite sharing the same name, are actually quite different.

Regarding the *mid-career* entry method, the most popular way to get a position in the UN Common System is to apply for a vacant post and after this, one can become a formal staff member. As mentioned previously in this chapter, whenever there is a vacancy after someone has retired, those posts are advertised among all the member countries and those who are qualified can apply for the post. This means that in order to get such a position, the candidates need to compete with candidates from all member countries. In this sense, the Japanese candidates face more competition than candidates in other countries when compared with recruitment via the YPP exam and/or JPO scheme.

Finally, recruitment missions take place when an International Organization plans to recruit staff members from specific countries at the mid and higher levels categories. For this reason, senior staff members of those organizations visit the country concerned and conduct the exam, which usually consists of a screening and an interview, after which process staff are recruited as formal staff members. In this case, the candidates with sufficient work experience and those who are considered ready to take up duties in the UN Common System are the target group of such missions.

Promotions and the Assignment of Staff Members

In the Japanese private sector the HR department is responsible for the relocation and promotion of staff members. As such the HR department is considered a highly influential section of the company. At the time of recruitment, the candidate's ability and performance is highly evaluated yet the number of year's service within the company and whether he/she is well balanced or not (*hitogara*)[8] are also evaluated.

According to a survey on employment management conducted by the Ministry of Health, Labour and Welfare[9], only 3% of companies replied that their company would allow staff members to be exempt from a transfer/relocation (*tennkin*) and ninety percent of companies would not allow such exemptions. The remaining 7% did not reply to the survey. From this survey, one can assume that almost all staff members employed by Japanese private companies accept the transfer request given to them by their employers. In addition, at the promotion panel in Japanese companies, not only is a candidate's performance evaluated but also his/her years of service and/or age. Therefore, if a staff member says 'no' to the requests of the HR department, the HR department has the power to negatively influence their future promotions.

On the contrary, in International Organizations in the UN Common System the decision to transfer or the desire to apply for a higher graded post lays entirely with the staff member not the HR department. Since all the vacant posts at the professional and higher categories are advertised all over the world, those who seek a promotion need to apply for a vacant post by increasing their abilities to be selected. One ought to make efforts to enhance their abilities in order to be selected for a higher-grade post. If necessary, staff should apply for a higher graded post after holding different posts at the same grade level. In this sense, staff members ought to make their own efforts to meet their personal goals by drawing their own future career plan. On the other hand, if staff members are satisfied with the status quo and if they don't seek promotion or transfer, although they cannot get an increase in salary, they are able to stay at the same grade for as long as they wish.

In this way, professional development paths in the UN Common System are implemented based on one's own ability, performance and personal wish and not their age or attitude to work. In the UN Common System, the process of promotion and assignment of staff starts with each staff member as he or she applies for a higher graded post or a post different from the present one. It is mandatory that all vacant posts in the professional and higher categories be advertised all over the world. If a staff member wishes to get promoted or to expand his or her field of work, he or she must apply for such higher graded posts or other applicable posts using her or his own initiative. If a staff member is satisfied with the present work, he or she can remain at the same post without applying for any vacant posts.

The Recruitment Policies of the Major International Organizations in the UN Common System by Organizational Characteristics

As was previously mentioned, International Organizations in the UN Common System all apply the same regulations (conditions of work, salary, job classification, etc). As the recruitment policy is significantly different for each organization, we will discuss the recruitment policies of each of the major International Organizations. The author visited the UN Secretariat, ILO, UNHCR, FAO and WFP in 2009, and interviewed the HR staff members in those organizations. The following analysis is based on these interviews and the interviews with Japanese formal staff members made in 2008. It was found that the recruitment policy can be classified into the following four channels: 1) UN Secretariat; 2) UNDP; 3) Humanitarian Assistance Organizations; 4) Specialized Organizations.

The Recruitment Policy of the UN Secretariat

In the UN Secretariat, members aged less than 32 years old are recruited via the YPP exam. Every year, the UN Secretariat announces the candidate countries for this exam. Nationals whose home country's contribution is lower in comparison with the number of staff employed by the UN Common System and/or countries that have a number of nationals retiring from employment in the system, are often invited to the YPP exam. Eligible candidates take a written exam and an interview and those who pass these exams are registered in the roster. When the UN Secretariat fills the posts at the P-1 and P-2 level they will select staff members from the above-mentioned roster. Those who pass this exam and who work for the UN Secretariat for a few years normally get indefinite contracts and they can work until the mandatory retirement age. When employees wish to be promoted to a P-3 or above graded post, they need to apply for vacant posts, competing with other candidates from all over the world. As those who are recruited via this exam have long-term job security, these people tend to be promoted within the UN Secretariat and continue to work until the mandatory retirement age instead of applying for positions in other International Organizations. In the UN Secretariat, for the posts at P-3 or higher level, the recruitment procedures are the same as those used at other International Organizations in the UN Common System. Recently, the numbers of Japanese who become formal staff members via the YPP exam are low.

The Recruitment Policy of the UNDP

The UNDP recruits members via the JPO and vacancy announcements. Thus, the recruitment is based on an American-style, performance-based recruitment process. The UNDP makes full use of young JPOs in their workforce but few JPOs become formal staff members in the UNDP. In addition, at the vacancy announcements for P-3 level and above, candidates with prior work experience in the UNDP are considered, yet, they need to compete with other candidates with qualifications. Also, if one cannot find their position within the limit of their contract, their contract will end. Employees must take responsibility for finding their own position thus surviving in a career in the UNDP is considered to be very tough.

The Recruitment Policy of Humanitarian Assistance Organizations

Recruitment policy of humanitarian assistance organizations such as the UNICEF and WFP are different from that of the UN Secretariat, the UNDP and specialized organizations (which will be discussed later). Staff in humanitarian assistance organizations must often work in developing countries and as these organizations have a rotation policy, they need to change their duty stations every 2-4 years. As the living conditions at the duty stations can be tough, it is difficult for people to work for these organizations for an extended period unless they have strong motivation. Therefore, these humanitarian assistance organizations select their core staff members both from the JPO scheme and internally, by upgrading qualified JPOs to formal staff members. In these organizations, the HR department has a strong influence on the relocation of staff members, which is very similar to HR departments in Japanese companies.

The Recruitment Policy of Specialized Organizations

Staff members in specialized organizations are mainly recruited via advertisements to staff in the middle of their career. As there are only a few positions at P-2 or P-3 levels for young staff members, it is difficult to be recruited as a formal staff member via the JPO route. At the time of recruitment, the division responsible for the employee plays a very strong part in the recruitment decision and thus, the influence of the HR department is very limited.

Discussion

This chapter provided an overview of HRM practices in International Organizations in the UN Common System. The first section defined international civil servants and introduced major characteristics of HRM practices in the UN Common System. The next section explained the Diversity Management strategies executed by the UN Common System. The third section explained the general recruitment policies in the UN Common System including recruitment method to International Organizations and promotion/assignment of staff members. The fourth section discussed the major characteristics of International Organizations in the UN Common System, classifying them into four groups; 1) The UN Secretariat; 2) UNDP; 3) Humanitarian Assistance Organizations and 4) Specialized Organizations.

From the studies in the first to the fourth sections of this chapter, it was found that there are shared Human Resource Management practices throughout the 35 International Organizations within the UN Common System. Among the system, the transfer of staff members is frequent, however, recruitment policies are considerably different.

Table 11: Comparison of HRM between the UN Common System and traditional Japanese companies

	The UN Common System	Japanese Traditional Companies
Transfers	Application to vacant posts by individual staff member	Mainly unilateral order from the HR department
Employment Security	Low	High
Discretion of Staff Members	High	Low

Table 11 summarizes the HRM practices between International Organizations in the UN Common System and the Japanese private sector. As can be seen in this table, at the International Organizations, although job security is low for the first few years, the discretion of staff members is high compared to those in Japanese private companies. For example, in International Organizations, staff must apply for vacant posts of their own choosing and not at the request of an HR department, which is what occurs in Japanese organizations. In addition, work at International Organizations is measured by quality and not by the number of hours employees stay in the office. Thus, staff members in International Organizations do not tend to stay at their workplace until late in the evening, which is different to the attitude of many employees in Japan.

Main Findings and Recommendations

Below are the main findings from this chapter and a list of recommendations for Japanese companies to follow to improve their HRM practices.

1. Individual staff members are responsible for managing his/her working hours.
Recommendation:
- ✓ Japanese companies should establish a more flexible system for managing working hours that encourages employees to develop a more favorable work-life balance, using more of their annual paid leave.

2. At International Organizations staff members continued to work outside their home country until their mandatory retirement age, sacrificing the comforts of living in their own home country. To reward their dedication to overseas assignments, International Organizations provide a favorable pension scheme to their staff members.
Recommendation:
- ✓ Japanese companies should provide attractive incentives for those who take on overseas assignments.

3. Over 40% of female staff members are working in professional categories. Women are core resources in the organization.
Recommendation:
- ✓ To implement affirmative action programs in the UN Common System it took 40 years, therefore Japanese companies need to create a long-term

strategy to implement such programs.

4. UN organizations utilize various human resources by using *early-career* entry method and *mid-career* entry method.
Recommendation:
- ✓ Japanese companies should utilize more human resources from various entry methods, not just relying on employing graduates in spring each year.

5. Recruitment policies differ among organizations.
Recommendation:
- ✓ Japanese companies should have their own recruitment policies and should not feel restricted by the academic calendar.

6. In the UN Common System, staff members take their own initiative when seeking promotions and/or relocation.
Recommendation:
- ✓ Japanese companies should give staff greater flexibility in designing their own career path, for example, by introducing internal application systems for promotion and/or relocation.

Notes:
1. As of 31 December 2011.
2. The World Bank Group offers loans, advice and array of customized resources to more than 100 developing countries and countries in transition. The World Bank is a general term of the International Bank for Reconstruction and Development (IBRD), International Finance Corporation (IFC), International Development Association (IDA), Multinational Investment Guarantee Agency (MIGA), International Center for Settlement of Investment Disputes (ICSID). Although the World Bank Group is not a member of the UN Common System, this Group is considered as an International Organization in some cases. The major difference with the UN Common System is the salary level of staff members.
3. The paramount consideration in the employment of the staff and in the determination of the conditions of service shall be the necessity of securing the highest standards of efficiency, competence, and integrity. Due regard shall be paid to the importance of recruiting the staff on as wide a geographical basis as possible.
4. Compiled from Personal Statistics Data, (CEB/2012/HLCM/HR/16) United Nations

system Chief Executives Board for Coordination (compiled on 31 December 2011).
5. Source: http: www.mofa.go.jp/mofaj/toko/tokei/hojin/09/index.html (Retrieved on 1 October 2007).
6. Staff Rules and Staff Regulations of the United Nations Secretary General's bulletin (ST/SGB/2011/1) United Nations PP47, Rule 6.3 Maternity and paternity leave (a).
7. Survey on the employment management by course in Japan by the Ministry of Health and Welfare. This survey was conducted to 123 companies that implement the management by course between April 2007 and March 2008. (http://www.mhlw.go.jp/houdou/2008/12/h1224-1.html) (Retrieved on 1 October 2010).
8. In Japan, harmonious manner without conflicting others is well respected.
9. Survey on the employment management by course in Japan by the Ministry of Health and Welfare, p.32. This survey was conducted to 123 companies that implement the management by course between April 2007 and March 2008. (http://www.mhlw.go.jp/houdou/2008/12/h1224-1.html) (Retrieved on 1 October 2010).
10. The level of salaries for Professional staff is determined on the basis of the Noblemaire principle, named after the Chairman of a committee of the League of Nations. This principle states that the international civil service should be able to recruit staff from all its Member States, including the highest-paid (http://users.ictp.it/~staff/psalaries.html#level_of_salaries, (Retrieved on 10 October 2012).
11. UN Conditions of Service Salaries (http://www.un.org/Depts/OHRM/salaries_allowances/salary.htm (Retrieved on 16 September 2012).
12. The Ministry of Health, Labor and Welfare (2008). Summary of Comprehensive Survey on Working Conditions in Japan. The Ministry of Health, Labor and Welfare, p.8.

Chapter 3

The First Survey Conducted on the Careers of Japanese International Civil Servants

This chapter provides an overview of the preliminary survey conducted on Japanese employees in International Organizations. The first section of this chapter introduces the survey, the second section explains the data collection employed, the third section reports the results of the email survey based on the responses from 170 Japanese formal staff members, the fourth section is a summary of the results and the fifth section is a list of the main findings and recommendations.

Introduction

Focusing on Japanese UN staff stationed in Geneva, New York and Tokyo, 25 preliminary interviews were conducted in 2001 and 2002. The respondents were selected via a snowball sampling method when the author conducted a mission at the request of an outside organization. During the interviews, it was found that the respondents responded positively to the pre-defined questions prepared by the author. Research notes taken during these interviews and additional information from a report entitled *The 4th Survey Results on Occupation and Life of Japanese Workers Seconded to Work Overseas* formed the basis of the question items designed for the first email survey.

Data Collection

A survey delivered by postal mail was initially considered as the most efficient way to collect data. However, on reflection, since the majority of staff members were working in developing countries where the postal service was not reliable, it was decided to conduct the survey by email.

Through trial and error, the author was able to establish artificial email addresses for the Japanese staff members employed by International Organizations. Firstly, the target staff members were identified from a directory of Japanese staff members employed by International Organizations. This information was only available in Japanese. Therefore, the author scanned the data and transformed it into *Romaji* (Roman alphabet form). Following the organizational rules[4] for developing email addresses for each organization, the author developed provisional email addresses. In order to verify these email addresses, in May 2003, the author sent an email to 741 addresses in English and Japanese, introducing the recipients to the forthcoming survey and asking for their cooperation. Those who declined to participate in the survey or whose email addresses were wrong were deleted from the survey list. Subsequently, a questionnaire consisting of 57 items both in English and Japanese was sent to 541 Japanese staff members employed by 23 International Organizations in June 2003.

In the UN Common System, staff members whose contract duration is equal to one year or longer are considered as formal staff members. This definition is the same as the definition provided by the Chief Executive Board for Coordination in their documentation (CEB/2010HLCM/HR/24, page vii). JPOs whose contract duration is longer than one year but whose fund is paid for by their respective Governments as well as consultants of various contract durations, are also working alongside formal staff members at duty stations. These people are employed for a limited-term and for a specific purpose and as such, they do not tend to have long-term careers in International Organizations.

Two hundred and fifty staff members from 20 organizations replied to the questionnaire within two months. The response rate was 46%, which was considerably high compared with other such surveys. This is due, in part to the preliminary introduction email and two subsequent email reminders. Among the two hundred fifty respondents, there were responses from 80 staff members who were not formal staff members: 34 Associate Experts (AE) or Junior Professional Officers (JPO) and who were funded by the Japanese government on a limited two-year contract, 21 Young Professional Programme participants (YPP) who were employed as trainees on a limited contract, and 25 regular staff members who were assigned by the Japanese government.

As previously mentioned, the purpose of this research is to examine the career development of Japanese formal professional staff members who develop their professional career in International Organizations. As such, it was decided that JPOs and consultants on limited-term contracts would be excluded from the target group. Therefore, there were 170 final respondents.

Findings
Overview

Table 1 is a summary of the 170 Japanese formal staff members who responded to the survey. It shows the average features of these Japanese staff members in the UN Common System. The breakdown of staff members by gender shows that 52% of the respondents were female and 48% were male. Table 2 shows the number and percentage of the respondents by gender and organizational category. Table 2 shows that the respondents were distributed proportionately among the UN Secretariat, organizations established by the General Assemblies of the United Nations, Specialized Agencies, the World Bank Group, the World Trade

Table 1: 170 Japanese respondents in the UN Common System

	Total	Male	Female
Number	166*	79 (48%)	87 (52%)
Average Age	43	46	39
Average Grade	P-4	P-4, Step IV	P-4, Step V
Married Staff Members	110	66 (84%)	44 (51%)
Highest Academic Level			
PhD or ABD**	40	22	18
Master Degree	98	40	58
BA, BSc	16	11	5
Total of staff with prior work experience in Japan	134	67	69
Years of work in Japan	7 years	9 years	4 years
Number of countries of duty station	2.4 countries	2.5 countries	2.3 countries

* 4 respondents did not report their sex
** ABD means those PhD candidates who are all but dissertation

Organization, etc. This means that a number of Japanese staff members answered the survey, irrespective of their organizational category and gender.

The average grade of Japanese formal staff members was P-4 as shown in Table 1 and the grade distribution by gender is shown in Table 2. As of December 2011 and according to the Personnel Statistics compiled by the Chief Executive Board for Coordination (CEB/2012/HLCM/HR/16,2012, page 11), P-4 is the average grade among professional staff employed by the UN Common System.

Table 2: Respondents by Gender and Organizational Category

	Male	Female	Total
UN Secretariat	8 (10%)	22 (26%)	30 (19%)
Subsidiary Organization*	22 (29%)	26 (31%)	48 (30%)
Specialized Agencies	31 (40%)	25 (29%)	56 (35%)
World Bank Group	12 (16%)	12 (14%)	24 (15%)
WTO etc.**	4 (5%)	0 (0%)	4 (2%)
Total	77 (100%)	85 (100%)	162 (100%)

* Organizations established by the decisions of the UN General Assemblies
** World Bank Group

The average age of the respondents was 43 years old. Eighty-four percent of male respondents were married, however, only 51% of female respondents were married and 44% were single (although 5% did not disclose their marital status). The author assumes that those who did not disclose this information were female and deemed it irrelevant to specify their gender.

As can be seen in Table 1, the Japanese staff members employed by the UN Common System have a higher level of education compared with those Japanese who are employed by the Japanese government and the private sector. The Japanese respondents in this survey had had an average of seven years work experience in Japan before being recruited into the UN Common System. Since being recruited, these Japanese have worked in an average of 2.4 countries (male 2.5 countries and female 2.4 countries).

There were significant differences between male and female staff members in age, marital status, years of service in Japan, and grade. However, there were no significant differences in academic qualifications, whether they had prior work experience in Japan or not and the number of counties they have worked in.

Cross Tabulation and Results
Educational Background

When the data were cross-tabulated, it was found that the biggest differences were related to gender. For ease of reference, the tabulation by gender together with each question item is included in Appendix 2. As seen in Table 1, 64% of the respondents (98 respondents) had a master's degree and 26% had a PhD or were ABD (40 respondents). As for PhDs and ABDs, almost twice the number of male staff members had these degrees compared to female staff members. In addition, Specialized Organizations employed more PhDs and ABDs. It is also worth noting that 10% (16 respondents) of the respondents only had a BA or BSc. It could be suggested that these members are now nearing the mandatory retirement age and that higher degrees were not required when the UN Common System initially employed them. In relation to their specialized field of study at their last degree held (Appendix 2, Q57), male staff members tended to specialize in business administration, economics, international relations, law, and engineering while female staff members tended to concentrate on international relations, MPA and development studies.

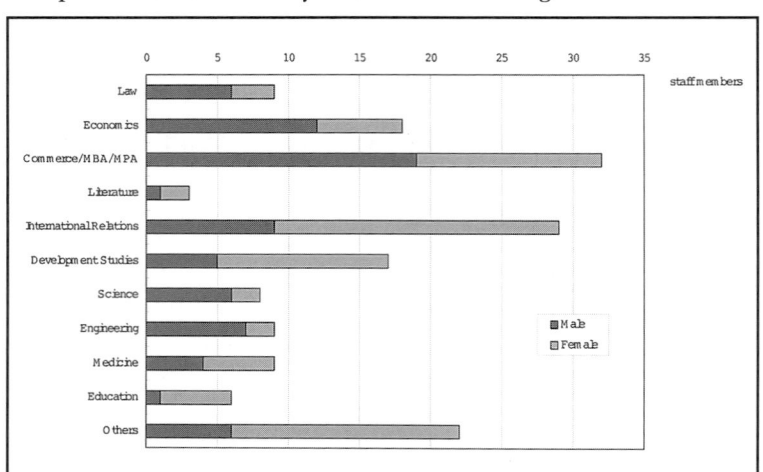

Figure 1: Specialized field of study related to the last degree held

[Bar chart showing staff members by specialized field of study, broken down by Male and Female, for categories: Law, Economics, Commerce/MBA/MPA, Literature, International Relations, Development Studies, Science, Engineering, Medicine, Education, Others]

As shown in Figure 1, with regard to their last degree held, about 60% of Japanese staff members (both men and women) pursued studies in commerce (MBA/MPA), international relations, economics or development studies. However, when the specialized fields were broken down by gender, it was found that the specialized fields of male staff members were widely spread out: 25% chose commerce (MBA, MPA), 16% economics, 12% international relations, 9% engineering, and 8% law. On the other hand, among female staff, 23% chose international relations, 15% commerce (MBA/MPA) and 14% development studies. When looking at degrees in 'commerce' specifically, it was found that the majority of male staff members have an MBA while the majority of female staff members have an MPA.

Occupational Field

More than 50% of respondents were working in the field of social economic development and project management, which are considered to be 'generalist' fields (Table 3). Yet, over 30% of the respondents worked in a field that required a high level of professional skills: politics, human rights, environment, IT, legal affairs, finance, public health, etc.

Table 3: Current occupational field(s)

(Multiple answers accepted, maximum of 2)

Occupational Field	%
Politics	5%
Economic/Social Development	20%
Humanitarian Assistance	10%
Human Rights	2%
Environment	3%
Project Management	20%
Information Technology (IT)	4%
Administration/Personnel	4%
Legal Affairs	3%
Public Information	2%
Finance	8%
Public Health	5%
Education	3%
Engineering	2%
Others (Please specify)	8%

Approximately 40% of the respondents changed their occupational field after being recruited by the UN Common System. In Japanese organizations, staff members are assigned to various occupational fields every three to five years, the idea being that this helps to identify their potential. However, Table 4 indicates that only 37% of the respondents have changed their occupational fields since the UN Common System recruited them and the remaining 59 % have not changed their occupational field. As will be discussed later in Chapter 4, the percentage of staff members who changed their occupational fields in the second survey was 38% (See Appendix 2, Q51).

Table 4: Change of occupational field upon recruitment by the UN Common System

Change of occupational Field	No. of staff members	Percentage
Yes	63	37%
No	100	59%
No answer	7	4%
Total	170	100%

Therefore, between the first and second surveys, approximately 60% of the respondents have continued to work in the same occupational fields during the course of their career in the UN Common System.

Grade

The average grade of formal Japanese staff members (male and female) surveyed was P-4. When this grade is broken down by gender, the average grade of the male staff was P-4, while that of the female staff was P-3, as shown in Figure 2. All International Organizations strive to achieve equal opportunities in the workplace, and they are encouraging the recruitment and promotion of more female staff members. However, this research shows that male staff members occupy higher grades than female staff members. It should be noted that the average age of male staff members was 46 years old and the average age of female staff members was 39 years old, as shown in Table 1.

Figure 2: Grade distribution of female and male staff members

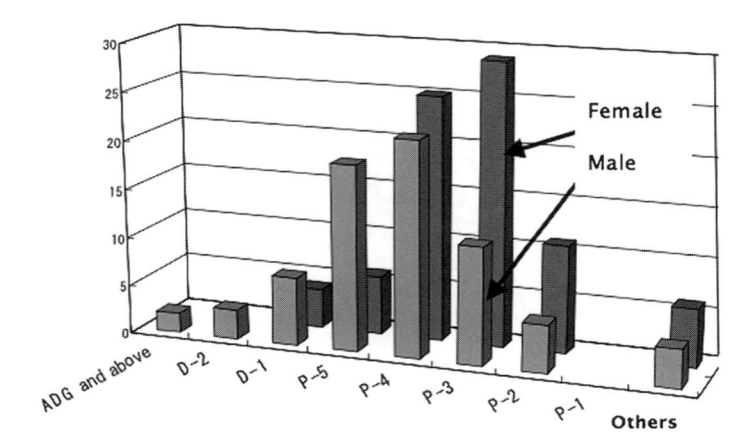

Preparation

When considering how people prepare for employment in the UN Common System, this research shows that 67% of respondents made preparations in their twenties. People are often advised to start career planning at an early stage in life. Yet, it was found that only 5% of the respondents decided to work for an International Organization of the UN Common System before they studied at university (Table 5).

Table 5: Time when first considered working for the UN Common System

	Male	Female	Total
Below 18 (High School Student)	4 (5%)	4 (5%)	8 (5%)
University Student/Graduate Student	19 (25%)	39 (45%)	58 (36%)
After graduation-29	26 (34%)	25 (29%)	51 (31%)
33-34	11 (14%)	14 (16%)	25 (15%)
35-39	3 (4%)	2 (2%)	5 (3%)
40-44	7 (9%)	2 (2%)	9 (6%)
45-49	5 (7%)	0 (0%)	5 (3%)
More than 50	1 (1%)	0 (0%)	1 (1%)
Total	76 (100%)	86 (100%)	162 (100%)

The situation is a little different when we examine the gender of respondents. Only 34% of the male staff members started their preparation in their twenties, i.e. upon completion of their undergraduate or post-graduate studies. On the other hand, 45% of the female staff members made up their minds to work for the UN Common System while in university or graduate school. As a result, over 40% of female staff members became formal staff members in the latter part of their twenties as compared to 20% in the case of male staff.

Motivations for Working in the UN Common System

When considering what motivates people to work in the UN Common System, more than half of the respondents expressed a desire to help people in developing countries and to utilize their special skills.

As can be seen in Table 6, looking at the data in more detail, 26% of respondents wished to help people in developing countries and refugees, 25% wished to utilize their specialist skills, 20% wished to work with people of different cultural backgrounds and 15% wished to contribute to world peace. It is evident that these respondents supported the missions of International Organizations in the UN Common System.

Table 6: Motivations for applying for a UN Common System post
(Multiple answers accepted, maximum of 3)

	Male	Female	Total
To contribute to world peace	26 (14%)	30 (15%)	56 (15%)
To help people of developing countries/refugees	50 (26%)	50 (26%)	100 (26%)
To utilize special skills	54 (28%)	43 (22%)	97 (25%)
To live overseas	22 (11%)	17 (9%)	39 (10%)
To work with people of different cultural backgrounds	33 (17%)	44 (23%)	77 (20%)
Other motive (please specify)	7 (4%)	10 (5%)	17 (4%)
Total	192 (100%)	194 (100%)	386 (100%)

However, some degree of difference was noted between male and female staff members. A greater number of male staff members expressed their wish to use their specialist skills while more female staff members expressed their wish to work with people of different cultural backgrounds.

Age

Table 7 shows the age of Japanese employees in different positions in the UN Common System. Forty percent of Japanese respondents became formal staff members at the UN Common System between the ages of 30 to 34.

Table 7: Age when became a formal staff member in the UN Common System

Age	Male	Female	Total
20-24	1 (1%)	6 (7%)	7 (4%)
25-29	18 (23%)	36 (41%)	54 (33%)
30-34	33 (42%)	33 (38%)	66 (40%)
35-39	9 (12%)	7 (8%)	16 (10%)
40-44	10 (13%)	5 (6%)	15 (9%)
45-49	5 (6%)	0 (0%)	5 (3%)
Older than 50	3 (4%)	0 (0%)	3 (2%)
Total	78 (100%)	87 (100%)	166 (100%)

However, a breakdown by gender shows a different picture. Over 80% of female staff members became a formal staff member before 35 years old; 70% were 20-24 years old, 41% were 25 to 29 years old and 38% were 30 to 34 years old. From 35 years old, the percentage of female staff members who became a formal staff member decreased significantly and no female staff members became a formal staff member after the age of 45.

On the contrary, in the case of male staff members, the largest age group to become a formal staff member was between 30 to 34 years old (42%). This shows that male staff members became formal staff members when they were older than female staff members. One significant characteristic is that 35% of male staff members became formal staff members after 35 years old and 10% of male staff members became formal staff members after 45 years old. Since the upper age limit of the JPO Programme is 35 years old in the case of Japanese nationals, those who became formal staff members after 35 years old are assumed to have been recruited by responding to vacancy announcements or through specific recruitment missions.

Prior Work Experience

Also of interest to the author was what kind of organizations formal staff members worked in while in Japan, prior to taking their post in the UN Common System. As is shown in Table 8, 51% of the respondents had worked in private companies in the private sector before the UN Common System. They worked for various organizations, which included governmental and ODA agencies, research institutes, NPOs/NGOs and other International Organizations located in Japan. It can be said that a larger number of male staff members had work experience in the government while female staff members tended to have prior experience working in an NGO/NPO. However, there are no other significant differences between male and female staff members.

Table 8: Prior work experience in Japan

	Male	Female	Total
Private company/companies	41 (49%)	44 (54%)	85 (51%)
Research institute/institutes	13 (15%)	11 (13%)	24 (14%)
Government/ODA Agency	19 (23%)	9 (11%)	28 (17%)
NPO/NGOs	4 (5%)	7 (9%)	11 (7%)
Self-employed	1 (1%)	0 (0%)	1 (1%)
UN Agency/Agencies located in Japan	3 (4%)	7 (9%)	10 (6%)
Others	3 (4%)	4 (5%)	7 (4%)
Total	84 (100%)	82 (100%)	166 (100%)

Entry Method

As already mentioned in Chapter 2, there are four channels for a Japanese national to take to become a formal staff member in the UN Common System:
1. Apply for a vacant post
2. Take an exam during a recruitment mission
3. Enter the JPO Scheme
4. Take the YPP exam (former UN competitive exam)

Table 9: Entry method by gender*

		Male	Female	Total
EC (*Early-career* entry)	JPO Programme	21 (27%)	37 (41%)	58 (34%)
	YPP (former UN Competitive Exam)	6 (8%)	14 (15%)	20 (12%)
	YPP	5 (6%)	6 (7%)	11 (6%)
	Total	32 (41%)	57 (63%)	89 (52%)
MC (*Mid-career* entry)	Vacancy Announcements	24 (30%)	13 (14%)	37 (22%)
	Recruitment Mission	7 (9%)	8 (9%)	15 (9%)
	Total	32 (41%)	57 (63%)	89 (52%)
Others		16 (20%)	13 (14%)	29 (17%)
Grand Total		79 (100%)	91 (100%)	170 (100%)

* As the YPP (Former UN Competitive Exam) was not included in 'the entry method' question in the survey, the author redeveloped a new table checking the original data.

Among those who responded the survey, found in Table 9, 34% of the respondents became a formal staff member upon completion of the JPO scheme and this occupies the highest ratio among the aforementioned recruitment channels. At the same time, 22% of the respondents became formal staff members by applying for a vacant post advertised by the UN Common System.

Table 10 shows the comparison between entry methods and gender. Male staff members were recruited almost equally by the *mid-career* entry method and *early-career* entry method. On the contrary, 63% of female staff members became a formal staff member through the *early-career* entry method, which is almost three times more than through the *mid-career* entry method (23%). Therefore, one can generalize that the entry method differs by gender.

Table 10: Summary of entry method by gender

Male staff members	EC (*Early-career* Entry Method)	(41%)
	MC (*Mid-career* Entry Method)	(39%)
Female staff members	EC (*Early-career* Entry method)	(63%)
	MC (*Mid-career* Entry Method)	(23%)

Important Factors to Consider When Working for the UN Common System

In this survey, the Japanese staff members were asked to choose three out of a possible ten most important factors to consider when working for the UN Common System (Table 11). These included adaptability/flexibility, specialty/specialties, ability to negotiate, language ability, positive attitude, leadership, work experience in the relevant field of UN activities, experience of having lived overseas, coordination skills with local staff/people, understanding/knowledge of the programs implemented at the UN, and others. A majority of the respondents chose adaptability/flexibility, language ability and specialty/specialties. However, when the responses were classified by gender, female staff members evaluated adaptability/flexibility (26%) and language ability (21%) and male staff members evaluated specialty/specialties (21%) and language ability (21%).

Table 11: The most important factors when working in the UN Common System (Multiple answers accepted maximum of 3)

	Male	Female	Total
Adaptability/Flexibility	41 (18%)	63 (26%)	104 (22%)
Specialty/Specialties	48 (21%)	30 (12%)	78 (17%)
Ability to negotiate	22 (10%)	17 (7%)	39 (8%)
Language ability	47 (21%)	50 (21%)	97 (21%)
Positive attitude	21 (9%)	28 (12%)	49 (10%)
Leadership	13 (6%)	8 (3%)	21 (4%)
Work experience in the relevant field of the UN Common System	9 (4%)	12 (5%)	21 (4%)
Experience of having lived overseas	3 (1%)	5 (2%)	8 (2%)
Coordination skills with local staff/people	10 (4%)	10 (4%)	20 (4%)
Understanding/knowledge of the programs implemented in the UN Common System	4 (2%)	5 (2%)	9 (2%)
Others	9 (4%)	14 (6%)	23 (5%)
Total	227 (100%)	242 (100%)	469 (100%)

Job Satisfaction

As shown in Table 12, over 80% of the respondents were very satisfied or satisfied with their job.

Table 12: Job satisfaction at the UN Common System

	Male	Female	Total
Very satisfied	30 (38%)	27 (31%)	57 (34%)
Satisfied	33 (42%)	46 (53%)	79 (48%)
Average	12 (15%)	10 (11%)	22 (13%)
Somewhat unsatisfied	2 (3%)	2 (2%)	4 (2%)
Very unsatisfied	2 (3%)	2 (2%)	4 (2%)
Total	79 (100%)	87 (100%)	166 (100%)

Staff members cited the substance of their work (25%), the feeling of accomplishment (14%), the contribution to society (13%), the work environment (13%) and the utilization of their capabilities (12%) as reasons for the job satisfaction (Table 13).

Table 13: The reasons for job satisfaction
(Multiple answers accepted, maximum of 3)

	Male	Female	Total
Substance of the job	55 (27%)	56 (23%)	111 (25%)
Work environment	26 (13%)	30 (13%)	56 (13%)
Working hours	7 (3%)	10 (4%)	17 (4%)
Equal work for both sexes	2 (1%)	22 (9%)	24 (5%)
Development of specialty/specialties	12 (6%)	22 (9%)	4 (8%)
Room for discretion	7 (3%)	6 (3%)	13 (3%)
Feeling of accomplishment	38 (19%)	23 (10%)	61 (14%)
Contribution to the society	28 (14%)	30 (13%)	58 (13%)
Utilization of abilities	24 (12%)	30 (13%)	54 (12%)
Others	6 (3%)	10 (4%)	16 (4%)
Total	205 (100%)	239 (100%)	444 (100%)

Working Hours

When evaluating working hours, there was no significant difference by gender in the evaluation of working hours. Over 40 % of the respondents thought that working hours in the UN Common System were about the same as those in Japan and 34% of the respondents thought them shorter (Table 14).

Table 14: Comparison of working hours with those in Japan

	Male	Female	Total
About twice as long or longer	1 (2%)	0 (0%)	1 (1%)
50% longer	2 (3%)	7 (11%)	9 (7%)
20 ~ 30% longer	5 (8%)	10 (16%)	15 (12%)
About the same	28 (47%)	24 (39%)	52 (43%)
20 ~ 30% shorter	22 (37%)	19 (31%)	41 (34%)
About half as long	1 (2%)	1 (2%)	2 (2%)
Less than half as long	1 (2%)	0 (0%)	1 (1%)
Total	60 (100%)	61 (100%)	121 (100%)

Salary

Over 40% of respondents considered their salary level to be 'very high' or 'somewhat high' as shown in Table 15.

Table 15: Evaluation of salary in the UN Common System

	Male	Female	Total
Very high	0 (0%)	6 (7%)	6 (4%)
Somewhat high	22 (28%)	43 (49%)	65 (39%)
Average	39 (50%)	29 (33%)	68 (41%)
Somewhat low	16 (21%)	8 (9%)	24 (14%)
Very low	2 (3%)	1 (1%)	2 (1%)
Total	78 (100%)	87 (100%)	166 (100%)

Focusing on gender, it was found that female respondents highly evaluated the salary they received. In fact, 53% of the female staff members replied that their salary increased upon entry at the UN Common System. As for the male staff members, it was difficult to draw conclusions as their answers were widely spread out. Over 40% of male respondents stated they had a 20%–50% decrease in their salary when they began working for the UN Common System (Table 16).

Table 16: Comparison of the present salary with that received in Japan

	Male	Female	Total
More than double	7 (13%)	10 (21%)	17 (17%)
About double	0 (0%)	3 (6%)	3 (3%)
20 to 50% more	13 (23%)	12 (26%)	25 (24%)
About the same	13 (23%)	11 (23%)	24 (23%)
20 to 50% less	16 (29%)	9 (19%)	25 (24%)
About half	7 (13%)	0 (0%)	7 (7%)
Less than half	0 (0%)	2 (4%)	2 (2%)
Total	56 (100%)	47 (100%)	103 (100%)

Fringe Benefits

Sixty-five percent of respondents considered that the fringe benefits in the UN Common System were at a high or very high level. The fringe benefits, particularly in pension, annual paid leave and education grants were higher or equal compared with those in leading Japanese companies (Table 17).

Table 17: Fringe benefits in the UN Common System

	Male	Female	Total
Very high	4 (5%)	21 (24%)	25 (15%)
Somewhat high	40 (52%)	42 (48%)	82 (50%)
Average	25 (32%)	19 (22%)	44 (27%)
Somewhat low	6 (8%)	4 (5%)	10 (6%)
Very low	2 (3%)	1 (1%)	3 (2%)
Total	77 (100%)	87 (100%)	164 (100%)

Satisfaction at Duty Station

Sixty-six percent of the respondents replied that their level of satisfaction at duty station was 'somewhat high' or 'very high'. When considering the level of satisfaction at duty station by gender, both males and females evaluated their satisfaction as 'very high'. Twenty-four percent of females stated their level of satisfaction was 'very high'. While only 9% of male staff chose 'very high' (Table 18).

Table 18: Satisfaction at duty station

	Male	Female	Total
Very high	7 (9%)	21 (24%)	28 (17%)
Somewhat high	42 (53%)	40 (46%)	82 (49%)
Average	26 (33%)	23 (26%)	49 (30%)
Somewhat low	3 (4%)	3 (3%)	6 (4%)
Very low	1 (1%)	0 (0%)	1 (1%)
Total	79 (100%)	87 (100%)	166 (100%)

Overall Satisfaction

Overall satisfaction was very high for both male and female staff members. More than 80% of the respondents stated 'somewhat high' or 'very high' as shown in Table 19. Also, as seen in Table 20, both male and female staff members selected 'substance of work' (25%), 'work environment' (12%) and 'contribution to society' (12%) as a reason for their overall satisfaction. There was not a big difference between male staff members and female staff members, however some female staff members appreciated 'equal work for both genders' (female 9%, male 0%) as an important reason for their level of satisfaction.

Table 19: Overall satisfaction

	Male	Female	Total
Very high	23 (29%)	27 (31%)	50 (30%)
Somewhat high	45 (57%)	45 (52%)	90 (54%)
Average	9 (11%)	12 (14%)	21 (13%)
Somewhat low	1 (1%)	2 (2%)	3 (2%)
Very low	1 (1%)	1 (1%)	2 (1%)
Total	79 (100%)	87 (100%)	166 (100%)

Table 20: Evaluation of overall satisfaction

	Male	Female	Total
Substance of work	57 (27%)	60 (24%)	117 (25%)
Work environment	26 (12%)	29 (12%)	55 (12%)
Remuneration	9 (4%)	14 (6%)	23 (5%)
Working hours	11 (5%)	5 (2%)	16 (3%)
Fringe benefits (pension, annual leave, etc.)	11 (5%)	14 (6%)	25 (5%)
Equal work for both genders	1 (0%)	23 (9%)	24 (5%)
Development of specialty/specialties	11 (5%)	12 (5%)	23 (5%)
Room for discretion	6 (3%)	6 (2%)	12 (3%)
Feeling of accomplishment	26 (12%)	26 (10%)	52 (11%)
Contribution to the society	27 (13%)	27 (11%)	54 (12%)
Utilization of abilities	12 (6%)	14 (6%)	26 (6%)
Work environment where political decisions often take place	6 (3%)	6 (2%)	12 (3%)
Too many transfers among duty stations	0 (0%)	0 (0%)	0 (0%)
Unfair treatment at the workplace	3 (1%)	2 (1%)	5 (1%)
Low salary	0 (0%)	2 (1%)	2 (0%)
Poor utilization of specialty/specialties	2 (1%)	1 (0%)	3 (1%)
Others (Please specify)	6 (3%)	8 (3%)	14 (3%)
Total	214 (100%)	249 (100%)	463 (100%)

Future Increase of Japanese International Civil Servants

When asked whether or not they thought the number of Japanese staff members in the UN Common System would increase in 10-15 years time, approximately 70% of respondents replied positively (as shown in Table 21). However, 14% of the respondents expressed doubts about an increase in Japanese staff members because employment practices in Japan are considered quite different to those in the UN Common System. Also, they stated that the Japanese government does not have strong political power internationally and that this may have an impact on the number of Japanese who join (as shown in Tables 21, 22 and 23).

Table 21: Opinions on the increase of Japanese staff members in the UN Common System in the future

	Male	Female	Total
Yes, of course numbers will increase	19 (24%)	16 (18%)	35 (21%)
Yes, but to some extent	36 (46%)	43 (49%)	79 (48%)
I do not know	10 (13%)	17 (20%)	27 (16%)
I doubt it	12 (15%)	11 (13%)	23 (14%)
I definitely do not think so	1 (1%)	0 (0%)	1 (1%)
Total	78 (100%)	87 (100%)	165 (100%)

Table 22: Reasons for the answers given in Table 21
(when the answer was positive, multiple answers accepted, maximum of 3)

	Male	Female	Total
The language proficiency of Japanese has increased	35 (38%)	31 (32%)	66 (35%)
It is easier to find an appropriate job in Japan, after working for the UN for a considerable number of years	3 (3%)	3 (3%)	6 (3%)
More young Japanese have shown interest in working for the UN Common System	43 (47%)	45 (47%)	88 (47%)
Others (Please specify)	11 (12%)	17 (18%)	28 (15%)
Total	92 (100%)	96 (100%)	188 (100%)

Table 23: Reasons for the answers in Table 21
(when the answer was negative, multiple answers accepted, maximum of 3)

	Male	Female	Total
The qualifications/requirements are very high	4 (11%)	9 (19%)	13 (15%)
The remuneration is rather low at the UN Common System	6 (16%)	6 (13%)	12 (14%)
The Japanese Government does not have strong political power internationally	8 (22%)	9 (19%)	17 (20%)
It is exhausting to work overseas for so many years	1 (3%)	2 (4%)	3 (4%)
Employment practices in Japan are quite different from those at the UN Common System	13 (35%)	15 (31%)	28 (33%)
Others (Please specify)	5 (14%)	7 (15%)	12 (14%)
Total	37 (100%)	48 (100%)	85 (100%)

Difficulties at Duty Stations

The respondents experienced life in an average of two countries (Table 1). Staff members must go through the process of various adjustments at each duty station. To the question of which element they considered most difficult to deal with, about 40% of the respondents, both male and female, chose 'general matters not directly related to work' (Table 24).

Table 24: Adjustment difficulties when assigned to a new duty station

	Male	Female	Total
Substance of work	13 (18%)	11 (14%)	24 (16%)
Relationship with local staff	8 (11%)	16 (20%)	24 (16%)
General matters, not directly relating to work such as security, access to reliable medical facilities, food, etc.	31 (44%)	28 (35%)	59 (39%)
The language used at the duty station	8 (11%)	5 (6%)	13 (9%)
Others (Please specify)	11 (15%)	19 (24%)	30 (20%)
Total	71 (100%)	79 (100%)	150 (100%)

Continuing to Work at the UN Common System until the Mandatory Retirement Age

Seventy percent of the respondents expressed their wish to work for the UN Common System until they reach mandatory retirement age. These respondents wished to continue to work because they could continue to use their expertise and or because the work environment was considered to be very comfortable. Some respondents stated they may find difficulty in finding appropriate jobs outside the UN Common System and 30% did not wish to continue working in the UN Common System until the mandatory retirement age (Table 25).

Table 25: Desire to work for the UN Common System until the mandatory retirement age

	Male	Female	Total
Yes	50 (69%)	57 (70%)	107 (70%)
No	22 (31%)	24 (30%)	46 (30%)
Total	72 (100%)	81 (100%)	153 (100%)

Those who would not continue to develop their career within the UN Common System stated that they would be able to better utilize their expertise outside the UN Common System. However, that does not necessarily mean that they were not happy with the work or treatment at the workplace at the UN Common System. In particular, staff members employed by specialized agencies did not express their wish to continue working for their organization until the mandatory retirement age. This was likely to be because these staff members were considered to have high-level transferable skills that would make them employable elsewhere. Forty-nine percent expressed a wish to use their skills outside of the UN Common System.

When the author asked respondents to choose three out of nine reasons why they wanted to stay in the UN Common System, they expressed that at their present work place they could develop their specialist skills, gain knowledge about their professional field and enjoy a good working environment. At the same time, 13% of staff members expressed that it is difficult to find an appropriate job outside the UN Common System (Appendix 2, Q33, H).

Finding a Job in Japan

A quarter of the Japanese staff interviewed had given serious consideration to returning to Japan. The reasons why they wanted to return to Japan and to find a job there, were 1) they needed to look after their elderly parent(s) back in Japan, 2) that they could not get along with their boss or 3) they had complaints about their present work. However, these people did not actually resign from the UN Common System either because they could not find a suitable job in Japan or they could not make the final decision to leave as the work environment in Japan was so different from that in the UN Common System (Table 26).

Table 26: Staff members who have given serious consideration to resigning and to finding a job in Japan

	Male	Female	Total
Yes	26 (33%)	14 (16%)	40 (24%)
No	53 (67%)	72 (84%)	125 (76%)
Total	79 (100%)	86 (100%)	165 (100%)

Current Concerns

The major concerns of the Japanese staff employed in the UN Common System were promotion/career development, care of elderly parent(s) and the education of their children. It was noted that male staff members were more concerned about the education of children, highlighting that they wanted their children to be educated in Japan in order to acquire Japanese culture, language and values as they felt it was difficult to obtain them living overseas for an extended period during childhood. On the other hand, female staff members placed more emphasis on promotion and the care of elderly parents (Table 27).

Chapter 3 The First Survey Conducted on the Careers of Japanese International Civil Servants

Table 27: The most pressing concerns of respondents
(Multiple answers accepted, maximum of 3)

	Male	Female	Total
Renewal of contract	8 (6%)	5 (4%)	13 (5%)
Promotion	26 (19%)	39 (28%)	65 (24%)
Education of children	28 (20%)	11 (8%)	39 (14%)
Care of parents	24 (17%)	22 (16%)	46 (17%)
Life after retirement	18 (13%)	10 (7%)	28 (10%)
Getting a job in Japan	4 (3%)	4 (3%)	8 (3%)
I do not have any pressing concerns	19 (14%)	22 (16%)	41 (15%)
Others (Please specify)	11 (8%)	24 (18%)	35 (13%)
Total	138 (100%)	137 (100%)	275 (100%)

Discussion

In the first section, the author explained the preliminary interviews and the second section detailed how the survey was carried out. The third section presented the findings of data collected from the first survey. The author selected 170 formal staff members as respondents to make up the target group. Through analyzing the data obtained from the first survey, the following characteristics were observed: first, female staff members started their preparation for working in the UN Common System earlier than male staff members. As a result, it was found that female staff members started their career in the latter half of their twenties, however male staff members started their career in their early thirties at the UN Common System. However, when we compare their grade, the average grade of male staff members was P-4, Step IV and female staff members were P-3, Step V.

In the case of male staff members, 35% of male staff members became formal staff between the ages 35-44 (Table 7). Those people were recruited via the *mid-career* entry method to a higher graded post. The relationship between gender and the grade is clearly illustrated in Figure 2. In addition to this *mid-career* entry method, the specialized degree of study at their last degree held was widely spread. On the contrary, female staff members started their preparations at an earlier stage and were recruited through the YPP exam or JPO schemes, which encourage an *early-career* entry method. Thus, they became a formal staff member when they were younger than their male counterparts. In addition, the females' specialized field of study at the last degree held was focused on three main fields: international relations, commerce (MPA), and development studies.

The survey showed that both male and female staff members were satisfied with work at the UN Common System and life at duty stations. In particular, one quarter of female staff members evaluated their satisfaction at duty stations very high. The level of overall satisfaction was high for both male and female. Female staff members evaluated equal work for both genders, in addition to the substance of their work and work environment as reasons for the high evaluation. Despite the fact that in the case of male staff members, over 40% of respondents experienced a 20%-50% decrease in their salary (when they began working at the UN Common System), they didn't cite this as a complaint.

With regard to working hours, 34% of male and female staff members expressed that their working hours reduced by 20–30% when they began working at the UN Common System. The most difficult adjustments to make when assigned to a new duty station were those matters not directly related to their work, such as medical facilities, security, access to reliable medical facilities and food. The language used at duty stations and the relationships with local staff were not so problematic. According to Nagai's (2002) study, which surveyed cross-cultural adjustment factors of Japanese expatriates located in 53 countries and regions, the most influential factor is the ability to develop satisfying relationships with local people. Besides, according to Black (2001), the most difficult adjustment at a new duty station is developing strong human relations with local people and general matters not pertaining to work. The easiest factor for adaptation to the new environment was work itself. At the workplace in the UN Common System, the working language is English or French regardless of the duty station, therefore, adjusting to work itself is not a major concern. Even if employees face difficulties with local people the degree of difficulty would be far less than those assigned from the private companies in Japan. Therefore, when the UN Common System assigns staff overseas, it is important to provide those assigned and their family with sufficient information relating to general issues that are outside the workplace.

Since the average age of the respondents was 43 years old, a quarter of respondents and a third of male staff, have seriously considered returning to Japan, in order to take care of their elderly parents or the education of their children. However, these respondents didn't resign from their post because they couldn't find an appropriate job in Japan or they couldn't make a final decision to work within a Japanese working environment.

Main Findings and Recommendations

Below are the main findings from this chapter and a list of recommendations for Japanese companies to follow to improve their HRM practices.

1. In general, female staff members started their career in the UN Common System in their twenties, while male staff members started working in the UN Common System in their thirties.
Recommendation:
- ✓ In order to develop a successful career path, both male and female Japanese job seekers should start planning their career from an earlier age. And, Japanese companies and educational organizations should support this initiative.

2. There were differences in the specialized fields of study between male and female staff members.
Recommendation:
- ✓ Japanese females should choose more specialized and highly technical fields of study.

3. The most difficult adjustments to make when assigned to a new duty station are not directly related to work.
Recommendation:
- ✓ Prior to being dispatched overseas, Japanese companies should give sufficient pre-departure training to not only staff members but also their families. This will enable them to better adjust to the basics of living overseas.

4. Both male and female staff members were satisfied with work in the UN Common System and life at duty stations. Male staff members appreciated the reduction of working hours. Female staff members appreciated the level of equality in the workplace.

Recommendation:
- ✓ Companies should create better work environments for female staff members so they feel equally treated and respected. Additionally, companies should give employees more personal freedom and more flexible working hours.

5. Many Japanese women are holding core managerial and professional positions in organizations in the UN Common System. The organizations are making full use of their skills and abilities.

Recommendation:
- ✓ Japanese companies should make better use of female human resources in their companies. They should develop systems that enable women to achieve a satisfactory work-life balance. Additionally, companies in Japan should develop return rights for women to return to their previous post after leaving work for maternity leave. Maternity leave is a right of a woman. It should be written in the staff regulations. It should be part of the long-term strategy of the company.

6. Staff members employed in the UN Common System do not work for money but to help people in developing countries using their specialist skills.

Recommendation:
- ✓ Japanese companies should clearly communicate their contribution to society. This can be influential in attracting future employees.

Notes:
1. Also referred to as chain sampling, a non-probability sampling technique where respondents are recruited from among the initial respondents acquaintances.
2. The Japan Institute for Labour Policy and Training. (2001). The 4th survey results on occupation and life of Japanese workers seconded to work overseas. The Japan Institute for Labour Policy and Training.

3. The Ministry of Foreign Affairs, Japan (2001). Shuyo Kokusaikikann no Nihonnjinn Shokuinn Meibo.
4. The structure of email addresses by International Organization is shown in page 253 of Telephone Directory, United Nations Office, Geneva, 2000.

Chapter 4
A Statistical Analysis of the First Survey - Characteristics of Japanese Formal Staff Members

This chapter provides a more detailed statistical analysis of the characteristics of Japanese formal staff members previously shown in Chapter 3. This chapter consists of five sections: the first section introduces the results of the t-test[1] analysis; the second section reports the results of the factor analysis; the third section provides the results of the factor analysis by gender; the fourth section reports the results of the multiple regression analysis; the fifth section includes a summary of the results and further discussion and the sixth section is a summary of the whole chapter.

t-test

The cross-tabulation discussed in Chapter 3 showed a significant difference between male and female staff members. In order to identify the variables with a significant difference, a t-test analysis was conducted. The results of a Levine's test, for the equality of variance, are shown in Table 1. The descriptive statistics for the key variables are shown in Table 2. From the results in Table 1 and 2, the following variables showed a significant difference:

a) **Age of recruitment:** male staff members score higher than female staff members;
b) **Evaluation of Salary:** female staff members score higher than male staff members;
c) **Fringe benefits:** female staff members score higher than male staff members;
d) **Satisfaction at duty stations:** female staff members score higher than male staff members;
e) **Grade:** male staff members score higher than female staff members;
f) **Age at the time of survey:** male staff members score higher than female staff members.

Table 1: t-test for the means of male and female formal staff members

T-test for the means of male and female formal staff members		Levene's Test for equality of variance		t-test for equality of variance						
		F value	Significance level	t-value	Degree of freedom	Significance level Two tails	Mean difference	Standard error difference	95% Confidence Interval of the difference	
									Lower limit	Upper limit
Year of service in the present organization	Equal variances assumed	1.36	0.245	0.97	168	0.333	0.181	0.187	-0.187	0.55
	Equal variances not assumed			0.966	160.587	0.335	0.181	0.187	-0.189	0.551
Number of job changes	Equal variances assumed	0.097	0.756	-0.939	163	0.349	-0.2	0.213	-0.622	0.221
	Equal variances not assumed			-0.944	161.446	0.347	-0.2	0.212	-0.62	0.219
Satisfaction at prior organizations	Equal variances assumed	6.59	0.011	1.428	168	0.155	0.108	0.076	-0.041	0.258
	Equal variances not assumed			1.433	165.294	0.154	0.108	0.076	-0.041	0.258
Age of recruitment to the UN Common System	Equal variances assumed	9.021	0.003	4.329	166	0.000	0.804	0.186	0.438	1.171
	Equal variances not assumed			4.211	135.593	0.000	0.804	0.191	0.427	1.182
Job satisfaction in the current position	Equal variances assumed	1.473	0.227	0.027	167	0.979	0.004	0.137	-0.266	0.274
	Equal variances not assumed			0.027	156.788	0.979	0.004	0.138	-0.269	0.276
Comparison of working hours with those in Japan	Equal variances assumed	0.183	0.669	-1.708	121	0.09	-0.3	0.176	-0.647	0.048
	Equal variances not assumed			-1.711	120.767	0.09	-0.3	0.175	-0.647	0.047
Evaluation of Salary	Equal variances assumed	4.194	0.042	-3.554	167	0.000	-0.426	0.12	-0.663	-0.189
	Equal variances not assumed			-3.58	165.436	0.000	-0.426	0.119	-0.661	-0.191
Comparison of Salary with that in Japan	Equal variances assumed	0.449	0.504	-1.851	146	0.066	-0.314	0.17	-0.649	0.021
	Equal variances not assumed			-1.858	145.981	0.065	-0.314	0.169	-0.648	0.02
Fringe benefits	Equal variances assumed	0.01	0.922	-2.576	165	0.011	-0.344	0.133	-0.607	-0.08
	Equal variances not assumed			-2.592	161.623	0.01	-0.344	0.133	-0.605	-0.082
Satisfaction at Duty Station	Equal variances assumed	0.035	0.852	-2.354	168	0.02	-0.283	0.12	-0.52	-0.046
	Equal variances not assumed			-2.366	166.097	0.019	-0.283	0.12	-0.519	-0.047

Chapter 4 A Statistical Analysis of the First Survey - Characteristics of Japanese Formal Staff Members

Variable	Assumption									
Overall satisfaction	Equal variances assumed	0.227	0.635	0.056	168	0.955	0.007	0.119	-0.229	0.242
	Equal variances not assumed			0.056	165.588	0.955	0.007	0.119	-0.228	0.241
Wish to work in the UN Common System until mandatory retirement age	Equal variances assumed	0.09	0.764	-0.151	168	0.88	-0.011	0.074	-0.157	0.135
	Equal variances not assumed			-0.151	163.043	0.88	-0.011	0.074	-0.157	0.135
Grade	Equal variances assumed	1.408	0.237	4.567	154	0.000	0.849	0.186	0.481	1.216
	Equal variances not assumed			4.507	139.379	0.000	0.849	0.188	0.476	1.221
Number of Organizations employed in (within the UN Common System)	Equal variances assumed	2.835	0.094	-1.252	165	0.212	-0.192	0.153	-0.495	0.111
	Equal variances not assumed			-1.279	164.991	0.203	-0.192	0.15	-0.488	0.104
Number of posts	Equal variances assumed	4.696	0.032	1.347	143	0.18	0.548	0.407	-0.256	1.353
	Equal variances not assumed			1.297	109.471	0.197	0.548	0.422	-0.289	1.385
Years of service in the UN Common System	Equal variances assumed	4.168	0.043	0.61	167	0.543	0.11	0.18	-0.246	0.466
	Equal variances not assumed			0.603	153.489	0.547	0.11	0.182	-0.25	0.47
Age (at time of survey)	Equal variances assumed	2.902	0.09	5.539	153	0.000	6.657	1.202	4.283	9.031
	Equal variances not assumed			5.506	143.882	0.000	6.657	1.209	4.267	9.047
Country of Duty Station (developed versus developing)	Equal variances assumed	4.921	0.028	1.11	168	0.269	0.068	0.061	-0.053	0.188
	Equal variances not assumed			1.098	154.454	0.274	0.068	0.062	-0.054	0.19
Entry Method	Equal variances assumed	12.753	0	-1.906	168	0.058	-0.137	0.072	-0.278	0.005
	Equal variances not assumed			-1.889	156.279	0.061	-0.137	0.072	-0.279	0.006

A significant Levene's test ($p \leq 0.05$) suggests that the variance in the two groups of mail and female staff members are not equal. Thus, one needs to see the test statistics in the raw labeled *Equal variances not assumed*.

Table 2: Descriptive statistics of key variables

(N=170, 1: Male formal staff members, 2: Female formal staff members)

Variables	Gender	N	M	SD	Standard error of the means
Years of service in the present organization	1	78	3.33	1.245	0.141
	2	92	3.15	1.185	0.124
Number of job changes prior to UN Common System	1	76	1.47	1.321	0.152
	2	89	1.67	1.404	0.149
Satisfaction at prior organizations	1	78	0.64	0.483	0.055
	2	92	0.53	0.502	0.052
First employment age at UN Common System	1	76	3.5	1.381	0.158
	2	92	2.7	1.024	0.107
Job satisfaction in the present position (at time of survey)	1	78	4.1	0.934	0.106
	2	91	4.1	0.844	0.088
Comparison of working hours with those in Japan	1	59	3.76	0.953	0.124
	2	64	4.06	0.99	0.124
Evaluation of salary	1	77	3.05	0.742	0.085
	2	92	3.48	0.805	0.084
Comparison of salary with that in Japan	1	71	2.8	0.98	0.116
	2	77	3.12	1.076	0.123
Fringe benefits	1	75	3.49	0.828	0.096
	2	92	3.84	0.881	0.092
Satisfaction at duty station	1	78	3.64	0.755	0.086
	2	92	3.92	0.802	0.084
Overall satisfaction	1	78	4.12	0.756	0.086
	2	92	4.11	0.791	0.082
Wish to work in the UN Common System until the mandatory retirement age	1	78	0.64	0.483	0.055
	2	92	0.65	0.479	0.05
Grade	1	71	4.37	1.245	0.148
	2	85	3.52	1.076	0.117
Number of organizations employed in (within the UN Common System)	1	75	1.37	0.866	0.1
	2	92	1.57	1.072	0.112
Number of posts	1	65	3.92	2.896	0.359
	2	80	3.38	1.99	0.222
Years of service in the UN Common System	1	78	3.54	1.256	0.142
	2	91	3.43	1.087	0.114
Age (at time of survey)	1	75	46.51	8.174	0.944
	2	80	39.85	6.758	0.756
Country of Duty Station (developed versus developing)	1	78	1.23	0.424	0.048
	2	92	1.16	0.371	0.039
Entry Method	1	78	1.6	0.493	0.056
	2	92	1.74	0.442	0.046

These results match the initial findings presented in Chapter 3:

- Female staff members evaluated salary and fringe benefits in the UN Common System more highly than male staff members;

- The age of recruitment and grade of male staff members were higher when compared to female staff members;
- More male staff members were recruited via *mid-career* entry methods

Factor Analysis[2]

This section examines the factor structure of Japanese formal staff members employed in the UN Common System who responded to the first survey. A factor analysis with a maximum likelihood estimation was conducted and three factors were extracted. The items included in the factor analysis were: satisfaction at prior organizations (before recruitment in the UN Common System); job satisfaction in the present position (at time of survey); comparison of working hours with those in Japan; evaluation of salary; comparison of salary with that in Japan; fringe benefits; satisfaction at duty station; overall satisfaction; wish to work in the UN Common System until the mandatory retirement age and finding a job in Japan.

The following variables were considered independent and as such were excluded from factor analysis:
- years of service in the present organization;
- number of job changes;
- age when began preparing to enter the UN Common System;
- age of recruitment in the UN Common System;
- entry method;
- grade;
- number of organizations employed in (in the UN Common System);
- number of posts;
- number of countries of duty stations;
- years of service in the UN Common System;
- gender;
- age (at time of survey);
- academic qualification and
- country of duty station (developed country vs. developing country).

Table 3: Total variance explained

Factor	Initial Eigenvalues			Extraction sums of squared Loadings			Rotation sums of squared Loadings		
	Total	% of Variance	Cumulative %	Total	% of Variance	Cumulative %	Total	% of Variance	Cumulative %
1	2.313	28.912	28.912	1.987	24.838	24.838	1.897	23.713	23.713
2	1.461	18.259	47.171	0.886	11.071	35.908	0.972	12.151	35.864
3	1.343	16.783	63.954	0.664	8.301	44.209	0.668	8.346	44.209
4	0.882	11.029	74.983						
5	0.681	8.514	83.497						
6	0.638	7.974	91.471						
7	0.520	6.506	97.977						
8	0.162	2.023	100.000						

(Extraction method: Maximum Likelihood)

The cumulative variance explained by the first factor was 23.713%, the cumulative variance explained by the second factor was 35.864%, and the cumulative variance explained by the third factor was 44.209% (Table 3). The results of the factor analysis with Promax rotation[3] are shown in Table 4. The same analysis with Varimax rotation[4] produced similar results. Based on the content of the items included in each of the three factors, they were termed: (1) Career-satisfied, (2) Treatment-satisfied and (3) Dissatisfied.

Table 4: Factor analysis with Promax rotation of the staff members

	Factor		
	1	2	3
Overall satisfaction	0.999	0.007	0.033
Job satisfaction	0.823	-0.007	-0.01
Wish to work until mandatory retirement age	0.339	-0.135	0.289
Fringe benefits	-0.055	0.616	0.118
Comparison of salary (with that in Japan)	-0.01	0.607	0.069
Satisfaction at duty station	0.321	0.376	-0.212
Comparison of working hours	0.093	0.053	0.663
Satisfaction at prior organizations	0.132	-0.232	-0.314

Extraction method: Maximum likelihood.
Rotation method: Promax with Kaiser normalization.

The above results suggest that there are three types of Japanese staff members employed in the UN Common System: those who are highly satisfied with their career in the UN Common System; those who are highly satisfied with the treatment provided by the UN Common System (e.g., fringe benefits, salary); and those who feel dissatisfied with the present conditions at the work place.

The correlations among variables excluded from the factor analysis and the three factors extracted by the factor analysis are shown in Table 5.

Table 5: Correlation matrix among variables in the study

	Years of service in the present organization	Number of jobs changed	Age at initial recruitment to the UN Common System	Evaluation of Salary	Grade	Number of organizations employed	Number of posts	Years of service in the UN Common System	Gender	Age at the survey	Country of Duty Station (developed vs. developing)	Entry Method (early-career entry vs. mid-career entry)	The first Factor-Career satisfaction	The second Factor-Treatment satisfaction	The third Factor-Dissatisfaction
Years of service in the present organization	1	-0.136	-.292(**)	0.075	-.347(**)	-.171(*)	.402(**)	.822(**)	-0.075	.506(**)	-0.132	0.01	.205(**)	0.028	0.041
		0.081	0	0.333	0	0.027	0	0	0.333	0	0.085	0.899	0.007	0.719	0.594
Number of jobs changed	-0.136	1	.217(**)	-0.026	-.232(**)	0.13	-.173(*)	-.167(*)	0.073	0.008	.205(**)	-0.034	-0.069	-0.078	.321(**)
	0.081		0.005	0.744	0.004	0.099	0.041	0.032	0.349	0.919	0.008	0.665	0.376	0.322	0
Age at initial recruitment to the UN Common System	.292(**)	.217(**)	1	-.188(*)	0.132	-0.037	-.292(**)	-.388(**)	-.319(**)	.380(**)	0.12	-.312(**)	-0.132	-.184(**)	.236(**)
	0	0.005		0.015	0.102	0.639	0	0	0	0	0.122	0	0.089	0.017	0.002
Evaluation of Salary	0.075	-0.026	-.188(*)	1	-0.098	0.055	0.046	0.038	.265(**)	-.180(*)	-0.119	0.073	0.076	.666(**)	-0.107
	0.333	0.744	0.015		0.226	0.484	0.582	0.627	0	0.026	0.124	0.346	0.329	0	0.168
Grade	-.347(**)	-.232(**)	0.132	-0.098	1	-0.024	.543(**)	.486(**)	-.345(**)	.710(**)	-.177(*)	-.189(*)	.164(*)	-0.081	0.059
	0	0.004	0.102	0.226		0.772	0	0	0	0	0.027	0.018	0.041	0.317	0.466
Number of organizations employed	-.171(*)	0.13	-0.037	0.055	-0.024	1	0.152	0.026	0.097	0.015	.211(**)	0.076	0.022	-0.06	0.044
	0.027	0.099	0.639	0.484	0.772		0.071	0.736	0.212	0.851	0.006	0.327	0.78	0.443	0.572
Number of posts	-.402(**)	-.173(*)	-.292(**)	0.046	.543(**)	0.152	1	.607(**)	-0.112	.420(**)	-0.046	0.085	0.138	0.08	-0.062
	0	0.041	0	0.582	0	0.071		0	0.18	0	0.58	0.308	0.097	0.34	0.458
Years of service in the UN Common System	.822(**)	-.167(*)	-.388(**)	0.038	.486(**)	0.026	.607(**)	1	-0.047	.620(**)	-.177(*)	0.037	.255(**)	0.022	0.056
	0	0.032	0	0.627	0	0.736	0		0.543	0	0.021	0.637	0.001	0.773	0.471
Gender	-0.075	0.073	-.319(**)	.265(**)	-.345(**)	0.097	-0.112	-0.047	1	-.409(**)	-0.085	0.145	0.008	.248(**)	-0.021
	0.333	0.349	0	0	0	0.212	0.18	0.543		0	0.269	0.058	0.919	0.001	0.789
Age at the survey	.506(**)	0.008	.380(**)	-.180(*)	.710(**)	0.015	.420(**)	.620(**)	-.409(**)	1	-0.129	-.287(**)	0.129	-0.118	.231(**)
	0	0.919	0	0.026	0	0.851	0	0	0		0.111	0	0.11	0.144	0.004
Country of Duty Station (developed vs. developing)	-0.132	.205(**)	0.12	-0.119	-.177(*)	.211(**)	-0.046	-.177(*)	-0.085	-0.129	1	0.117	-0.006	-.268(**)	0.086
	0.085	0.008	0.122	0.124	0.027	0.006	0.58	0.021	0.269	0.111		0.129	0.935	0	0.267
Entry Method (early-career entry vs. mid-career entry)	0.01	-0.034	-.312(**)	0.073	-.189(*)	0.076	0.085	0.037	0.145	-.287(**)	0.117	1	0.09	0.082	-0.019
	0.899	0.665	0	0.346	0.018	0.327	0.308	0.637	0.058	0	0.129		0.242	0.286	0.803
The first factor-Career satisfaction	.205(**)	-0.069	-0.132	0.076	.164(*)	0.022	0.138	.255(**)	0.008	0.129	-0.006	0.09	1	0.136	0.024
	0.007	0.376	0.089	0.329	0.041	0.78	0.097	0.001	0.919	0.11	0.935	0.242		0.078	0.756
The second factor-Treatment satisfaction	0.028	-0.078	-.184(**)	.666(**)	-0.081	-0.06	0.08	0.022	.248(**)	-0.118	-.268(**)	0.082	0.136	1	-.173(*)
	0.719	0.322	0.017	0	0.317	0.443	0.34	0.773	0.001	0.144	0	0.286	0.078		0.024
The third factor-Dissatisfaction	0.041	.321(**)	.236(**)	-0.107	0.059	0.044	-0.062	0.056	-0.021	.231(**)	0.086	-0.019	0.024	-.173(*)	1
	0.594	0	0.002	0.168	0.466	0.572	0.458	0.471	0.789	0.004	0.267	0.803	0.756	0.024	

The results of the correlation matrix in Table 5 showed that factor one, the *career-satisfied* group, was positively correlated ($p<=.01$ and $p<=.05$) with years of service in the present organization, years of service in the UN Common System, and grade (high grade/rank). Factor two, the *treatment-satisfied* group, positively correlated with evaluation of salary and gender (i.e., female staff members), but negatively correlated with age of recruitment, and duty station (i.e., working in a developing country). Factor three, the *dissatisfied* group, was positively correlated with age of recruitment (older age), age at the time of survey (older age), and number of changing jobs prior to the UN Common System. The features of Japanese staff members based on the above results are summarized in Table 6.

Table 6: Major characteristics of formal staff members extracted via factor analysis

Career Satisfied	Treatment Satisfied	Dissatisfied
Long-term employment at the present organization	Female staff members	*Mid-career* entry Staff (middle-aged when recruited)
Long-term employment in the UN Common System	*Early-career* entry staff	*Mid-career* entry Staff (middle-aged at the time of survey)
	Evaluation of salary	
Mid-career entry staff (high grade/rank)	Staff employed in a developing country show low treatment satisfaction	Changed jobs numerous times prior to recruitment in the UN Common System

Factor Analysis by Gender

In order to identify the differences by gender, the same factor analysis was conducted separately for the two groups of male staff members and female staff members. The extraction method of the maxim likelihood with Promax rotation was used separately to identify a viable structure of factors for both categories. After four rotations for the male sample and five rotations for the female sample, three factors with slightly different items in each of them were extracted. The results of the factor analysis for the male sample are shown in Table 7 and the results for the female sample are shown in Table 8. The same analysis with Varimax rotation produced similar results.

Table 7: Factor analysis with Promax rotation of <u>male</u> formal staff members

	Factor		
	1	2	3
Satisfaction at prior organization	0.100	-0.326	-0.059
Job satisfaction	0.788	-0.003	-0.024
Comparison of working hours with those in Japan	0.095	0.987	0.107
Comparison of salary with that in Japan	0.029	0.151	0.436
Fringe benefits	0.128	0.146	0.797
Satisfaction at duty station	0.206	-0.321	0.506
Overall satisfaction	0.996	-0.016	0.019
Wish to work until mandatory retirement age	0.231	0.200	-0.224

N=78
Extraction method: Maximum likelihood.
Rotation method: Promax with Kaiser normalization. Factor analysis was repeated four times.

With regard to the male sample (n=78), the first factor of 'high career satisfaction' included items such as job satisfaction and overall satisfaction. This suggests that job and overall satisfaction of this group was very high. The second factor of 'dissatisfaction with the previous duty station' included items such as dissatisfaction with prior organizations before joining the UN Common System, an increase in working hours compared to those in Japan, and low satisfaction at duty station. The third factor of 'treatment satisfaction' included items such as salary increase compared to the salary received before entering the UN Common System, high appreciation for fringe benefits, and high satisfaction at the duty station. Job satisfaction for this group was low.

Table 8: Factor analysis with Promax rotation of <u>female</u> staff members

	Factor		
	1	2	3
Satisfaction at prior organizations	0.115	-0.230	-0.137
Job satisfaction	1.038	-0.178	-0.121
Comparison of working hours with those in Japan	0.036	0.108	-0.292
Comparison of salary with that in Japan	0.092	0.092	0.636
Fringe Benefits	0.020	0.107	0.497
Satisfaction at duty station	0.545	0.015	0.251
Overall satisfaction	0.873	0.085	0.011
Wish to work until mandatory retirement age	0.044	0.959	-0.083

N=92
Extraction method: Maximum likelihood.
Rotation method: Promax with Kaiser normalization. Factor analysis was repeated four times.

With regard to the female group (n=92), the first factor of 'high satisfaction with career and duty station' included items such as significantly high job satisfaction, high overall satisfaction, and high satisfaction at duty station. The second factor of 'dissatisfaction with the status quo,' but a wish to work long-term with the UN Common System included items such as a strong wish to work in the UN Common System until the mandatory retirement age, low job satisfaction, and low satisfaction at duty station. The third factor of 'treatment satisfaction' included items such as a comparison of salary with that in Japan, a high appreciation for fringe benefits, and low satisfaction at the duty station. Job satisfaction for this group was low.

The order of the factors of analysis of both male and female respondents was as follows: 1) career satisfaction, 2) treatment satisfaction and 3) dissatisfaction. Yet, the order of the second and third factors was reversed for both male and female categories.

The above results suggest that there are three types of staff members employed by the UN Common System: 1) those who are happy with their career and work, 2) those who are content with the treatment provided by the organization and 3) those who are dissatisfied with the present situation.

Multiple Regression Analysis

This section examines which variables influence an employees overall satisfaction using the tool of multiple regression analysis. The dependent variable is overall satisfaction. The independent variables include:
- years of service in the present organization;
- number of job changes before recruitment to the UN Common System;
- satisfaction in prior organization(s) before entering the UN Common System;
- age of recruitment to the UN Common System;
- job satisfaction in the present postition;
- comparison of working hours with those in Japan;
- evaluation of salary;
- comparison of salary with that in Japan;
- fringe benefits;
- satisfaction at duty station;
- wish to work in the UN Common System until the mandatory retirement age;
- grade;
- number of organizations employed in within the UN Common System;
- number of posts;
- gender;
- age at time of survey;
- country of duty station (developed vs. developing);
- entry method (*early-career* entry vs. *mid-career* entry).

The results of the multiple regression analysis are shown in Table 9.

Table 9: Multiple regression analysis for overall satisfaction

Model		Non-standardized coefficients		Standard coefficients	t	Significance level
		B	Standard error	β		
1	(Constant)	0.601	0.779		0.772	0.444
	Years of service in present organizations	-0.023	0.087	-0.038	-0.269	0.789
	Number of job changes	-0.063	0.055	-0.113	-1.152	0.254
	Satisfaction at prior organization	0.12	0.118	0.084	1.015	0.314
	Age at initial recruitment to the UN Common System	-0.006	0.106	-0.009	-0.052	0.959
	Job satisfaction	**0.621**	**0.09**	**0.659**	**6.876**	**0.000**
	Change of working hours	-0.009	0.067	-0.014	-0.14	0.889
	Evaluation of salary	-0.073	0.116	-0.072	-0.628	0.533
	Comparison of salary with that in Japan	-0.019	0.072	-0.027	-0.265	0.792
	Fringe benefits	0.124	0.076	0.154	1.635	0.108
	Satisfaction at Duty Station	0.081	0.091	0.086	0.892	0.376
	Wish to work in the UN Common System until the mandatory retirement age	**0.301**	**0.132**	**0.194**	**2.276**	**0.027**
	Grade	-0.028	0.073	-0.048	-0.389	0.699
	Number of organizations employed in the UN Common System	0.02	0.062	0.03	0.322	0.748
	Number of posts	0.004	0.035	0.015	0.124	0.902
	Years of service in UN Common System	-0.031	0.171	-0.047	-0.181	0.857
	Gender	0.008	0.141	0.006	0.058	0.954
	Age at the survey	0.01	0.022	0.101	0.473	0.638
	Country of duty station (developed versus developing)	0.081	0.146	0.05	0.552	0.583
	Entry Method	0.045	0.153	0.029	0.296	0.768

The results suggest that only job satisfaction and a wish to work in the UN Common System until the mandatory retirement age were significantly related with overall satisfaction ($p<.01$ and $p<.05$ respectively). As shown in Table 10, the variance explained by the variables in the study was high (adjusted $R^2=.553$). In summary, job satisfaction and employment security can be strong predictors of overall satisfaction.

Table 10: Model summary

Model	R	R^2	Adjusted R^2	Standard error of the estimate
1	.815(a)	0.665	0.553	0.472

Discussion

The purpose of this chapter was to statistically examine the characteristics of Japanese formal staff members. In section one, the results of the t-test analysis suggested that more male staff members were recruited via a *mid-career* entry method. This is because the age of recruitment to the UN Common System, age at the time of survey, and grade of the male staff members were higher than those of the female staff members. In addition, female staff members showed a stronger appreciation for the treatment provided by the UN Common System. In section two, the factor analysis identified three types of Japanese staff members employed by the UN Common System namely: (1) the *career-satisfied* group, which included those who are satisfied with their work, have high overall satisfaction, and who wish to work for the UN Common System until the mandatory retirement age; (2) the *treatment-satisfied* group, which included those who appreciate and enjoy the treatment provided by the UN Common System (e.g., salary and fringe benefits) to a large extent; (3) those *dissatisfied*, which included those who were dissatisfied with their organization(s) before entering the UN Common System and who had complaints against the long working hours at their workplace at the time of the survey. The correlation analysis indicated that the *career-satisfied* group is engaged in long-term employment at the present organization, have worked long-term in the UN Common System, and have a high rank within the present organization. The features of the *treatment-satisfied* group are that they are female, were recruited via an *early-career* entry method, and work at a duty station in a developed country. The features of the *dissatisfied* group are that they were older at the time of recruitment, they were older at the time of survey, and they had changed jobs many times prior to starting to work for the UN Common System.

In the third section, the results of the factor analysis by gender indicated that the level of satisfaction of female staff members in the *career-satisfied* group is higher than that of male staff members. With regard to the *dissatisfied* group, although the satisfaction of female staff members is low, they still wish to continue to work in the UN Common System until the mandatory retirement age. With regard to the *treatment-satisfied* group, no significant differences were found between male staff members and female staff members.

In the fourth section, the results of the multiple regression analysis indicated that job satisfaction and employment security are the only predictors of overall satisfaction.

In order to increase the understanding of the findings of the empirical results, a qualitative study was utilized as a complementary research strategy. Interviews with 23 Japanese staff members and one non-Japanese staff member employed by the UN Common System were conducted. The results of the qualitative study are shown in Chapter 6 and summaries of the interviews are provided in Appendix 1. You can find that Case G in Appendix 1, is representative of an employee who exhibits characteristics of being from the *career-satisfied* group. Case J represents an employee of the *treatment-satisfied* group.

In addition, the findings of the empirical analysis provide support for the findings discussed in Chapter 3. According to the t-test results, gender does have an influence on the entry method. More specifically, more male staff members are recruited via the *mid-career* entry method compared to female staff members.

The results of the factor analysis indicated that gender does have an effect on the determinants of satisfaction. More specifically, job satisfaction was indicated as the only determinant of career satisfaction for male staff members. On the contrary, satisfaction at the duty station in addition to the job satisfaction, were both indicated as determinants of career satisfaction for female staff members. These results are summarized in Table 11.

Table 11: Satisfaction determinants by gender

	Male formal staff Members	Female formal staff members
Components of satisfaction	Job satisfaction only	Job satisfaction and satisfaction at Duty Station

The three groups of Japanese staff members identified by the factor analysis were further examined using Hertzberg's motivation-hygiene theory. According to Hertzberg (1966) there are factors in the work place that result in job satisfaction and factors that cause job dissatisfaction. Job satisfaction and dissatisfaction were said to act independently of each other.

Based on Hertzberg's theory, career-satisfaction is classified as a motivation factor and treatment-satisfaction is classified as a hygiene factor. Dissatisfaction is also seen as a hygiene factor. The relationship between career satisfaction (motivation factor) and treatment satisfaction (hygiene factor) is shown in Table 12.

Table 12: The relationship between career satisfaction and treatment satisfaction

		Career satisfaction (Motivation Factor)	
		High	**Low**
Treatment Satisfaction (Hygiene Factor)	**High**	Promotion and/or continue to work	Continue to work at the same place
	Low	Exit to other workplace or continue to work at the same place	Continue to work at the same place or forced exit (end of contract)

The cross tabulation between these two factors indicates that those who have high career-satisfaction and high treatment-satisfaction tend to advance to higher ranks and/or continue to work in the same place. Those who have high career-satisfaction and low treatment-satisfaction, try to move to another organization within or outside the UN Common System. Those who have low career satisfaction and high treatment satisfaction tend to continue to work in the same working place. Those who have low career satisfaction and low treatment satisfaction tend to continue to work in the same place or they are forced to exit the UN Common System at the end of their contract.

To summarize, it is not possible to motivate staff members only by increasing treatment satisfaction (hygiene factor). Therefore, if organizations within the UN Common System want to motivate their staff members, it is important to increase the career satisfaction of their staff members (motivation factor).

Main Findings and Recommendations

Below are the main findings from this chapter and a list of recommendations for Japanese companies to follow to improve their HRM practices.

1. Female staff members tended to come from a generalist background, while male staff members tended to specialize in hard social sciences.
Recommendation:
- ✓ Japanese companies should recruit more female staff with specialist backgrounds.

2. In the *career-satisfied* group, female staff members had higher levels of satisfaction than male staff members.
Recommendation:
- ✓ Japanese companies should create a long-term strategy for staff professional development, particularly for female staff members.

3. Overall satisfaction comes from job satisfaction and employment security.
Recommendation:
- ✓ Japanese companies should focus on their employees' job satisfaction and reevaluate the importance of employment security.

4. There is a difference between males and females when looking at the determinants of satisfaction. Male staff members only evaluate job satisfaction, while female staff members evaluate job satisfaction and satisfaction at duty station.
Recommendation:
- ✓ Japanese companies should send more female staff members on overseas assignments, as they are able to adapt to new conditions and find a way to enjoy their life in different countries.

5. In the UN the salary is not so attractive, yet fringe benefits such as education grants and pensions are attractive. These are hygiene factors not motivation factors.

Recommendation:
- ✓ Japanese companies should develop programs to improve motivation factors i.e. job satisfaction, instead of hygiene factors such as fringe benefits, etc.

Notes:
1. The t-test assesses whether the means of two groups are statistically different from each other. In this study, the means of male Japanese staff members (respondents) and female Japanese staff members (respondents) were compared.
2. Factor analysis is a statistical method used to describe variability among observed, correlated variables in terms of a potentially lower number of unobserved variables called factor.
3. Promax Rotation is an alternative rotation method that is often used for large datasets. More details about Factor Analysis can be found in Thompson, B. (2004). Exploratory and confirmatory factor analysis: Understanding concepts and applications. Washington, DC: American Psychological Association.
4. Varimax Rotation is an orthogonal rotation of the factor axes. It is used to identify each variable with a single factor. More details about Factor Analysis can be found in Thompson, B. (2004). Exploratory and confirmatory factor analysis: Understanding concepts and applications. Washington, DC: American Psychological Association.
5. Multiple regression analysis indicates the relationship between several independent or predictor variables and a dependent variable. In this study, the dependent variable is 'overall satisfaction'.

Chapter 5

The Second Survey Conducted on the Careers of International Civil Servants — Comparative Analysis between Japanese Formal Staff Members and Non-Japanese Staff Members

International Organizations, including the United Nations, consist of staff members from more than 190 member states. Japanese staff members occupy only 3% of such UN Common System employees. Since the first survey was conducted in 2003, the author has been trying to draw comparisons between these Japanese formal staff members and non-Japanese formal staff members. When the author made a presentation to the researchers at JIL, currently the *Japan Institute for Labor Policy and Training* (JILPT) in December 2006, the author received the suggestion from one researcher that in order to draw accurate comparisons, a survey should be conducted on all the international civil servants.

Following this advice, the first questionnaires used in the 2003 survey were reviewed, restructured, and the second survey, with revised question items, was conducted on both Japanese and non-Japanese staff members at the end of May 2007. In this chapter a comparative analysis will be made on the differences and similarities of the two groups.

The first section of this chapter defines the target group and methods of data collection. The second section explains the relationship between the first and the second surveys and the third section introduces the findings of the comparative analysis. The fourth section provides a discussion and the fifth section lists the main findings and recommendations.

Target Group and Data Collection

The target group of this research was formal staff members employed by the

UN Common System and who were on contracts of more than one year (as in Chapters 3 and 4). In the first survey, questionnaires were sent to all formal staff members working in the UN Common System, the World Bank and the World Trade Organization, but in the second survey, respondents were restricted to the formal staff members who worked in the UN Common System. In the first survey, 17% of responses were from the World Bank and the World Trade Organization and their data were included to conduct a more accurate factor analyses. However, the second survey was conducted to explore career development paths of those who work in the UN Common System. As a result, the second questionnaires were not sent to staff members who work in the World Bank and the World Trade Organization. It must be pointed out that there is a discrepancy between the respondents of the first survey and those of the second survey.

Two additional problems arose before conducting the second survey via email. The first was the difficulty in obtaining personal information of Japanese International Civil Servants and the second was the difficulty of approaching non-Japanese staff members.

The first survey was conducted via email on July 10th 2003. In Japan, around the same time, a movement to protect an individual's personal information had become heated. On May 23rd 2003, a personal information protection law was formed and in April 2005 it was enforced. When the first survey was conducted in 2003, with cooperation from the respective organizations concerned, it was possible to obtain personal information about Japanese staff members. However, by 2007 when the second survey was conducted, the most up-to–date personnel data was extremely difficult to acquire because of the *Private Information Protection Law*. As a result of this, the same respondents as those in the first survey were asked to cooperate with the second survey. The questionnaire was sent to them via email. In order to increase the number of responses, the cover letter of the questionnaire asked respondents to assist in obtaining additional members' cooperation for the project. In addition to this, a copy of the questionnaire was displayed on the author's homepage to make the questionnaires easily accessible to download and complete.

As for non-Japanese staff members, the UNDP JPO Service Centre in Copenhagen, Denmark helped the author get in touch with possible respondents. This centre controls all the personnel information of the present UNDP staff and ex-JPO members around the world. About 50% of the Associate Experts (AE) or JPO are currently working either in an international organization or in the field of international cooperation. The JPO service Centre offered to send the second questionnaire out through their network. The content of the second survey was largely the same, but as a result of feedback from respondents in the first survey, the question items in the second survey were reduced from 57 to 40 and new question items about actual annual income and the number of subordinates were added (Appendix 3, Q1.13 and Q1.14).

The Relationship between the First Survey and the Second Survey

Almost 30% of the emails that had been sent had not been received. This was due to people retiring from the organization, being transferred or for other reasons. Additionally, some Japanese staff members had become cautious of disclosing personal information and so were reluctant to complete the survey.

Only ninety responses from the Japanese staff members were received. The responses differed little from those received in the first survey. The main difference observed was that some of the staff members' duty stations were different from the first survey. Additionally, only twenty-nine responses were received from non-Japanese members. Yet, since no previous comparative research had been conducted on the professional development of Japanese and non-Japanese staff members, a comparative analysis based on the second survey was still considered meaningful.

Problems Encountered during Data Collection

Table 1 shows the basic demographic features of the Japanese and non-Japanese staff that were employed in the UN Common System. There were some differences between the two groups. Fifty percent of the 29 non-Japanese staff member respondents were employed by the UNDP. Therefore, their responses were highly influenced by the characteristics of their organization. In the case of Japanese staff members, in the first survey, 15% of the respondents worked in the

UN Secretariat, whereas in the second survey, this percentage rose to 30%. Additionally, there were only two out of 61 Japanese respondents employed by the UNDP. As a result, the ability to conduct a truly fair comparison is affected by the above disparity. From Table 1, however, looking at their bio-data, there are no outstanding differences between Japanese and non-Japanese staff members.

Table 1: Responses to the second survey

		Japanese staff members	Non-Japanese staff members	Total
Number		61	29	90
Gender	Male	28 (46%)	18 (62%)	46 (51%)
	Female	32 (52%)	11 (38%)	43 (48%)
	No response	2 (2%)	0 (0%)	2 (1%)
Average Age		44	41	43
Average Grade		P-3 Step IX	P-4 Step VI	P-4 Step IV
Married		5 (60%)	20 (69%)	57 (63%)
Highest Academic Level	Ph.D.*	6 (10%)	7 (24%)	13 (14%)
	MA/MSc	43 (70%)	30 (69%)	63 (70%)
	BA/MSc	7 (11%)	1 (3%)	8 (9%)
	Others	5 (8%)	1 (3%)	4 (4%)
Number of organizations employed in the UN Common System		1.6	2	1.8
Number of countries of duty station		2.1	3.3	2.4
Years of service in the UN Common System		12	11	12
Subordinates in professional category		5	6	5
Subordinates in general service category		6	9	7
Years of work experience prior to recruitment in the UN Common System		6	4	5
Number of organizations prior to recruitment in the UN Common System		1.5	1.7	1.6
Average age at time of survey		32	31	32
Annual base salary, including tax		US$100,816	US$106,898	US$103,549

* includes ABD

Overview — Comparison between Japanese Formal Staff Members and Non-Japanese Staff Members

In this section, the general characteristics of the two groups, Japanese formal staff members and non-Japanese staff members are presented. Further details of these can be seen in Appendix 3.

Age

The average age of Japanese staff members was 44, while for non-Japanese staff members it was 41, at the time of survey. For both groups, results showed that the older a person is, the more satisfied he/she is with his/her employment within the UN Common System.

Nationality

Only three respondents out of twenty-nine non-Japanese staff members were from developing countries; representing 10%. The data further shows that European staff members made up 78% of these respondents, signaling that the non-Japanese staff members in the second survey were mainly from developed countries.

Country of Duty Stations

Within the UN Common System, duty stations are classified into developed countries (member countries of the OECD) and developing countries (other countries which are non-members of the OECD). Thirty-four percent of Japanese staff members were based in developing country duty stations while 66% were in developed countries (as shown in Table 2). On the other hand, 69% of non-Japanese staff members worked in developing countries while 31% worked in developed countries.

Table 2: Country of duty stations

Country of duty stations	Japanese Staff Members	Non-Japanese Staff Members
Developed Countries	40 (66%)	9 (31%)
Developing Countries	21 (34%)	20 (69%)
Total	61 (100%)	29 (100%)

Number of Countries of their Duty Stations

Japanese staff members have worked in an average of 2.1 countries, whereas non-Japanese members have worked in 3.3 countries. In the case of non-Japanese staff members, results showed that the greater the number of duty stations experienced, the more satisfaction they had with their job, although their level of satisfaction was not shown in Appendix 3.

Years of Service

The average number of years of service (in the UN Common System) for the two groups was almost the same; Japanese formal staff members had, on average, 12 years of service and non-Japanese staff members 11 years. As for their levels of satisfaction, it was shown that the greater the number of years of service, the more satisfied both groups were with their employment.

Academic Qualifications

The biggest difference observed between the two groups was seen in their academic qualifications. Only ten per cent of Japanese formal staff members were either PhD holders or who were considered all but dissertation (ABD) while 25% of non-Japanese staff members had obtained some form of doctorate.

Specialized Field of Study at the Last Degree Held

As shown in Table 3, with regard to the specialized field of the last degree held, 23% of Japanese respondents had studied international relations. The remaining Japanese staff members engaged in studies in a variety of subjects, such as legal affairs, science, economics, commerce, MBA/MPA, medicine, including public health, etc. It could be said that the reason why a particularly high percentage of Japanese studied international relations is that a greater number of staff members from the UN Secretariat responded to the second survey. On the other hand, the specialized fields at the last degree held of non-Japanese staff members were concentrated in three fields: economics 24%, international relations 17% and commerce, MPA, MBA, 14%.

Table 3: Specialized field of study of last degree held

	Japanese Staff Members	Non-Japanese Staff Members
International Relations	14 (23%)	5 (17%)
Legal Affairs	6 (10%)	1 (3%)
Science	6 (10%)	2 (7%)
Economics	4 (7%)	7 (24%)
Commerce/MBA/MPA	4 (7%)	4 (14%)
Medicine/Public Health	4 (7%)	3 (10%)
Other	23 (38%)	7 (24%)
Total	61 (100%)	29 (100%)

Organizations

Japanese respondents were employed by 21 organizations of the UN Common System and 30% worked in the UN Secretariat. Non-Japanese respondents worked in eight organizations and 50% worked in the UNDP.

Grade

The average grade of Japanese staff members was P-3, Step IX, while that of Non-Japanese was P-4, Step VI, as shown in Table 1. Results showed that the higher the grade was, the more satisfaction both non-Japanese and Japanese staff members felt.

Salary

In the second survey, with regard to salary, respondents were only asked about their grade and step, and so their annual base salaries after tax were calculated based on this information (as can be seen in Table 9 of Chapter 2). The average base salary for Japanese staff was approximately US$100,816 whereas that of non-Japanese staff was US$106,898. As discussed in Chapter 2, about 30% of the base salary, including tax is called staff assessment and this amount is considered as the tax that one would pay to one's country if they worked in their home country. Therefore, actual annual salary can be calculated as follows:

actual base salary including tax x 0.7 + post adjustment + education grant
(maximum amount per child, outside the USA is approximately US$15,668 per year)
(See UN Education Grant for further details and a downloadable table)

As an example, take a married staff member as of January 2012, who is P-4, Step III with two children working in New York, his annual salary after tax is US$116,436.

In the case of a staff member at the same grade working in Geneva it would be US$141,834. In Bangkok the salary would be US$104,616. If a staff member has a child under 22 years old, the maximum annual amount of education grant, outside the USA is US$15,668 per person and in the USA US$34,895 per person would be added. The salary for those working in the UN Common System is not considered to be low, unless compared with those who work in banks or financial organizations.

We may well say that for those who have school-age children, the salary received from working in the UN Common System is very attractive.

Subordinates

As can be seen in Table 4, on average, Japanese staff members had five subordinates in the professional category, whereas non-Japanese members had six. No significant differences were observed with regard to this. The average number of subordinates in the general service category was six for Japanese and nine for non-Japanese. It was observed that non-Japanese staff members had more general service subordinates in duty stations in developing countries.

Table 4: Number of subordinates in professional category and general service category

	Japanese Staff Members	Non-Japanese Staff Members
Professional and Higher Categories	5	6
General Service Category	6	9

Field of Specialization and Occupational Field

Japanese formal staff members' occupational fields were fairly scattered at the time of survey, and included economic/social development, management and HR, project management, humanitarian assistance, etc. The occupational fields of non-Japanese members were mostly focused in two areas: economic/social development and project management. The difference can be explained by looking at which organizations within the UN Common System they work for. Japanese members worked in 21 different organizations whereas half of non-Japanese members worked within the UNDP.

Organization Prior to Recruitment in the UN Common System

As seen in Table 5, thirty-one percent of Japanese staff members had worked in private enterprises, 23% in government/governmental organizations, and 20% in universities or research institutes before joining the UN Common System. On the other hand, in the case of non-Japanese staff members, 45% were from government or ODA related agencies and 17% had previously worked at a university or research institute. Those who had been working in a private company occupied only 10 %, which was only a third of Japanese staff members.

Table 5: Organizations prior to recruitment in the UN

	Japanese Staff Members	Non-Japanese Staff Members
Private Company/companies	19 (31%)	3 (10%)
Government/ODA Agency	14 (23%)	13 (45%)
University/Research Institute(s)	12 (20%)	5 (17%)
NPO/NGOs	7 (11%)	4 (14%)
Other	9 (15%)	4 (14%)
Total	61 (100%)	29 (100%)

Age on Becoming a Formal Staff Member

When looking at the age when employees became formal staff members, we can see that both groups share similar characteristics. Japanese staff members tended to become a formal staff member at the age of 32, while non-Japanese staff members at the age of 31.

Entry Routes

Approximately 80% of Japanese staff members entered the UN Common System through the following routes: the JPO scheme (38%), YPP exam (former UN Competitive Exam) (21%), or by applying for a vacancy announcement (18%). On the other hand, the majority of non-Japanese staff members entered either through the JPO scheme (62%), or by applying for vacancy announcements (28%). Half of the non-Japanese respondents worked in the UNDP and this is where many of the staff members become formal members through the JPO scheme as shown in Table 6. Japanese respondents who entered the UN Secretariat through the YPP exam occupied 21%. Only one non-Japanese staff member (3%) joined the UN Common System through the same exam.

Table 6: Entry routes to the UN Common System

	Japanese Staff Members	Non-Japanese Staff Members
Vacancy Announcements	11 (18%)	8 (28%)
JPO scheme	23 (38%)	18 (62%)
YPP exam*	13 (21%)	1 (3%)
Other	14 (23%)	2 (7%)
Total	61 (100%)	29 (100%)

* YPP is the former UN Competitive Exam

Motivations for Working in the UN Common System

Staff members of both groups applied for a UN Common System post with the desire to help developing countries as shown in Table 7. They also both wanted an opportunity to make use of their professional skills. The motivation to contribute to world peace was ranked third among Japanese staff members. The same motivation was ranked fifth among non-Japanese members. Both Japanese and non-Japanese staff members wish to help developing countries or refugees and to utilize their specialized skills.

Table 7: Motivations for working in the UN Common System

	Japanese Staff Members	Non-Japanese Staff Members
First Place	To help people of developing countries/refugees	To help people of developing countries/refugees
Second Place	To utilize special skills	To utilize special skills
Third Place	To contribute to world peace	To live overseas
Forth Place	To work with people of different cultural background	To work with people of different cultural background
Fifth Place	To live overseas	To contribute to world peace

Preparation

As shown in Table 8, in preparation for entering the UN Common System, some Japanese staff members felt it important to obtain an MA at graduate school (25%). On the other hand, 23% of Japanese made no specific preparation. Twenty-eight percent of non-Japanese staff members gained some relevant work experience in a position related to the field of International Organizations, while 24% of non-Japanese made no such specific preparations.

Table 8: Preparation for working in the UN Common System

	Japanese Staff Members	Non-Japanese Staff Members
Studied abroad	6 (10%)	5 (17%)
Mastered English and/or other UN working/official languages	2 (3%)	1 (3%)
Post-graduate degree	15 (25%)	0 (0%)
Relevant Work Experience	5 (8%)	8 (28%)
Internship	3 (5%)	3 (10%)
No preparation	14 (23%)	7 (24%)
Other	16 (26%)	5 (17%)
Total	61 (100%)	29 (100%)

Utilization of Professional Skills

To the question as to what extent the staff members felt their professional, specialized skills were utilized in their workplace, 75% of Japanese staff and 69% of non-Japanese staff answered they felt their skills were 'very highly' or 'somewhat highly' utilized (Table 9).

Table 9: Degree of using specialized skills in the workplace

	Japanese Staff Members	Non-Japanese Staff Members
Very high	22 (36%)	9 (31%)
Somewhat high	24 (39%)	11 (38%)
Average	10 (16%)	6 (21%)
Somewhat low	2 (3%)	3 (10%)
Very low	2 (3%)	0 (0%)
No answer	1 (2%)	0 (0%)
Total	61 (100%)	29 (100%)

Professional Development

Thirty-nine percent of Japanese staff members tried to develop their professional skills by attending workshops and/or training programs inside and outside of their workplace, while 27% attended a language course. Forty-four percent of non-Japanese staff members attended workshops and/or training programs and 22% attended a language course. There is no significant difference between Japanese and non-Japanese in terms of such professional development (Appendix 3, Q3.3).

Working Hours

Regarding working hours, 39% of Japanese staff members answered that they were 'very satisfied' and 30% of them 'somewhat satisfied' with the amount of hours they worked (Table 10). On the other hand, 21% of non-Japanese members were 'very satisfied' and 38% 'somewhat satisfied'. Therefore, as far as working hours are concerned, Japanese staff members were more satisfied than non-Japanese staff members.

Table 10: Satisfaction of working hours

	Japanese Staff Members	Non-Japanese Staff Members
Very satisfied	24 (39%)	6 (21%)
Somewhat satisfied	18 (30%)	11 (38%)
Average	12 (20%)	8 (28%)
Somewhat unsatisfied	2 (3%)	3 (10%)
Very satisfied	4 (7%)	1 (3%)
No answer	1 (2%)	0 (0%)
Total	61 (100)	29 (100%)

Fringe Benefits

Both groups showed a high level of satisfaction with the fringe benefits provided within the UN Common System. Forty-eight percent of non-Japanese staff members and 31% of Japanese responded that they were 'very satisfied'.

Overall Satisfaction

As for Japanese staff members, over 80% of respondents were either 'very satisfied' or 'somewhat satisfied' (very satisfied 36%, somewhat satisfied 48%). In the case of non-Japanese staff members, the results were slightly higher with 86% feeling 'satisfied' (very satisfied 41%, somewhat satisfied 45%) as can be seen in Table 11.

Table 11: Overall satisfaction

	Japanese Staff Members	Non-Japanese Staff Members
Very satisfied	22 (36%)	12 (41%)
Somewhat satisfied	29 (48%)	13 (45%)
Average	7 (11%)	3 (10%)
Somewhat unsatisfied	2 (3%)	1 (3%)
Very unsatisfied	1 (2%)	0 (0%)
Total	61 (100%)	29 (100%)

Important Factors to Consider When Working for the UN Common System

This was a multiple–response question. For Japanese staff members, the following were deemed important factors (in order of importance): the ability to make personal relations; adaptability/flexibility; specialized field and language competence. On the other hand, non-Japanese staff members answered that only the following two factors were most important: adaptability/flexibility and the ability to make personal relations (Appendix 3, Q3.10).

Difficulties at Duty Station

As for difficulties encountered when adapting to life at duty stations, both groups mentioned safety and access to reliable medical facilities as concerns. Both such concerns are not directly connected to the content of work. Only a small number of respondents from both groups cited the specific content of their work or relationships with colleagues as a difficulty. This is because in the UN Common System, the major working language is English (or French). Therefore, wherever staff members are assigned, language is not an issue (Appendix 3, Q3.11).

Current Concerns: Job-related and Outside the Workplace

Regarding the respondents' job-related concerns at the time of the survey (Table 12), although 41% of Japanese formal staff members answered that they had no particular concerns, 25% of them answered that promotion was a concern for them. With regard to non-Japanese staff members, 28% of them answered renewal of contract as a concern, similarly, 28% answered promotion and 24% answered nothing in particular. As mentioned previously, 50% of non-Japanese staff members worked in the UNDP and they were under a fixed-term contract.

Table 12: Most pressing job related concerns

	Japanese Staff Members	Non-Japanese Staff Members
Renewal of contract	4 (7%)	8 (28%)
Promotion	15 (25%)	8 (28%)
Getting a job outside the UN Common System	3 (5%)	1 (3%)
No pressing concerns	25 (41%)	7 (24%)
Others	11 (18%)	3 (10%)
No answer	3 (5%)	2 (7%)
Total	61 (100%)	29 (100%)

Regarding current concerns outside the workplace, a more significant difference was observed between the two groups, as shown in Table 13. Thirty-one percent of the Japanese staff members answered that taking care of parents or aging parents was their primary concern. Eighteen percent answered education of their children citing that if they worked overseas, their offspring may not speak their mother tongue and wouldn't have opportunities to nurture their national identity. Respondents who cited these as concerns were, at the time of the survey, considering returning to Japan. Conversely, in the case of non-Japanese staff members, 34% stated concerns over being separated from close family members who lived in a different country. Secondly, 28% they were concerned about educating their children. There were no non-Japanese staff members who expressed a pressing concern for the care of parents or aging parents. This discrepancy will be discussed further in the discussion and recommendation section of this chapter.

Table 13: Most pressing concerns outside the workplace

	Japanese Staff Members	Non-Japanese Staff Members
Education of children	11 (18%)	8 (28%)
Care of parents/aging parents	19 (31%)	0 (0%)
Country to live in after retirement	2 (3%)	0 (0%)
Activities after retirement	3 (5%)	0 (0%)
Separation from close family members who live in a different country	5 (8%)	10 (34%)
Current living condition	3 (5%)	3 (10%)
Personal health	1 (2%)	0 (0%)
No pressing concerns	12 (20%)	5 (17%)
Other	3 (5%)	3 (10%)
No answer	2 (3%)	0 (0%)
Total	61 (100%)	29 (100%)

Continuing to Work in the UN Common System until the Mandatory Retirement Age

Seventy percent of both groups were considering working in the UN Common System until they reach the mandatory retirement age, while slightly less than 20% showed more doubt about their intention to work until that time (Appendix 3, Q3.14).

Finding a Job Outside the UN Common System

Although eighty-four percent of Japanese and 86% of non-Japanese formal staff members showed job satisfaction in the UN Common System (Table 11), more than a third of these staff members (36% of Japanese and 38% of non-Japanese) had considered finding a job outside the UN Common System (Table 14).

Table 14: Respondents' thoughts on resigning and finding a job outside the UN Common System

	Japanese Staff Members	Non-Japanese Staff Members
Considered	22 (36%)	11 (38%)
Considered, but not seriously	21 (34%)	10 (34%)
Don't know	2 (3%)	0 (0%)
I doubt I will resign	3 (5%)	3 (10%)
I have definitely not considered	13 (21%)	5 (17%)
Total	61 (100%)	29 (100%)

Discussion

The first section of this chapter defined the target groups and explained the method of data collection used in the second survey. The second section explained the consistent relationship between the first and the second surveys. The third section explained the problems encountered in the analysis of Japanese formal staff members and Non-Japanese formal staff members employed by the UN Common System, due to the difference in the number of respondents. A comparison was then made between Japanese formal staff members and non-Japanese staff members; their differences and characteristics were compared across 27 different items.

When we examined the comparisons between Japanese and non-Japanese staff members, we could see that their biographical data were almost the same; both groups started working as formal staff members at a similar age (32 for Japanese and 31 for non-Japanese); their years of service in the UN Common System were almost the same and their average age of respondents was also similar (44 for Japanese and 41 for non-Japanese). However, if we look in more detail, there are more significant differences.

The first main difference was that two-thirds of Japanese formal staff members work predominately in developed countries. The proportion of Japanese staff members who worked in developed countries was high in both the first and second surveys. Only a third of Japanese staff members worked in developing countries. On the other hand, a greater proportion, two thirds, of non-Japanese staff members worked in developing countries.

The second difference was that non-Japanese staff members took more positive steps in forging their own career. They were on average three years younger than Japanese staff members, with an average rank of P-4 Step VI, whereas Japanese staff members' average rank was P-3, Step IX. In the UN Common System, promotion is generally achieved by applying and being accepted to a higher post in a different duty station. Coincidently, the numbers of countries the staff members have worked in also varied between the two groups. On average, non-Japanese staff members had worked in 3.3 countries, whereas Japanese staff members had worked in 2.1 countries. The basic annual salary is also different. Non-Japanese staff members received US$6000 more than Japanese formal staff.

The third difference was observed in the staff members' career paths, prior to entering the UN Common System. Non-Japanese staff members started preparation for work in the UN Common System from an early age. If we compare the organizations respondents had worked in prior to their recruitment to the UN Common System, 31% of Japanese staff members worked in private enterprises, 23% for the government or ODA related organizations and 20% worked at universities or research institutes. As the highest percentage of Japanese formal staff members had private sector experience, this means that they started preparation for work in the UN Common System in the latter half of their twenties or at the beginning of their thirties. Conversely, in the case of non-Japanese staff members, 45% worked in government or ODA related organizations, 17% in universities and research institutes, and only 10% had come from private enterprises. As a result, about half of the staff members started working for in the UN Common System after they had had relevant work experience in the field of international development at ODA-related organizations.

You can find two typical case examples, Case X. from Finland and Case B. from Japan in Appendix 1.

Case B developed his field of specialization while he worked in a private enterprise and this coincided with the field advertised by the UN Secretariat. On the contrary, Case X had a dream to pursue an international profession, and in the course of his preparation, he found a job in an International Organization and thus fulfilled his dream. When the careers paths of Case B and Case X are compared as shown in Appendix 1, it could be argued that non-Japanese, Case X, pursued his career path more positively.

Returning to the original argument, let us compare the respondents' last academic qualification for both groups. In the case of non-Japanese, 25%, were PhD holders or ABDs. In the case of Japanese staff members, according to the results of the second survey, only 14% held a doctoral qualification. This figure may reflect the fact that members of the World Bank were not included. In the first survey, the percentage of those who possessed a PhD (or who were ABD) was 26%, nearly the same as that of non-Japanese).

As for the field of study, studies in international relations were more common among Japanese staff members and as mentioned previously, the reason for this appears to be that many of those Japanese respondents work in the UN Secretariat. Non-Japanese staff mainly held qualifications in economics, international relations and business administration. Organizations that support developing countries, especially the UNDP, require specialists in more specific fields such as economics.

Regarding the questions about preparation for work in the UN Common System, one third of non-Japanese staff members mentioned they had obtained 'work experience in the relevant field'. On the other hand, a quarter of Japanese staff members answered that it was important to 'study at graduate school.' From the results above we might conclude that non-Japanese staff members started preparation at an earlier stage than Japanese staff members.

The fourth difference observed was that Japanese and non-Japanese had different concerns outside of the workplace. A third of Japanese staff members selected taking care of aging parents as a primary concern. A third of non-Japanese members pointed out separation from family members who live in different counties as a concern. No non-Japanese staff member cited the need to take care of elderly parents as a pressing concern. In Europe, individualism is a fundamental part of society and social security systems have been developed so that children do not need to worry about taking care of their aging parents in the same manner as people do in Japan.

The fifth difference was seen when respondents were asked about whether they had contemplated changing jobs to a position outside of the UN Common System. According to Table 11, more than 80% of staff members of both groups were satisfied with both work and life. However, about 40% of both groups answered that they had once thought of changing their workplace. In the first survey aimed only at Japanese staff members, their response on changing their workplace was the same. The main motivation was that they wished to utilize their ability and knowledge in a different work environment. Many Japanese staff members have left the UN Common System and have pursued careers in higher education. The author is one of them. Both Japanese and non-Japanese staff members are not overly concerned about working in the UN Common System but they are prepared to change their job if there is an opportunity to make better use of their ability.

Main Findings and Recommendations

Below are the main findings from this chapter and a list of recommendations for Japanese companies to follow to improve their HRM practices.

1. Two-thirds of Japanese formal staff members work in developed countries.
Recommendation:
- ✓ Japanese companies should develop attractive packages to encourage staff members to work in developing countries.

2. Non-Japanese staff members took more positive steps in forging a career than Japanese staff members.
Recommendation:
- ✓ Japanese higher education institutions should develop better career development programs and guidance at an earlier stage in a student's career.

3. Generally, non-Japanese staff members have a higher level of academic qualifications than Japanese staff members.
Recommendation:
- ✓ In order to compete globally, Japanese companies should develop an HRM strategy which allows the recruitment of graduates with advanced level academic qualifications (such as PhDs) in more specialized fields.

4. Japanese graduates tended to study international relations to work for the UN Common System, while non-Japanese staff members studied subjects such as economics and business administration.
Recommendation:
- ✓ To work successfully on the global stage, individuals should focus their studies in a more specialized field such as economics or business administration.

5. Japanese and non-Japanese staff members had different concerns outside the workplace.
Recommendation:
- ✓ Japanese companies should try to establish company-wide systems that provide support for the care of elderly parents whose children are working overseas. Creating such policies and support networks can allow Japanese staff working overseas to work with a clearer mind.

6. Staff members in the UN Common System are prepared to change their job if there is an opportunity for them to make better use of their abilities outside.
Recommendation:
- ✓ Japanese companies should encourage greater job mobility to ensure that people with sufficient qualifications are used to the best of their ability in jobs that stimulate them.

7. Non-Japanese staff members make decisions about their careers earlier than Japanese staff members. They make and implement plans to meet their goals.
Recommendation:
- ✓ Japanese companies should select candidates for overseas assignments at an earlier stage in their career in order for them to develop the necessary skills such as language skills and intercultural communication skills.

Chapter 6

Job Satisfaction by Occupational Field Results from Interviews with Japanese Formal Staff Members Employed by the UN Common System

In the previous chapters the results of a quantitative analysis of surveys carried out on Japanese formal staff members employed by the UN Common System were presented. Through the course of the research, it was thought that in order to gain a richer and deeper understanding of these staff members, a mixed-methods approach should be taken. Thus, this chapter presents the results of the qualitative interviews with Japanese formal staff members working in the UN Common System. Interviews were undertaken while the author took a sabbatical and visited The Graduate Center, City University of New York, USA, between April and August 2008. Similar interviews were also carried out in Geneva and Rome in August of the same year.

The major theme of this chapter is the relationship between job satisfaction and the staff members' occupational fields. This chapter consists of eight sections. The first section clarifies the purpose of the research explaining how interviews with the target groups were prepared and executed. The second section provides an overview of the interview respondents and a brief picture of the interview survey. The third section examines the respondents' experiences of studying abroad, while the fourth section discusses the relationship between job satisfaction and their occupational fields. The fifth section examines the possibility of respondents being able to change their specialized field. The sixth section tries to deepen understanding of the career anchors which Japanese formal staff members have while working in a multi-cultural environment. The seventh section lists the main findings and recommendations.

Purpose of Interviews and Methods

A description and analysis of the first and second surveys that were conducted by email was discussed in Chapter 3, Chapter 4 and Chapter 5. Through the course of conducting these surveys it was thought that a quantitative analysis alone would not provide a deep enough understanding of the complexities of the career development of Japanese formal staff members employed by the UN Common System. In order to provide a richer account of these staff members and their experiences, face-to-face interviews were deemed essential. However, as duty stations where target groups of Japanese formal staff members were working were primarily outside Japan, the only way to conduct interviews with them in Japan was if returned to Japan on home leave. After much thought, the author decided to apply to take a sabbatical abroad for a period of five months in order to carry out extensive research. During this period, the author worked from a base in the Graduate Center of the City University of New York, as it was a convenient and neutral place to meet with UN Common System staff. In December 2007, when the respondent were notified of the results of the second survey, the author asked them if they would be interested in cooperating in face-to-face interviews.

The hypothesis of this section of the research was that work experience in Japan would be helpful when establishing a career in International Organizations in the UN Common System. With this in mind, respondents were selected according to the following criteria:
1. They should be a Japanese national employed by the UN Common System
2. They should have had work experience in Japan.

However, it was soon realized that if the condition of having worked in Japan were to be strictly imposed, the number of qualified candidates for interview would drop significantly. Therefore, those who showed interest in cooperating and who gave consent for publication of their interview record were selected.

Due to time restraints, the author was unable to visit developing countries[1] and some interviews were conducted on return from sabbatical leave. As an example, at the time of interview, Case W was working as a medical officer employed by the WHO and he had been stationed in Egypt for fifteen years. The interview with Case W was made possible by interviewing him during his home leave to Japan. His case is included as a representative case of a staff member employed in a developing country.

After further consideration, the criteria for interview was developed and the respondents were selected when <u>one</u> of the following three conditions was met:
1. Formal Japanese staff members employed by the UN Common System who answered the Second Survey <u>and</u> who have work experience in Japan.
2. Formal Japanese staff members employed by the UN Common System who were interviewed in the International Forum <u>and</u> where work experience in Japan was mentioned in their brief profile on the website.
3. Formal Japanese staff members employed by the UN Common System selected via a snowball[2] sampling technique.

Regarding number 2, candidates were selected from <u>the UN Forum</u>, a website run by volunteers of UN officials, graduate school students, researchers and journalists mainly based in New York. Profiles of UN staff members appear on this website and if the staff profile indicated that the staff member had work experience in Japan, the author approached them by email, asking for an interview. Once a request for interview was accepted, it would take place outside their office, often during a lunch break and would last for one and a half to two hours.

Thirty-two interviews, including two JPOs and one non-Japanese staff member were conducted. Seven members (approximately 20%) declined to publish the content of their interviews. As a result, there are twenty-two Japanese formal staff members and one non-Japanese formal staff member employed by the UN Common System included in this chapter. One of the respondents had just retired and a second had just resigned before the interviews took place.

The majority of the collaborators were between 40-60 years old. Most of those who declined to publish their interviews were between 30-40 years old. When asked their reasons for not wishing to publish their interviews, some felt that they had not yet achieved enough professionally in the UN Common System to comment, others thought that they had yet to establish a concrete plan for their future and some collaborators stated that they wanted to protect their privacy.

According to the factor analysis presented in Chapter 4, Japanese formal staff members employed by the UN Common System were divided into the following three types: *career-satisfied* group, *treatment-satisfied* group and *dissatisfied* group. It is thought that the respondents introduced in Chapter 6 are likely to be from the *career-satisfied* group and those who declined are thought to be from the *treatment-satisfied*{/italic} or *dissatisfied* groups.

Overview of Interview Respondents and Summary of Interviews

A summary of interview respondents is shown in Table 1. Interview records of Case A through to Case X (with the exclusion of Case T, who withdrew from publishing) are included in chronological order (of date of interview) in Appendix 1.

Data used to prepare the tables in Chapter 6 represent the staff members at the time of interview. Changes after interview, if any, are added as a note at the end of each individual interview record in Appendix 1. Table 1 shows basic details of the respondents, including their job title, occupational field, grade and their level of satisfaction based on a Likert scale. As can be seen in Table 1, 60% of the collaborators were working in New York; 20% in Geneva; 13% in Rome and 4% in developing countries.

Table 1: Summary of respondents

Name	Sex	Age	Organization	Job Title (at time of interview)	Field of Occupation	Grade	Satisfaction 1-5	Duty Station
A	F	31	UNDP	Evaluation Analyst	Specialist (Evaluation)	P-2	5.0	New York
B	M	42	UN	Senior Investment Office	Specialist Investment	P-5	5.0	New York
C	M	41	UNDP	Chief, Administrative Service Division	Specialist (Finance)	P-5	4.0	New York
D	F	47	UN	Deputy Cashier (Treasury)	Administration	P-3	2.0	New York
E	F	33	UN	Political Affairs Officer	Specialist (Political Affairs)	P-3	5.0	New York

Chapter 6 Job Satisfaction by Occupational Field — Results from Interviews with Japanese Formal Staff Members Employed by the UN Common System

F	F	54	UNDP	ASG (Assistant Secretary General)	Administration	ASG	5.0	New York
G	F	50	UN	Social Affairs Officer	Specialist (Social Affairs)	P-4	5.0	New York
H	M	41	UNDP	Regional Programme Specialist	Coordination	P-4	4.0	New York
I	F	60	UN	Chief, Collection and Information processing Section	Specialist (Library)	P-5	5.0	New York
J	M	58	UN	Programme coordinator	Coordination	P-4	4.0	New York
K	F	53	UNFPA	Deputy Director, Division for Oversight Services	Specialist (Auditing)	D-1	4.0	New York
L	M	42	UN	Project Coordinator	Coordination	L-3	4.0	New York
M	F	53	UNFPA	Senior Advisor	Coordination	P-5	2.5	New York
N	M	45	WFP	Logistics Officer	Specialist (Logistics)	P-3	4.0	Rome
O	F	51	WFP	Chief, contributions and Project Accounting Branch	Specialist (Finance)	P-5	4.0	Rome
P	F	45	ILO	Senior Human Resource Officer	Specialist (HR)	P-4	5.0	Geneva
Q	F	45	WHO	Medical Officer	Specialist (Medical)	P-5	5.0	Geneva
R	F	41	WHO	Budget and Resources Coordination Officer	Specialist (Finance & Budgeting)	P-4	4.0	Geneva
S	F	54	ILO	Chief Internal Auditor	Specialist (Auditing)	D-1	5.0	Geneva
T	F	45	UN-HABITAT	Coordinator, Rapid Response for Settlements in Crisis	Supporting Developing Countries	P-4	4.0	Geneva
U	M	50	UNIDO	Industrial Development Officer	Coordination	L-4	4.0	Tokyo
V	M	50	IFAD	Treasurer	Specialist (Finance)	D-1	4.0	Rome

W	M	48	WHO	Coordinator, TB, AIDS and Malaria	Specialist (Medicine)	P-6	5.0	Cairo
X*	M	51	UNDP	Senior Evaluation Advisor	Specialist (Environment)	P-5	3.0	New York

* non-Japanese

Table 2 shows a summary of interview respondents by gender, including age at the time of interview; grade; years of service in the UN Common System; age when they became a formal staff member; the number of countries they were assigned to; age at the time of recruitment in the UN Common System and their level of satisfaction. As indicated in Table 2, the percentage of male and female interview respondents was 40% and 60% respectively.

Table 2: Summary of interview respondents

	Male	Female	Total
Number of respondents	10	14	24
Average age at the time of interview	47	47	47
Average grade	P-4 Step V	P-4 Step VI	P-4- Step V
Average years of service in the UN Common System	11 years	16 years	16 years
Age when became a formal staff member	35	32	34
Number of countries assigned to	2.0	2.5	2.3
Age at initial recruitment to the UN Common System	33	31	32
Level of satisfaction	4.1	4.3	4.2

The average age at the time of interview was 47 years old for both male and female interview respondents. The average grade was P-4 for both respondents. However, male staff members became formal staff members at 35 years old and females at 32 years old. In addition, male formal staff members had been employed in the UN Common System for an average of 11 years while females had worked in the system for 16 years. Thus, we can conclude that even though male respondents started working for the UN Common System later than female respondents, the grade given to men at the time of recruitment was higher than that of females or male respondents were promoted faster than female respondents, this matches the findings in Chapter 3 and Chapter 4. Additionally, female staff members tended to work at more duty stations than male staff members. It could be interpreted that female respondents were more likely to be employed by organizations that have a rotation policy such as humanitarian assistance organizations. Both male and female staff members showed a high level of satisfaction with their work.

Table 3 supports the fact that there are various ways to obtain a position as a formal staff member in the UN Common System. The most common way to enter the UN Common System was via the JPO scheme (50%), after which the employee became a formal staff member (Cases A, C, E, F). Seventeen percent of staff members applied to vacancy announcements (Cases B, T, V, W). On the other hand 21% of staff members were recruited via other routes (Cases I, J, L, Q, S): Case J was seconded by the Japanese Government; Case L was recommended to a Japanese trust funded post by a senior ranked official of the Japanese Government; Case I directly applied to the UN Secretariat; Case S was directly recruited by UNDP and Case Q was originally seconded by the Japanese Government and later became a formal medical officer in the WHO, resigning from her post in the Japanese Government.

Table 3: Entry Routes to the UN Common System

Entry Route	Male	Female	Total
JPO scheme	5 (56%)	7 (47%)	12 (50%)
YPP exam	0 (0%)	1 (7%)	1 (4%)
Vacancy announcement	3 (33%)	1 (7%)	4 (17%)
Recruitment mission	0 (0%)	2 (13%)	2 (8%)
Others	1 (11%)	4 (27%)	5 (21%)
Total	9 (100%)	15 (100%)	24 (100%)

Table 4 summarizes the timing of entry to the UN Common System. Sixty-seven percent entered via an *early-career* entry method, becoming formal staff members through the JPO scheme or via passing the YPP exam (former UN Staff members competitive exam). On the other hand, 33% of the respondents were recruited via a *mid-career* entry method, either applying to vacancy announcements or to recruitment missions.

Table 4: Entry method

Entry method	Male	Female	Total
Early-career	7 (70%)	9 (64%)	16 (67%)
Mid-career	3 (30%)	5 (36%)	8 (33%)
Total	10 (100%)	14 (100%)	24 (100%)

Table 5 shows where the staff members were educated and to what level (as one of the 24 respondents was a non-Japanese national, this case was excluded from Table 5). Additionally, when a staff member obtained degrees from more than one academic institute/university, each of them was counted.

Table 5: Where staff members were educated

	Japan	Overseas
Before university (Elementary school, junior high school, senior high school)	18 (78%)	5 (22%)
University	15 (65%)	8 (35%)
Graduate school	6 (27%)	16 (73%)

What we can learn is that 65% of the staff members completed their university education in Japan and 73% obtained post-graduate degrees overseas. Twenty seven percent of the respondents were solely educated at Japanese academic institutes/universities.

Table 6 shows whether or not the staff member had had work experience in Japan prior to becoming a member of the UN Common System. Eighty-eight percent of the respondents had worked in Japan. Interestingly, all male staff members had had prior work experience in Japan.

Table 6: Work experience in Japan

	Male	Female	Total
Yes, I have	10 (100%)	11 (79%)	21 (88%)
No, I have not	0 (0%)	3 (21%)	3 (12%)

A further question sought to uncover the type of organizations that staff members had worked for in Japan. Table 7 shows that 43% of staff members worked in private companies, 24% worked for foreign-affiliated companies, 14% worked for the government or government related organizations and 5% worked in academia. The remainder included those who were self-employed, such as consultants. In contrast, as indicated in Chapter 5, 45% of non-Japanese staff members who worked in their home country prior to recruitment in the UN Common System worked in government organizations, including the ODA.

Table 7: Type of organization worked for in Japan

	Male	Female	Total
I have work experience in Japan	10 (48%)	11 (52%)	21 (88%)
Private company	4 (44%)	5 (56%)	9 (43%)
Foreign affiliated company	2 (40%)	3 (60%)	5 (24%)
Government/Government related organization	2 (67%)	1 (33%)	3 (14%)
Academic or research institution(s)	0 (0%)	1 (10%)	1 (5%)
Others	2 (67%)	1 (33%)	3 (14%)

The respondents were also asked whether their prior work experience in Japan proved useful or helpful in developing their career in the UN Common System. As is clearly shown in Table 8, there was a significant discrepancy between male respondents and female respondents. All the male respondents evaluated their work experience in Japan as *very useful*. For example, Case U said that the procedures and steps needed to process work that he learned in the Japanese company were useful when working in UNIDO. Case N said that the way of processing work and the international standards and regulations used at the Japanese shipping company, were the same as those used in the WFP. Case N also mentioned that the Japanese company trained him how to be a good businessperson. Case W mentioned that the technical and business skills acquired at a Japanese institute served him well in his present work.

Table 8: Evaluation of work experience in Japan prior to recruitment in the UN Common System

	Male	Female	Total
Useful	10 (100%)	6 (60%)	16 (80%)
Not useful	0 (0%)	4 (40%)	4 (20%)
Total	10 (100%)	10 (100%)	20 (100%)

(Four female respondents did not have work experience in Japan, they were not included in Table 8.)

On the contrary, female respondents answered quite differently. Forty percent of female respondents answered that their work experience in Japan was *not useful* in their present work in the UN Common System. Although 60% of the female respondents answered that it was useful, the meaning of term *useful* was considered differently to the male use of the term. Case R said that the work environment in Japan was harsh for women and that this made her tough in the face of adversity. Case Q answered that her work experience in Japan was useful in developing technical skills for the job but it was not useful for surviving in the UN Common System. Case Q stated that in contrast to working in a purely Japanese organization, work experience in a foreign-affiliated company in Japan *was* useful for work in the WFP.

As discussed in Chapter 1, mentors play an important role in career development. The term 'mentor' refers not only those who guide people in the right direction to solve problems at work but also people who are good advisors for life in general. They are usually senior members of staff or supervisors in the workplace. During the preliminary survey conducted in 2001, more than one respondent mentioned such comments as '*If it wasn't for him I wouldn't be here now*' and '*Thanks to him, I could learn the basics of working in an international work environment.*'

If employees meet a mentor or mentors at the initial stage of their career, the mentor will likely affect the employee's later working life. When asked about mentors, about 60% of staff members responded that they had met their mentor or mentors in their first workplace (Table 9) and 46% still had their mentors. The mentors came from a variety of nationalities: Dutch, Finnish, South African, American and Japanese. Most of them were direct supervisors or experienced senior members in the same department. In some cases, such as Case Q, the staff member was proactive in seeking out a mentor herself. It was concluded from the interviews that those who had a mentor at the beginning of their career were more successful in making career decisions than those who did not have one and that male staff members evaluated the role of mentors more highly than females.

Table 9: Mentor(s)

	Male	Female	Total
I met (a) mentor(s) at my first job	8 (57%)	6 (43%)	14 (58%)
I now have (a) mentor(s)	7 (64%)	4 (36%)	11 (46%)

When asked about working until the mandatory retirement age, 40% of staff members expressed that they were not able to foresee their future (Table 10). For example, Case Q answered that she will consider leaving the UN Common System if a stimulating job were to be offered elsewhere. Case X answered that he will consider leaving if an interesting job relating to his specialized field is on offer. Many respondents were keen to make better use of their professional skills and/or knowledge.

Table 10: Desire to work for the UN Common System until the mandatory retirement age

	Male	Female	Total
Yes, I would like to	5 (50%)	8 (57%)	13 (54%)
No, I don't want to	1 (10%)	1 (7%)	2 (8%)
I do not know	4 (40%)	5 (36%)	9 (38%)
Total	10 (100%)	14 (100%)	24 (100%)

With regard to salary, although some of the respondents faced a drastic decrease in salary when taking a post in the UN Common System, all except one respondent answered that the amount they received was not important to them (Table 11).

Case G said that whether or not the job is challenging and stimulating is more important to him. Case K also said that as long as a certain amount of salary is guaranteed, job satisfaction is more important than the amount of money earned. Case W answered that he could not complain when he knew how much money civil servants in developing countries received.

Table 11: Importance of salary

	Male	Female	Total
Yes, it is important	0 (0%)	1 (7%)	1 (4%)
No, it is not important	10 (100%)	13 (93%)	23 (96%)
Total	10 (100%)	14 (100%)	24 (100%)

Finally, a comparison was made between the Japanese interview respondents and non-Japanese respondents. The data for the non-Japanese respondents in Table 12 was extracted from Chapter 5, Table 5. When asked to participate in an interview conducted by the author, these Japanese staff members were positive and did not show any hesitation to take part. As can be seen from Table 12, the average grade of these Japanese respondents was P-4, Step V, which was higher than the average grade of the Japanese respondents in the second survey (P-3, Step IX) in Chapter 5. It could be interpreted that those who participated in an interview were from the *career-satisfied* group.

Table 12: Japanese Interview respondents and non-Japanese respondents during the second survey

	Japanese interview respondents	Non-Japanese respondents
Average age	47	41
Average grade	P-4 Step V	P-4 Step VI
Age at recruitment	32	31

Study Abroad Experience

This section discusses whether or not the respondents had studied abroad and how their experience of studying abroad influenced them to work in the UN Common System.

Table 13 shows how a total of 23 respondents were educated overseas, (excluding one non-Japanese respondent from the table). Thirty-five percent graduated from a graduate school overseas either by supporting themselves financially or through a scholarship. Twenty-six percent of respondents had been educated abroad, as so-called expatriate Japanese children, during their early school years. Thirteen percent had been to the USA and obtained an MA with the support of a scholarship from the private companies that employed them at that time. The remaining 13% had no experience of studying abroad before becoming employed by the UN Common System. All their education had taken place in Japan.

Table 13: Sources of education overseas

Source	Percentage
Scholarship/ Study at one's own expense	35%
Children of Japanese who lived overseas (Returnees)	26%
Company sponsored overseas study	13%
No overseas study	13%
Other	13%

As the author mentioned in Chapter 2, the UN Common System is a qualifications-based society. When selecting a new staff member, the level of applicants' qualifications is given serious evaluation but the name of the university they graduated from is not given so much consideration. The applicants' nationality, their field of specialization, relevant work experience, and the level of academic qualifications are considered together as a package. On the contrary, when a private company in Japan recruits a new employee, the major concern is which university the applicant graduated from. The applicant's specialized field studied at university is not a major factor in determining their eligibility and suitability for the position. Thus, in Japan after graduating from high school, the university the student was accepted into and graduated from heavily determines the young applicants' working life. In comparison, International Organizations in the UN Common System has taken quite a different course of recruiting and utilizing human resources. Case O, Case S and Case T are all female. These three female respondents had obtained degrees in the United States or had acquired a global professional qualification such as CPA or MBA or they had had professional work experience before they were recruited to the UN Common System via a *mid-career* entry method. One can say that it is very rare to find people with similar backgrounds effectively utilized in a Japanese organization. Their cases show how degrees and experience obtained overseas enabled Japanese applicants to become staff members in the UN Common System (see Appendix 1 for further information).

We can see from the above cases that there are various ways to be employed by the UN Common System and these differ greatly from the Japanese way of recruiting human resources. Case N and Case W show that even without having an overseas education or overseas work experience it is still possible to be employed as a staff member in the UN Common System.

Job Satisfaction by Occupational Field

This section attempts to deepen understanding of the relationship between job satisfaction and occupational fields. The author was highly convinced of the importance of this relationship through the results of the first survey and second survey as well as the interviews.

In the course of cross tabulation analysis in the first survey and processing of interview data conducted in 2008, the author found some relationships between job satisfaction and occupational fields. After cross-examination and review, the interview collaborators were classified into the following five occupational groups. (Administration stands for administration work in general, including general affairs and other support tasks):

- Specialist Group
- Finance Specialist Group
- Program Management Coordination Group
- Administration and HR Group
- Assistance to Developing Countries Group

Table 14 shows, by group, the number of respondents and their percentage, average grade, average age at the time of interview and level of satisfaction broken down by gender.

Chapter 6   Job Satisfaction by Occupational Field — Results from Interviews with Japanese Formal Staff Members Employed by the UN Common System

Table 14: Interview respondents by occupational group

Occupational group	Total	Male	Female	Average grade	Average Age	Satisfaction Level (1-5) (M: Male, F: Female)
Specialist	10 (41%)	4	6	P-4 Step VII	48	4.7 (M=4.25, F=5.0)
Finance Specialist	4 (17%)	2	2	P-4 Step VII	46	4.25 (M=4.0, F=4.5)
Program Management Coordination	5 (21%)	4	1	P-4 Step I	49	4.0 (M=4.0, F=2.5)
Administration and HR	3 (13%)	0	3	P-4 Step V (*)	46*	4.5 (M=**, F=4.5)
Assistance to developing countries	2 (8%)	0	2	P-3 Step V	39	4.5 (M=-**, F=4.5)

* : One case was excluded as this case highly deviated from the average.
** : As there were no male respondents, the male satisfaction level is not available.

The following section details the major findings and characteristics of the above five occupational groups.

Specialist Group

The *Specialist* group uses their professional skills to fulfill their duties.   Their specialized fields are widely varied, including medicine, evaluation, social development, logistics, library science, and investment operation, etc. The collaborators were all confident of their skills in their specialized fields and their level of satisfaction was very high.   Their average grade was rank P-4, Step VII, which was high or higher than other groups. Their level of satisfaction was the highest of all the groups, of which their score was 4.7 out of 5. It is worth mentioning that all six female collaborators in this group answered 5, the full score. Most of the females in the *Specialist* group were either employed via a *mid-career* entry method or were recruited via an *early-career* entry method such as the JPO scheme or YPP exam.   They had built their career as a specialist before being employed in the UN Common System. Case B and Case K are good examples of employees in the specialist group (Appendix 1).

Finance Specialist Group

The *Finance Specialist* group shows the same characteristics of the *Specialist* Group. These groups could be combined together, however, as there were a considerable number of staff members in this group, they were divided to show they are independent. Their average level of satisfaction was high (4.25) and their average grade was also high, at P-4 Step VII, which is the same level as that of the *Specialist* group. Regarding the level of satisfaction, the male respondents marked 4.0 and female respondents marked 4.5. Female respondents marked higher scores and this shows the same tendency as shown by the *Specialist* group. As indicated in Table 14, there are four respondents in the *Finance Specialist* group and one of them was recruited via an *early-career* entry method, the JPO scheme, but the remaining three had worked as finance specialists in the private sector. These three respondents were recruited to the UN Common System via a *mid-career* entry method. This could have been through a recruitment mission or via a direct recruitment procedure. Case C and Case O are good examples of employees from the Finance Specialist Group.

The Program Management Coordination Group

The *Program Management Coordination* group comprises of respondents engaged in coordination duties and this group appears to be having difficulties when compared with other groups. The average age of this group was 49, which is the highest among the groups, but their average grade was at P-4 Step I, which is the lowest. Regarding the level of their satisfaction, all four male respondents scored it 4.0 out of 5. There was only one female respondent in this group. As the score of this respondent is highly deviated from the mean of the other respondents, her score was excluded. Generally speaking, Japanese are considered to be good coordinators in the field of programs and management. However, it is not easy to continue competing with colleagues whose mother tongue is a Germanic language, for a higher graded post. It was found that the UN Common System employed many of the respondents in this group when they were still young. The entry method of this group was varied, some entered the UN Common System via the JPO scheme and others were recruited via *mid-career* entry methods. Case H is a good example of an employee from the Program Management Coordination Group.

Administration and HR Group

Three respondents were classified into the *Administration & HR* group. One was the Head of Administration Bureau and the remaining two were in Finance and HR departments. As there are only three cases in this group and their specialized fields are all different, it is not possible to evaluate the characteristics of this group in a fair manner. All three of them were female and their average level of satisfaction was 4.0. Judging from the author's experience, duties of this group are mostly based on routine work, so it is assumed that Japanese respondents would receive high recognition and a good reputation for their work. Yet it seems difficult for those in this group to get the same high level of satisfaction as those in the *Specialist* group or *Finance Specialist* Group. Case P is a good example of an employee in the Administration and HR group.

Assistance to Developing Countries Group

The fifth group is the *Assistance to Developing Countries* group. The respondents in this group either work in the Headquarters of the UN Common System or in developing countries working to alleviate poverty or to improve economic conditions in developing countries. Work to assist developing countries is very rewarding, but at the same time, their work is often influenced by uncontrollable external factors, such as a coup d'état or a change in government regime. The level of satisfaction in this group varied significantly. Some respondents had a high level of satisfaction through their work in developing countries, whereas, others showed low satisfaction as their dedication and performance were not duly recognized because of the above-mentioned reasons. There were no male respondents in this group at the time of interview and the average level of satisfaction of all the female respondents in this group was 4.5. Case T is an example of an employee who is representative of the *Assistance to Developing Countries Group*, yet, Case T withdrew her interview record from publication in the English edition of this book.

Summing up the discussions in this section, we can conclude that Japanese formal staff members who are in higher graded positions and who have a high level of satisfaction are in the *Specialist* occupation group and the *Finance Specialist* group. The staff members in these groups are very often recruited via a *mid-career* entry method. As discussed in Chapter 3, the specialized fields at the last degree held of male Japanese staff members were widely spread and half of male staff was recruited via a *mid-career* entry method. This also confirms that many Japanese male staff members have been recruited as specialists.

Changing of Specialized Field and Transferring to other Occupational Groups

This section examines whether or not it is easy for staff members who are employed by the UN Common System to change specialized fields or to transfer to other occupational groups.

Table 15 was prepared in order to clarify the relationship between the employee's field of specialization at the last academic degree held and their present occupational post. The data indicates a close relationship between the field of specialization at the last academic degree held and staff members present occupational post. As already mentioned in Chapter 2, at the time of recruitment, promotion and transfer to another post, the selection committee always judged whether the short-listed candidates could carry out the duties required for the post, such as meeting technical qualifications. Therefore, it was not easy for staff members to make significant changes to their specialized field once they were recruited into International Organizations in the UN Common System.

Table 15: Interview respondent's field of specialization at their last academic degree and their present occupational post

	Field of Specialization at last Academic Degree	Present Occupational Post
A	Development Economics	Evaluation Analyst
B	Business Administration (MBA)	Senior Investment Officer
C	Finance	Chief, Administrative Service Division
D	Business Administration & Finance	Deputy Cashier
E	International Relations	Political Affairs Officer
F	International Economics	Assistant Secretary General (ASG)
G	Higher Education & Public Policy	Social Affairs Officer, Social Integration Branch
H	Development Studies	Programme Specialist (Crisis Prevention in Asia-Pacific Region, Reconstruction Assistance)
I	Library Science	Library Science, Chief Information Processing and Collecting Documents, Dag Hammarskjold Library

Chapter 6 Job Satisfaction by Occupational Field — Results from Interviews with Japanese Formal Staff Members Employed by the UN Common System

J	International Relations	Programme Coordinator, Socio-Economic Governance & Management Branch
K	Development Studies	Deputy Director, Division of Oversight Service
L	Law (LLM)	Project Coordinator, Conventional Arms Branch
M	Politics	Senior Advisor
N	International Studies	Logistics Officer, Distribution Section
O	Business Administration (MBA)	Chief, Contribution and Project Accounting Branch
P	International Relations	Senior Human Resource Officer
Q	Medicine (Infectious Diseases)	Medical Officer (World Influenza Programme)
R	Business Administration (MBA)	Budget and Resources Coordination Officer
S	Accounting	Chief, Internal Auditor
T	Development Economics	Coordinator, Rapid Response for Settlements in Crisis
U	Economics	Senior Industrial Development Officer
V	Business Administration (MBA)	Treasurer
W	Medicine	Coordinator, TB, AIDS and Malaria
X	Economic Geography	Senior Evaluation Advisor

As discussed in Chapter 2, Japanese private companies implement staff professional development by frequently rotating their staff members within the organization. At the time of selecting candidates for a position within the organization, an employee's potential, personality, age and the name of the university from which they graduated are considered to be the major criteria for selection. The specialized fields majored in at university are not so important.

The next question is whether it is easy to change their occupational field in the course of a career in the UN Common System. Figure 1 shows the relationship of transfers to another occupational field. The size of a circle shows the size of satisfaction and arrows show the possibility of moving to another field. As the figure shows, it is easy for those in a *Specialist* group and *Finance Specialist* Group to move to the *Program Management Coordination* Group but not vice versa. It is very difficult for those in the *Program Management Coordination* group or in the *Assistance to Developing Countries* Group to move to the *Specialist* Group or *Finance Specialist* group, including the *Finance Specialist* group, unless one had previous relevant experience or qualifications in that field. When a vacant post is advertised, selection is made among the short listed candidates based on their field of specialization, knowledge, achievements and their relevant work experience.

Figure 1: Change of specialized field and transferring to another occupational group

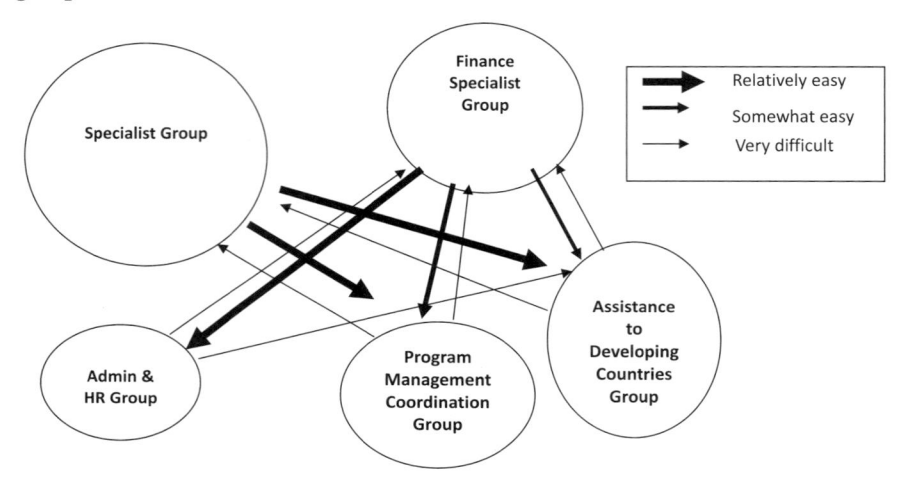

In Japanese private companies, the HR department is mainly responsible for staff relocation, staff development and training, observing their potential and their aptitudes in the workplace. On the contrary, the HR department in the UN Common System rarely decides the relocation of staff, except in the humanitarian assistance organizations such as UNICEF, UNHCR and WFP. In these humanitarian assistance organizations, there is a rotation policy, and the HR department encourages staff members to apply to vacancy posts in other duty stations every 4-6 years, unless they do not voluntarily apply for them as explained in a previous section.

People in Japan often say that they would like to get a job in the UN Common System after having sufficient work experience in Japan. However, selection criteria at both organizations are quite different, thus, it is not easy for Japanese to be selected for a post in the UN Common System after having a considerable amount of work experience in Japan.

Career Anchor

In the course of conducting a literature review of career development before writing this book, the author consulted *Career Dynamics* (the Japanese title) written by an American organizational psychologist Edgar H. Schien as first mentioned in Chapter 1. In his book, he stated that employees generally get to know themselves and can then develop a clearer image towards their career or their occupation in the course of their working life[3]. He used the term of 'Career Anchor' to explain the concept of self-image that one has of their occupation.

The career anchor consists of the following three elements[4]: 1) one's perception of one's talents and abilities; 2) one's basic values and 3) one's perceptions of motives and needs as they pertain to their career. In the three elements, there are various classifications in career anchors. In the English version of the book the career anchors were composed of five elements and later expanded to eight elements. The Japanese edition of Schien's book classified the career anchors into three elements. As the original version of this book was in Japanese, the author used the classification used in Schien's Japanese edition.

Schien stated that career anchors are discovered after working for several years.[5] Yet, the author has been interested in how staff members in the UN Common System handle their daily work when facing daily stressful political elements. Thus, the author redefined the idea of a career anchor as a symbol that employees have towards their work or words or phrases they use to describe their attitudes towards work; their credo. At the end of the interview, the author asked staff members to describe their own career anchor. When asked, most of them stopped for a moment to think before disclosing their personal career anchor or their credo. The respondents each had their own career anchor and credos that helped them to carry out their own duties within a multicultural and politically complex work environment. The career anchors provided by the interview respondents are shown in Table 16.

Table 16: Career Anchors of the Japanese staff members

Elements of Career Anchor	Career Anchor	Collaborator
One's perception of one's talents and abilities	*Respect for the workplace, positive thinking, mid and long-term plan*	E
	Respect for the workplace, closely look at patients and not at their illnesses	Q
	There is no other way for me than this, I go this way	S
	Respect for workplace, be good ears and eyes for the people who have no means to see, hear or speak	T
	Work technically correct, reflect them into administration; think the essence of the subject, simplify them and deliver the result	W
One's basic values	*Decide one's life on his own*	B
	Wish to contribute to people in developing countries	G
	Wish to help people in developing countries or betterment of their countries	H
	Work for others and be content with it	J
	Once one takes on a task, accomplish it to the end	L
One's perception of motives and needs as they pertain to one's career	*Work is a means to living and enjoying life*	D
	I believe in myself and am lucky being supported by family	F
	Dedicate yourself fully to your work	I
	Forget good and bad things and start from scratch every morning	K
	You can bend the rules as far as you can, so long as you don't break them; you can interpret them as you like as long as it is for the good of the country and program and not for yourself	M
	Hot heart, cool mind	N
	Work with a professional pride	O
	Be idealistic but be realistic	P
	Have conviction, if not continue thinking until one is convinced	R
	Have high serenity, distant ambition	U
	Go back to the basics when one is confused	V

Main Findings and Recommendations

Below are the main findings from this chapter and a list of recommendations for Japanese companies to improve their HRM practices and for individuals seeking to develop their own career path.

1. There are many ways to enter the UN Common System.
Recommendation:
   ✓ Japanese companies need to make better use of human resources from different backgrounds.

2. To change specialized field and/or to transfer to other occupational fields is difficult.
Recommendation:
   ✓ Japanese companies should select a group of staff members within their organization and train them as specialists to cope with overseas business.

3. Male respondents highly valued their work experience in Japan whereas female respondents did not necessarily value that experience.
Recommendation:
   ✓ Japanese companies need to develop some schemes and policies to support and nurture female employees.

4. Mentors play a very important role in professional development.
Recommendations:
   ✓ Japanese companies should reevaluate the roles and values of their mid-level staff and/or senior level staff, reconfirming the importance of the role of mentors in the organization.

5. Many Japanese UN employees have their own career anchor.
Recommendation:
   ✓ Japanese companies should include workshops about career anchors in their staff development program, especially for those staff members assigned overseas.

Notes:
1. Due to limitation of time and funding, it was only possible to interview only one staff

member working in the developing countries. To make a comprehensive analysis on the career development of International Civil Servants, an analysis on staff members working in developing countries will be a future research task.
2. Snowball sampling is a non-probability sampling technique where existing study subjects recruit future subjects from among their acquaintances. Thus the sample group appears to grow like a rolling snowball. As the sample builds up, enough data is gathered to be useful for research. This sampling technique is often used in hidden populations, which are difficult for researchers to access.
3. p. 143, Career Dynamics (Japanese Edition), 1991.
4. p. 143, Career Dynamics (Japanese Edition), 1991.
5. p. 143, Career Dynamics (Japanese Edition), 1991.

Chapter 7
Final Reflections and Recommendations

This chapter provides a summary of the results of this study. The first section summarizes the first six chapters of this book. The second section verifies the hypothesis proposed in Chapter 1. The third section discusses the results of the most recent survey of Japanese international civil servants employed by the UN Common System. The fourth section presents practical suggestions for the professional development of international civil servants. The fifth section provides recommendations for the globalization of Japanese private enterprises and the sixth section discusses future research.

Overview of Survey Results

In this section, the results of the two surveys are summarized. Chapter 1 of this book explored various human resource management trends in Japan. Companies have an increasing demand for staff who can handle difficult situations associated with globalization, individual employees have various attitudes to their profession and there is a general social trend towards equal employment opportunities for men and women. Ideas concerning national and international society and the concept of diversity management, particularly the way in which it has been employed within companies, was also explained and discussed.

Research in the fields of international managerial development and career studies provided the foundation of this book. Perlmutter (1969) claimed that the ultimate multi-national corporations would utilize the most appropriate employees, regardless of their nationality. According to his theory, the HRM of International Organizations is an example of such global management practice. Additionally, despite research in the field of career studies having an extensive history in the US, it has only garnered attention in Japan since around the end of the twentieth century. It was at this time that Japanese private enterprises began to introduce a performance-oriented HRM system.

The literature review in Chapter 2 made a comparison between the HRM practices within the UN Common System and Japanese HRM practices. The study of HRM practices in the UN Common System revealed that female staff members are better utilized in the UN Common System than in Japan. Instead of fulfilling the organization's demands, employees' individual needs and wants are given priority during promotion and relocation. Although job security could be regarded as low, the discretion of the individual is highly respected in the UN Common System. Additionally, each organization has its own recruitment policy. In accordance with the individual organization's recruitment policy, humanitarian assistance organizations make use of JPO resources.

Chapter 3 provided a look at the characteristics of Japanese international civil servants that emerged through the first survey. It was found that there were two clear differences between male and female staff members. First, a greater number of male staff members were employed via the *mid-career* entry method, that is, after having had some relevant work experience. Yet, many female staff members were employed via an *early-career* entry method, meaning that they had had less prior work experience than men when entering the UN Common System. Second, it was found that male staff members' specializations were spread across various fields whereas female staff members' field of specialization tended to be concentrated in just three main fields i.e. international relations, development studies and MPA.

Chapter 4 provided further evidence for the findings by presenting the results of a statistical analysis of the survey. From factor analysis, the author was able to ascertain that staff members could be divided into three groups: *career-satisfied* group; *treatment-satisfied* group and *dissatisfied* group. There was no discrepancy found between male and female members as far as the three categories were concerned. However, there was a slight difference in type and reason of their satisfaction. The satisfaction of male staff members arose from only by their job satisfaction whereas the satisfaction of female members originated in their job satisfaction and satisfaction at their duty station. In addition, female staff members showed greater satisfaction with their life at their duty stations than male staff members. Multiple regression analysis found that job satisfaction and job security were the two largest predictor variables that contributed to a staff members overall satisfaction.

In Chapter 5, comparisons were drawn between Japanese formal staff members and non-Japanese formal staff members. It became immediately apparent that the career paths between these two groups of staff members were different. Non-Japanese staff members became a formal staff member after having had relevant work experience in government-related work, such as the ODA or in the field of international development. In the case of Japanese staff members, results showed that they had worked for private enterprises before entering the UN Common System. Furthermore, non-Japanese staff members took more positive steps towards their professional development by working in developing countries to obtain promotion and this positive attitude lead to their higher-ranked grade and higher salary.

Chapter 6 discussed the evaluation of Japanese staff members by classifying their occupational fields with their work experiences in Japan. All male collaborators highly evaluated their work experience in their home country, Japan. On the contrary, only 60% percent of female staff members valued such experience. The female staff members stated that although the experience improved their technical skills, it lacked opportunities for professional growth. The remaining 40% of female staff members did not evaluate their previous work experience in Japan.

Following those discussions, the next stage was to classify formal staff members into groups based on their occupational field and their level of job satisfaction. It was clear through this classification that staff members working within highly professional fields had a higher level of satisfaction and were working at a higher grade. It was comparatively easy for them to move to a field of *Programme Management Coordination* or a field of *Assistance to Developing Countries* yet, it was not as easy to do this the other way around.

Test of the Hypotheses

The following two hypotheses were tested throughout this research:

Hypothesis 1: *Work experience in Japan is useful for career and professional development* within International Organizations the UN Common System.

Hypothesis 2: *There are no differences between Japanese males and Japanese females with regard to their satisfaction within International Organizations the UN Common System.*

Beginning with Hypothesis 1, 88% per cent of the interview collaborators had worked in Japan. Evaluation of that experience varied between men and women. All male interview collaborators had work experience in Japan and all of them highly valued that experience. However, many female collaborators did not value their work experience in Japan, particularly for improving their professional ability/capability. Japanese private enterprises invest a great deal of money into educating and training their employees; it can take a long time to recover the money invested over the course of an employee's career with the same company. From the results of the interview surveys discussed in Chapter 6, we can conclude that Japanese private enterprises provide male employees with a high level of professional development. Therefore, in the case of male staff members working in the UN Common System, the skills and experience they acquired while working in Japanese enterprises can be said to be useful for their job performance. However, in the case of women, Japanese private enterprises did not give the same level of education and in-house training, although those collaborators worked in Japan before the *Equal Employment Opportunity Law* was enforced. Therefore, Japanese female staff member could not see the value of their work experience in Japanese private enterprises in forming their skills for work as an international civil servant.

On reflection, in Hypothesis 1 the term '*work experience in Japan*' is not precise enough. If we refer to Japanese private companies, the hypothesis is supported but if we look in more detail, there are discrepancies between foreign-affiliated companies in Japan and Japanese enterprises. Foreign-affiliated companies in Japan follow performance-based HRM practices, thus working in such an environment is more similar to working in an international organization in the future. In conclusion, Hypothesis 1 was proved for male staff members but not for female staff members.

Looking at Hypothesis 2, it was found that there was no great difference in the degree of job satisfaction between male and female staff members, as shown in Table 1. As was clarified in Chapter 4, Japanese staff members were divided into three groups: *career-satisfied*, *treatment-satisfied* and *dissatisfied* (Table 1). These were also divided by gender and although there were some differences, they were not significant. In the factor analysis by gender, female staff members in the *career-satisfied* group, had higher levels of satisfaction than male staff members, as seen in Table 2. However, in the case of female staff members, overall satisfaction was determined by both job satisfaction and satisfaction at duty station. From the t-test analysis, it was shown that female staff members had a higher level of satisfaction at their duty station than male staff members (Table 1 in Chapter 4 and Table 3 in this chapter).

In conclusion, Hypothesis 2 was not proven as there were discrepancies based on gender; Japanese male staff members were only satisfied by their job whereas female staff members had job satisfaction and satisfaction at their duty station. Additionally, it was found that a staff member's occupational field has more influence on job satisfaction than gender (Table 3).

Table 1: Relationship between satisfaction and gender

	Job satisfaction	Satisfaction at duty station	Overall satisfaction
Male	High	Low	High
Female	High	High	High

Table 2: Relationship between satisfaction by group and gender

	Career-satisfied	*Treatment-satisfied*	*Dissatisfied*
Male	High	Low	Unknown*
Female	High	High	Unknown*

* Dissatisfaction levels are unknown as the number of cases in this category was small.

Table 3: Satisfaction and occupational group

Occupational group	Level of satisfaction
Specialist	High
Finance Specialist	High

Coordination	High (junior level)
	Low (senior level)
Administration and HR	Unknown*
Assistance to Developing Countries	High/Low
	(depends on assignments and political situations)

* Levels for Administration and HR are unknown as the number of cases in this category was small.

Characteristics of International Civil Servants

The following section summarizes the characteristics of international civil servants. Generally in Japan, staff members employed by International Organizations in the UN Common System are considered to be elite; they work energetically and efficiently in international society. However, as can be seen from the factor analysis discussed in Chapter 4, there are people who are *career-satisfied, treatment-satisfied and dissatisfied* with their work so it is fair to say that not all of them are happy with their work in the UN Common System.

A significant difference can be seen when comparing the HRM practices in the UN Common System with those in Japanese private enterprises. Figure 1 shows that staff members in the UN Common System make their decisions by taking their own initiative.

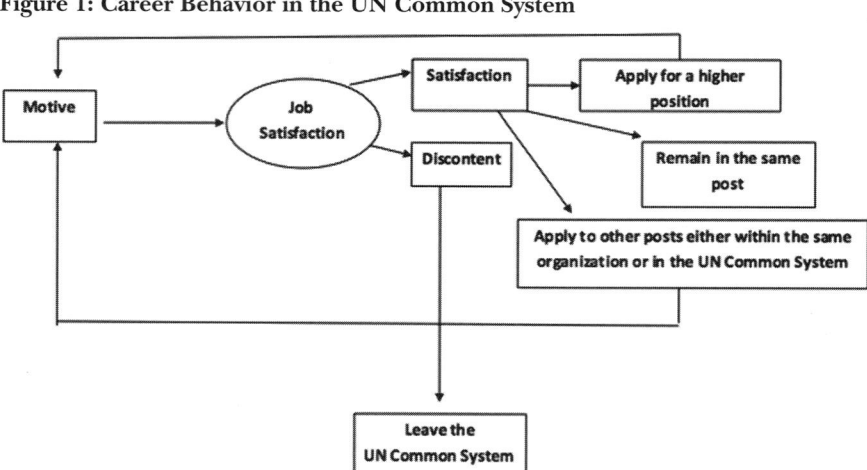

Figure 1: Career Behavior in the UN Common System

```
                 ┌──────────────────────────────────────────────┐
                 ↓                                              │
    ┌────────┐        ┌──────────┐    → Satisfaction ──→ Apply for a higher
    │ Motive │ ────→  │   Job    │                             position
    └────────┘        │Satisfaction│                      
         ↑            └──────────┘    → Discontent  ──→ Remain in the same
         │                                                     post
         │                                       ↘
         │                                        Apply to other posts either within the same
         │                                        organization or in the UN Common System
         │                                        
         └──────────────────────────↓
                                Leave the
                            UN Common System
```

Chapter 7 Final Reflections and Recommendations

In International Organizations of the UN Common System, a staff member has the freedom to design their own career path; if a staff member is satisfied with their present post, they can stay at that post or they can apply to a higher position. If one is dissatisfied with their current post or their career path, they can apply to a different post, find a job outside the UN Common System or accept the status quo and continue in their post. They take the initiative to make these decisions.

Conversely, in Japanese private enterprises, an individual's career is mainly determined by the long-term management policy of the organization and there is very little chance for individuals to craft their own career path. In performance-oriented International Organizations in the UN Common System, staff members are recruited on a contract basis meaning that job security may be low. Yet, in this modern age of globalization, where diversity is respected, it may be time for private enterprises to establish a new HRM system that respects diversity.

International Organizations within the UN Common System were established with the objectives to maximize the interests of related countries, to coordinate with other member states to avoid conflict and to achieve world peace. This means that in the UN Common System, problems are solved through consensus building among the countries involved.

The first difference between international civil servants and national civil servants is power. In the case of national civil servants, they are capable of executing their authority or discretion for the benefit of their country. However International Organizations and international civil servants are only authorized to recommend or advise the member states, having no authority to interfere with or get involved in the domestic policy or politics of the member countries. Ordinary Japanese might feel that as they are civil servants, international civil servants have the same authority as Japanese public servants, but in reality their authorities are widely different.

If a staff member joins the UN Common System with the belief that international civil servants can influence the member countries national policies, they may become disappointed and may suffer setbacks in their career. If they were appointed to a position that deals with the politics of member countries they would likely become frustrated with the gap between reality and their ideals. This is the reason, as mentioned in Chapter 6, why a staff member's career anchor is important. Many staff members try to take a realistic attitude towards work or have a career anchor to confirm the significance of their role. One should carefully consider whether they wish to realize their own personal ideals and if this is ones' goal, they should work in an NGO or NPO, not in International Organizations.

When the career of international civil servants is observed from the viewpoint of recognizing the intently political nature of the work, Japanese staff members who have higher satisfaction with their work, are those who are in highly specialized professional fields that are less influenced by politics.

Reflections on Methods

The results of the first and second surveys are shown in Appendix 2 and Appendix 3. When the first survey took place in 2003, email was not yet a popular survey method. As mentioned in Chapter 3, email addresses were artificially constructed, tested and used to send the questionnaire to qualified Japanese employed in the UN Common System. This method of constructing email addresses is now more problematic due to issues of privacy. If you were to replicate and extend this study, it is necessary to find a directory of UN Common System employees, yet this can prove difficult as not all the information you need can be found in one place.

There were 57 question items in the first survey and 40 in the second survey. In spite of the fact that there were many question items, 170 Japanese staff members responded to all questions in the first survey and 90 staff members of various nationalities responded in the second survey. As their answers were straightforward, the statistical tests, including t-test, factor analysis and regression analysis, clearly showed the characteristics of Japanese staff members employed in the UN Common System. Between the first survey and second survey, questions that were specifically related to Japanese staff members were deleted. Additionally, in the second survey, in order to compare Japanese and non-Japanese salaries, respondents were asked their step in addition to grade so that the salary could be constructed. Finally, to understand more about leadership experience, a question about the number of subordinates at the professional level and the general service level was added.

Consequently, these statistical analyses were helpful in choosing questions to clarify the issues in the second survey. The result of these tests also became the base of the complementary qualitative analyses by interview.

Value of Interview Records

The record of interviews with 23 international civil servants and their career paths can be found in Appendix 1. People are generally reluctant to disclose such personal information and their career path; therefore, it is with thanks that these 23 individuals have allowed us to gain a deeper insight into life working as an international civil servant. These staff members cooperated with interviews and in the publication of the contents in the belief that their comments would be useful to those who wish to serve as an international civil servant, a specialist in the field of international cooperation or a professional developing a career in international private companies. In this study it was difficult to interview staff members working in developing countries due to financial reasons and time constraints. To enhance the quality of this study some additional interviews would be useful, particularly interviews with staff members working in developing countries.

Final Recommendations for the Career Development of International Civil Servants

In this section, looking at the case of Ms. F highlights the key factors for successful career development in the UN Common System. As seen from Ms. F's career path, during the 30 years of her professional life she has worked in five countries and experienced nine posts in the UNDP. She also experienced three posts in Japan while taking two leaves of absence from the UNDP. She is a typical example of a staff member who is in the *career-satisfied* group. She has had long-term employment in her present organization; long term employment in the UN Common System and has worked at a high grade. Ms. F. is from Japan, from an under-represented country, she is female (and as such a target group for affirmative action), and she has been active in moving duty stations throughout her career, increasing her experience by working in three developing countries. Furthermore, she twice took a leave of absence from the UNDP, the first time to work in a research position and to work as an independent development consultant in Japan. These decisions widened her area of specialization. Additionally, she also had a second leave of absence and worked as a university professor, establishing a solid network with Japanese specialists in the field of international development.

The following are considered to be the key factors in Ms. F's success in her career in the UN Common System:

a) **Ms. F is Japanese**: The number of Japanese staff members in the UN Common System is under-represented.
b) **Ms. F. is a woman**: In order to fulfill the equal employment policy of the UN Common System, women are strongly encouraged to apply for a post and are actively recruited and promoted within the UN Common System.
c) **Ms. F. actively pursued work in different countries**: She worked in as many as or more different countries compared to other Japanese staff members. She had a very positive attitude towards her career. This positive attitude was the greatest factor that contributed towards her success.

Learning from Ms. F's example, young people, regardless of nationality who wish to embark on a career as a professional in the UN Common System should continually remember and take the following advice to find success:

- ✓ Choose a professional field or a specialist area of study during university or post-graduate school. Think of how to become a specialist in your field of study and what sort of training and international qualifications are necessary to become such a specialist in the field;
- ✓ Carefully consider which organization you wish to work for and find its recruitment policy;
- ✓ Find the appropriate entry method. Check to see if your country is invited to a YPP exam (former UN competitive exam) for employment in the UN Secretariat. Also check whether there is a JPO scheme in your country;

- ✓ Find opportunities to pursue higher-graded posts, regardless of the duty station. If promoted, you will gain greater satisfaction;
- ✓ Try to find a mentor at your first workplace and have a career anchor.

If you develop your career path by taking into account the points above, your path to becoming a successful international civil servant with a highly satisfying career will not prove too difficult. Even if you are over 30 years old, the door to the UN is still open to you.

Final Recommendations for the Globalization of Japanese Enterprises

In this section, recommendations for the successful globalization of Japanese enterprises as viewed from the perspective of the study of International Civil Servants are presented. As globalization accelerates, employees who are capable of working in English and who positively embrace work overseas will aspire to work in a workplace that respects and highly-evaluates their ability. From the interviews, we learned that staff members working for International Organizations in the UN Common System were not financially motivated; they were seeking to gain personal satisfaction out of their work. As such, Japanese private enterprises should establish a HRM system that nurtures such highly capable and motivated employees.

There are five recommendations for the successful globalization of Japanese enterprises:

- ✓ **Develop Specialists**: From the interviews with those Japanese collaborators who work in the UN Common System, we learned that highly professional specialists expressed the highest levels of satisfaction. Japanese private enterprises tend to be keen on training generalists, but outside Japan, organizations utilize highly professional specialists with high academic credentials and those who have work experience in a relevant field. If we realize that Japanese enterprises will have to compete with enterprises overseas, Japanese companies must select qualified staff, concentrating on educating them to become specialists to compete with their counterparts overseas.
- ✓ **Expand the mid-career employment market**: As explained in Chapter 3

many of the staff members who work in specialized organizations are considering pursuing work in a workplace where they can utilize their skills and ability. In order to better utilize the high capacity of specialists in society, it is necessary to enlarge the mid-career recruitment market that would enhance the mobility of professional human resources in Japan.

- ✓ **Select *global* candidates at an early stage in their career**: From the second survey it was clear to see that non-Japanese staff members were more positive towards career development than Japanese staff members. Many Japanese started working in private enterprises upon graduating from university and changed their career track to the UN Common System in the middle of their career. Non-Japanese staff members choose their occupational field at an earlier stage and developed their career path in accordance with their professional field. To develop human resources who can take an active global role, it is essential to acquire education in a specialized field; various work experience, including experience overseas; the ability to communicate in English and intercultural communication strategies. To acquire these skills, long-term preparation is essential. Therefore, Japanese enterprises need to select qualified individuals and train these global candidates from an earlier stage.
- ✓ **Increase the number of women in the workplace**: The average age of female collaborators in the interviews was 47 years old. It is not appropriate to simply compare this figure with the present situation in Japan, as these women worked in Japan before the *Equal Employment Opportunity Law* was enforced in Japan. However, from the survey conducted by the Ministry of Health, Labour and Welfare in 2007, the number of female managers above chief level in Japan was as low as 4.9%. It can be said that female human resources are not well utilized in Japan. It takes time to increase the number of women in the workforce. As an example, Scandinavian countries experienced a national labour shortage, as a result, a national referendum as to whether or not the country should make use of an immigrant labor force or their own female labor force took place. The country chose to use the female workforce and developed a social security system where women could work and raise their children. Labor shortages

are already being felt in Japan. Therefore, if enterprises wish to use women to cope with this demand, they need to seriously consider the adoption and improvement of similar policies so that women are encouraged to take an active part in society. Companies will have to guarantee women the right to return to the same or equivalent post to enable them to continue to work after they have taken maternity leave. Maternity leave is a right of a woman, and should be clearly stated in staff regulations.

- ✓ **Assist employees in achieving a work-life balance**: The fifth recommendation is the realization of a balance between work and life. Many collaborators pointed out that over the course of a long successful career, work-life balance is indispensable. Allowing employees to develop quality and satisfaction in their private life will surely support their performance in a performance-oriented workplace. It is necessary for the organization to seriously explore a work environment where work-life balance is materialized, as well as to effectively utilize human resources within the organization over longer periods of time.

Recommendations for Future Research

A study on career development is an emerging field of HRM. As discussed in Chapter 1, to cope with globalization, leading Japanese companies have changed their HRM practices to become more performance-oriented.

Consequently, highly talented Japanese who can also work in English will not hesitate to develop their careers outside Japan, using their skills accumulated in Japanese enterprises. In this research, the author focused on the case of Japanese international civil servants. However, there are qualified Japanese who work for private enterprises overseas or for foreign affiliated companies in Japan. These people have the potential to be interesting research subjects in the future.

In addition, when Japanese enterprises expand their market overseas, an essential issue will be whether or not Japanese companies are attractive to local elites in the recipient countries. Thus, it is meaningful to study what makes local elites want to select a Japanese company to work for over a foreign-affiliated company.

Future Prospects

This study on the career development of formal staff members in the UN Common System was done from the point of view of individuals who work as international civil servants.

As previously described, Japan is at the height of societal and structural change as a result of globalization, and it cannot steer around this change. Japanese-style management, that played an enormous role in Japan during the latter part of the twentieth century before the collapse of the bubble economy, is coming to an end. It is important to nurture new human resources and change systems so that these young employees can take an active part in a globalized society.

The author considers that there are some HR practices in Japan to be re-evaluated and some to be discarded; both have to be studied in more detail. For example there is an excellent system of teamwork in Japanese enterprises. Mid-level managers provide younger employees with opportunities for learning and leadership. They also play the role of a mentor leading younger members through problem solving strategies and providing guidance in the workplace. Studying the career paths of the international civil servants made the author reconfirm how such teamwork, leadership and mentoring are taken for granted in Japan and how much they contributed to the power of Japanese business organizations. These aspects of Japanese HRM practices should be emphasized. Conversely, the seniority-order wage system and management policy that places an importance on generalists, is not a good fit with global HRM. In order to survive in a globalized society now is the time for such Japanese HRM practices to be seriously reviewed.

It is the author's strong wish that readers who have strong qualifications and who want to take an active part in designing their future will enjoy a satisfying career as an international civil servant.

Finally, by looking at the UN Common System and its HRM practices, it is hoped that policy makers and managers will find the recommendations in this book useful for improving the HRM practices in Japan.

Appendix 1

The 23 Interviews from International Civil Servants and a Description of their Career Paths

Interviews were designed based on a set of pre-defined questions. The answers were written in sentence-form on two A4 sheets. Diagrammatic representations of the respondents' career paths were made from the interview data. Then, each record of interviews was sent back to the respective respondents by e-mail to be proofread. Prior to publication, the author asked all of the respondents for their approval to include their case in this book. The author also checked if the respondents had received any promotion or transfer of post, since the interviews and if this was the case, these facts were added to the end of each record.

Question Items
0. Name
1. Age
2. Gender
3. Marital status (1 single, 2 married, 3 other)
4. Birthplace (prefecture)
5. Education prior to university
6. Name of agency/organization where one works
7. Duty station (1 headquarters, 2 others)
8. Post
9. Grade
10. Time when first wished to work in an international organization
11. Work experience in Japan
12. Occupation in Japan
13. How employed by international organizations
14. Starting age at international organizations
15. Length of service thus far

16. Age when employed as a formal staff member
17. Years of service in the UN Common System
18. Number of countries worked in (duty stations under the UN Common System)
19. Professional development activities after starting work in international organizations
20. Level of satisfaction (1 low, 2 more or less low, 3 average, 4 more or less high, 5 high)
21. Presence or absence of a mentor in the initial position
22. Networks inside outside of the work place
23. Prospect of working in the international organization up to retirement age
24. Source of satisfaction (job satisfaction, satisfaction at duty stations, overall satisfaction)
25. Usefulness of work experience in Japan
26. Importance of salary when choosing an occupation
27. Attitude for work
28. Career Anchor

Appendix 1 The 23 Interviews from International Civil Servants and a Description of their Career Paths

Case A

Gender:	Female
Age:	31 years old (at time of interview)
Birthplace:	Japan
Position:	UNDP Headquarters, Evaluation Specialist (P-2)
Location:	New York (USA)

Ms. A. entered an international high school in Switzerland by her own initiative. She then went to a 4 year liberal arts college on the East coast of the USA, and majored in Development Studies. While studying at that college she went to study at a university in Senegal, Africa as part of an exchange program. After graduating from university, she obtained work experience at The Training Center of International Law in Washington, DC. She then went to Columbia University Graduate School and majored in Development Economics. When she was still at graduate school she worked as an intern and a consultant at the UN Secretariat. She also took an examination to become a Junior Professional Officer, sponsored by the Ministry of Foreign Affairs in Japan. She passed the exam and was employed by the UNDP as a JPO, that is, as a young expert. This enabled her to go to Malawi, Africa at the age of 25. Three years later she passed the organization's internal management re-assignment programme called the Quarry Exercise (which was later abolished). This exercise selected highly qualified young professionals for reassignment within the organization. After this exercise she became a formal professional staff member. Her responsibilities include the evaluation of an entire country program (not individual projects within the country) and the strategy of the organization as a whole. She presents evaluation reports to the Executive Board.

Ms. A. had began thinking about working in an international organization when she was at high school, during her experience engaging in refugee assistance programs in Switzerland and long-term volunteer activities in Eastern Europe. With that idea in mind she designed and established her career. Upon finishing her post-graduate course she was offered a position by an international finance corporation in Japan. At that point she wavered, thinking that the experience of working in the private sector might help further her future career in an international organization. However, after much deliberation, she chose to work directly in an international organization without prior private sector experience.

During her second year working in the UNDP headquarters, she became devoted to achieving actual results and performing well. Her present responsibility is to evaluate the projects she is in charge of, and that enables her to observe the overall activities of the UNDP. It is a highly responsible role and, as such, she is satisfied with this position. In the future she is hoping to be in a management position of a country office operation.

As for the location of her work, she said that an international organization was not the only possibility for her. She is also willing to work in JICA, a developmental aid organization, or a university, if the chance arises. However, it is difficult to obtain information about possible positions. In addition, the opportunity for a horizontal shift of job (between different systems) appears infrequent. As she is still young, Ms. A. is unconcerned about a potential decrease in income if she changes positions. She would appreciate a new role if the work provides a new challenge.

Regarding professional development activities, Ms. A. took a French language course offered by the UN Secretariat in New York and she attended a number of training programmes conducted within the organization. She also undertook an annual two-week training course on evaluation conducted by the World Bank and Carlton University. Currently, due to her travel missions, she scarcely has time for training. In order to develop one's career, one could get a PhD, but she doesn't feel that is necessary at this point.

In the UN system, staff, Japanese and non-Japanese alike, often have their hands full just to 'survive' in their post (in the UNDP, employment contracts are short; only one to two years, there are no new permanent contracts issued and job security is not very good). Employees seem to be unable to afford time to train young staff and focus on mentoring and nurturing a cohort of young professionals. Ms. A. is single, and hopes to find a partner who would respect her career, accepts potential job relocation requirements and who would be capable of moving with her if required. She also expressed that it is difficult for women to satisfy both their career and private life as there are few role models that combine the two successfully. In principle, such international organizations understand the concept of equality between the sexes. However, when we observe women who are trying hard to implement these principles, they seem to feel under extreme pressure from their work and difficult working conditions that come with this line of work often prevent women with a young family to be successful.

Additional Notes: Just after this interview, Ms. A. applied to a new system called Rank in Post within the UNDP. She passed the requirements for promotion and passed a competitive process of recruitment for the P4 post, and has now been promoted from rank P-2 to P-4.

Case A Career Path

Age	
16-18	• Attended international high school in Switzerland
18-22	• Attended university in the USA, majoring in Development Studies • Exchange Student in Senegal for 6 months
22-24	• Worked at a Washington-based think-tank
24-25	• Attended graduate school and obtained an MA in Development Economics
25-28	• JPO Malawi • Passed the Quarry Exercise Exam
29-present	• Evaluation Specialist(P-2), UNDP Headquarters, New York, USA

Appendix 1   The 23 Interviews from International Civil Servants and a Description of their Career Paths

Case B

Gender:	Male
Age:	45 years old at time of interview
Birthplace:	Tokyo
Position:	Senior Investment Officer (P-5), UN Joint Staff Pension Fund (UNJSPF)
Location:	New York, USA

Mr. B. was educated in Japan to university level, where he majored in economics. After graduation he joined a Japanese securities company and worked there for ten years. From 1991 to 1993, his company dispatched him to New York University. While there, he obtained an MBA (Master of Business Administration). One and a half years after returning to Japan he was transferred to his company's Hong Kong office. After working there for about four years, he left the company.

He then joined a foreign capital investment trust bank in Japan where he worked as a fund manager. In 2004, on finding an announcement for a vacancy in a P-4 post at the UN Pension Fund, he applied for the post, and was accepted. Three years later, the post was reclassified as P-5 and he was selected through a competitive selection process. The UN Pension Fund amounts more than four trillion yen in total. Mr. B. is in charge of a portfolio of the Japan and Asia-Pacific equity portfolio and he manages the resources of as much as 300 billion yen by himself. His primary responsibility at that time was in charge of international equities both in the Japanese securities company and foreign-capital bank. However, he wanted to expand his expertise in Japanese stocks so he changed his employment to the UNJSPF. He is now very pleased with his current position.

As to the sources of satisfaction, his main interest used to be job satisfaction when he worked for companies in Japan and when he started at the UN, but now, both his job-satisfaction as well as satisfaction at this duty station are fulfilled. Concerning his family life, he is 100% satisfied but with regard to his job-satisfaction, he is 70%

satisfied. This is because, although he is very content with the present duty, his duties, which have no direct relevance to investments, have increased due to political issues. The decision making process in the UN is sometimes very top-down and politically motivated. Also, he feels the rules and regulations are so tight and complicated, the procedure is very lengthy and inflexible, particularly in the area of the procurement and hiring.

Regarding a mentor, previously, he could learn from his former supervisor and senior members, however, he cannot name any mentors in the present office. There is no colleague or boss who could be a mentor. As for his personal networks, outside the office, he has business relations with his former securities colleagues and other professionals in the security field. To the question of whether he intends to work at the UN until retirement age, he didn't know. As each position is independent, it is difficult to work in another UN department. On the other hand, he has 20 more years before retirement, and he could not foresee whether he could carry on doing the same sort of work till retirement age. As to shifting jobs to another organization, he said it depended on the opportunity and timing.

When the author asked if his experience of working in a Japanese enterprise proved useful to his present job, he says the experiences at UNJSPF is very unique, so he does not have any specific career plan in Japan at this moment. However, the networks he has made so far in the Japanese context are certainly useful.

As for his own self and professional development, he attended various lectures and study meetings organized by universities and other research institutes that are financed by the UN. He attended a seminar on finance technology at Harvard University and a training course at Columbia University.

When he applied for a position in the United Nations, income was not so important. Actually, his income did drop substantially. However, he was pleased with his work, and he had long wanted that his children should be educated in the United States, that is, the quality of life in the United States was more important than financial gain.

At the end of his interview he mentioned his disapproval of the way Japanese personnel departments relocate staff members based on the needs of the company. Once an involuntary writ of appointment is issued as to the place to live, period, etc., one has to change all their life plans, including their children's education and other family plans. He said that individuals should make their life plans by themselves.

Additional Note: The year after the interview took place Mr. B. was selected as a Deputy Director of the newly established Investment Department (D-1).

Case B Career Path

- **18-22**: Graduated from university in Japan, majoring in Economics
- **22**: Employed by a Japanese Security Company, Tokyo, Japan
- **25-27**: Studied at the Graduate School of New York University USA, funded by the Japanese company
- **27-29**: Returned to the Japanese security company, Tokyo, Japan
- **29-33**: Transferred to the Hong Kong office of the same Japanese securities company
- **33-37**: *Fund Manager*, Foreign Capital Trust Investment Bank, Tokyo, Japan
- **37-40**: *Investment Officer* (P-4), UN Joint Pension Fund, New York, USA
- **41-present**: *Senior Investment Officer* (P-5), UN Joint Pension Fund, New York, USA

Case C

Gender:	Male
Age:	41 years old (at time of interview)
Birthplace:	Shizuoka Prefecture
Position:	Chief, UNDP (United Nations Development Programme), Chief, Financial Administration Section, Administration Department (P-5)
Duty Station:	New York, USA

Due to his father's work, Mr. C. was educated in the USA from high school, then studied Political Science at Columbia University. After graduation he was employed by a Japanese commercial bank in Japan. Three years later, he moved to a US investment bank, and stayed there for six years. Then, he entered LSE (London School of Economics) and obtained a Master's degree in Finance.

As he approached the age of 30, he began to question the meaning of working in a profit pursuing company, and thought of working for a place where he can contribute to society. He thought of working for an NGO, but he didn't pursue the idea as the salary level there was low. Finally, he decided to work for an international organization. He passed the AE (Associate Expert, presently JPO) Exam organized by the Japanese Ministry of Foreign Affairs. He started as an Associate Expert at the UNDP in Laos. He was 32 years old.

He started his career as an international civil servant in Laos, but his specialty was finance. He thought his chance of utilizing his ability would be limited if he worked with a relatively small programme. He got on well with the American deputy representative of the office, and when they were talking about his future in an international organization, he came to know that the New York headquarters of the UNDP was looking for finance specialists. When Mr. C. was an associate expert, his work period was for three years. Therefore, he negotiated with the Ministry of Foreign Affairs in Tokyo so that his third year assignment could be at the headquarters of UNDP in NY, and this worked out.

Since he moved to the headquarters in NY his supervisors recognized his strong ability in finance, thus he got a position as a P-3 regular finance officer at the UNDP at the age of 34.

After working three years at the headquarters, he became a deputy resident representative (P-4) in Tanzania for three years, and since 2007, his staff grade was P-5, although his post grade is D-1. He is 41, soon going to be 42. The number of higher posts in the United Nations Common System, including the UNDP, is limited. He does not feel the necessity of pursuing rapid career-advancement, when he thinks of his own age. Financing operations in the UNDP is not necessarily the main function of the UNDP in comparison with the programming division. Therefore, he is exploring the possibly of moving to such organizations as the DPKO (Department of Peace Keeping Operations) or WFP (World Food Programme) where the distribution and finance divisions have a more important place within the organization. Regarding his intention to work in an international organization, he answered that for the moment he intends to continue in the UNDP.

In answer to the question about mentors, he stated that mentors and other human networks play a very important role in his working life. During his days at the Japanese commercial bank he hadn't encountered any mentors, but in the second year after he started working for a US investment bank, he found two mentors, and their influence is still great in his life. At present, he has three mentors; one of them is his former boss.

Regarding networking at the office, as major decisions are usually made by consensus, prior consultation with colleagues is indispensable. Now, he has colleagues whom he trusts in other departments and he can share opinions with them. This networking is crucial for carrying out work successfully.

To the question of whether the amount of income is an important factor for choosing a job, he answered it didn't matter as far as one can maintain a relatively comfortable lifestyle. Actually, when Mr. C. changed his job from a US investment bank to the UNDP his income has reduced to less than one-third.

When asked if his work experience as a business man in Japan was useful for the present job, he answered that his experience and knowledge acquired in a Japanese bank and an American investment bank are fully utilized now. Although he has worked for a US bank, most of the customers were Japanese, so he needed to understand the mechanisms of decision-making in Japanese organizations. When working in an international organization Japanese staff should be more aware that he is Japanese, and should be able to explain to other non-Japanese staff members how decisions are made in Japanese organizations.

Case C Career Path

- **Childhood**: Spent Junior High School in Japan and High School in the USA
- **18-22**: Obtained BA Columbia University in the USA majoring in Politics
- **22-25**: Worked at a commercial bank, Tokyo, Japan
- **25-31**: Worked for a US Investment Bank, Tokyo, Japan
- **31-32**:
  - Studied at the School of Economics, London University, UK
  - Obtained an MSc in Finance
- **32-33**: *JPO (L-2)*, in charge of Finance, UNDP, Laos Office
- **33-34**: JPO (L-2) in charge of Finance, UNDP Headquarters, New York USA
- **34-37**: *Finance Specialist (P-3)*, UNDP, New York Headquarters, New York, USA
- **37-40**: *Deputy Resident Representative (P-4)*, UNDP, Tanzania Office
- **40-present**: *Chief, (P-5) Finance Administration Section, Administration Department*, New York Headquarters, New York, USA

Case D

Gender:	Female
Age:	47 years old (at time of interview)
Birthplace:	Kanagawa Prefecture
Position:	Deputy Cashier, Treasury Dept. (P-3), the UN Secretariat
Duty Station:	New York, USA

Ms. D was educated overseas from junior high to university due to her father's job. At university she obtained a BA majoring in Business Administration with an emphasis in Finance. As she contemplated of returning to Japan after graduation, she decided not to pursue a post-graduate degree (in those days it would have been difficult to find an entry-level job in Japan if one had a MA).

Once back in Japan, she was employed by a Japanese subsidiary of a US company, and was assigned to the personnel department. She worked there just over three years, but her main duties were clerical work and translation, which provided limited job-satisfaction. During that time, her father found a newspaper article advertising that a competitive examination for United Nations staff would be held in Tokyo, so he suggested her to send her application. Following her father's advice she submitted the application, and she was invited to participate in the written exam. Subsequently, she was invited for the interview and placed on a roster as a successful candidate for future opening. She was 24 years old at time. However, due to the hiring freeze resulting from the financial crisis in the UN, it was not until almost 3 years later that she was offered a job.

Her first duty station was Nairobi, the headquarters of the UNEP (United Nations Environment Programme). She was in charge of Cashier's Office there for six years. Then she applied and was selected for a post in the Cashier Office in Treasury at the Headquarters in New York. She has been working in that department until now.

At present, there are two professional staff members in the Cashier's Office, including herself. They supervise five clerical workers. The section is responsible for recording incoming payments, including government contributions, salary payments to New York-based staff and those working in the field offices, payments to vendors, consultants and various other entities. In addition, the section handles setting up banking details for the staff members and government entities in the in-house developed system. Accuracy and an eye for detail are expected as the section deals with actual payments and bank account details. Sometimes she feels frustrated as it is a low profile appointment, and that the section's contribution to the overall well-being of the organization is not fully appreciated.

She has thought of seeking another post at a different department, or another duty station, she has even considered the possibility of returning to the private sector, but eventually she decided to continue with her present responsibility. Had she been working in a budgeting or accounting department in the UN Common System, she might have been able to transfer to a different area within the same department since these departments are much larger in size than the Treasury. The cashier section is a small office and only one person, the Head Cashier, is above her, so unless her boss transfers to another post or retires, she cannot expect a promotion.

In response to the question of her credo towards work, she mentioned that working for the UN is not much different from working for any other internationally-based company, and it is a means to pay the bills and travel abroad for leisure.

Additional Notes: After the interview took place, Ms.D. was promoted to Chief Cashier (P-4)

Case D Career Path

Childhood
- Studied Junior and High School outside Japan

18-23
- Graduated from a university in the USA majoring in Business Administration with an emphasis in Finance

23-27
- Worked for a Japanese subsidiary of a US Company
- Passed the UN Competitive Exam

27-33
- *Assistant Finance Officer* (P-1) and then *Associate Finance Officer* (P-2) at UNEP Nairobi Headquarters, Nairobi, Kenya

33-50
- *Deputy Cashier* (P-3) at UN Secretariat, New York, USA

50-present
- *Cashier* (P-4) at UN Secretariat, New York, USA

Case E

Gender:	Female
Age:	33 years old (at time of interview)
Birthplace:	Tokyo
Position:	UN Secretariat, Political Affairs Officer, Best Practices Section, Department of Peacekeeping Operations (P-3)
Duty Station:	New York, USA

Ms. E. was educated partially overseas and partially in Japan due to her father's work. She graduated from the Sociology Department of Keio University, Tokyo, Japan. After graduation, she went to graduate school at Leeds University, UK, and obtained an MA in International Studies. After that, she went to Columbia University and got her second MA in International Relations.

After getting her degree in the United States, she applied for a job and went back to Japan to work in a private bank. When she was studying at graduate school, she took an exam to become an Associate Expert, which was a programme organized by the Ministry of Foreign Affairs in Japan. She passed it, and left the bank where she had worked for a year and a half. She started her career in the Department of Political Affairs of the United Nations Headquarters. At that time, Ms. E. was 27 years old.

In the Department of Political Affairs, she provided assistance to the desk officer, working on the Sudan for the first eighteen months as an Associate Expert. She was then deployed to Sudan in a formal staff position as a Special Assistant to the Special Representative of the Secretary-General in the Sudan. She worked in Sudan for one and a half years. During this period she had applied and was accepted for a new post in the UNOPS (United Nations Office for Project Services) Tokyo Liaison Office. By the time she was on this post for about 10 months, she received the news of having passed the National Competitive Exam for the UN. Through this process, she was offered a post in the Department of Peacekeeping Operations in New York. At the time of the interview, Ms. E. had worked in the United Nations for five years, in three countries and experienced four different posts. She said her variety of experience proved useful for her present post.

She said it was when she was at university that she seriously thought that working in the United Nations was a reality. When she was at graduate school she worked as an intern in the Electoral Affairs Division, in the Department of Political Affairs in the United Nations Secretariat. At that time, she came to know the actual content of such work, which strongly motivated her to work in the United Nations.

To the author's question of whether she met any mentor when she started to work, she mentioned two people. One was a Japanese UN staff member whom she met in her intern days. By coincidence, when she began working in the UN Headquarters as an Associate Expert, this person was working in the same bureau, so she was able ask her for various advice. As for the other person, she met him through the Mentorship System in the department also when she was an Associate Expert. At that time, a South African senior staff member offered to be her mentor, and she learned how to work in an environment such as the United Nations. At present, along with these staff members, she also has a few more whom she can ask for advice.

As for her networks inside and outside of her workplace, she has a few friends whom she can talk to about personal and other matters. She also tries to increase communication with her colleagues by going out for lunch, etc.

To the question of satisfaction, she answered that maintaining balance between job-satisfaction and personal life is important. When she was a Special Assistant to the Special Representative of the Secretary-General to the Sudan, she scarcely had time for herself. Having experienced this, she is convinced that the balance between work and private life is important.

As for her experience of working in Japan in the private sector, she answered that her experience was very helpful as Japanese companies invest in educating their employees. Although she didn't realize while working there, her supervisors took plenty of time to educate her about the basics of work. It has proved very useful for her present job to which she is appreciative. Since she enjoyed the working environment in the Japanese company, it was difficult for her to decide whether to work for the United Nations after having been informed that she was selected to become an Associate Expert.

To the author's question of whether or not she intends to work in the international organization until retirement age, she said she didn't know. Though she is satisfied with the present job, she might possibly leave and work in a different place if anything unreasonable or disappointing should arise. For that reason, she believes one should have many options in life.

Regarding the importance of salary in choosing a job, she answered that has never been the key factor in making decisions. In the future when she must decide whether or not she would want to be transferred to other international organizations, the key to her decision making would lie in whether the work would be interesting or not. Finally, she mentioned three important attitudes towards work; first, put importance on the actual work you do; second, think positively; and third, have your own mid- and long-term work plan.

Appendix 1　The 23 Interviews from International Civil Servants and a Description of their Career Paths

Case E Career Path

- **Childhood**: Spent Junior High School and High School both inside and outside Japan

- **18-22**: Studied and Graduated from Department of Sociology, Keio University, Japan

- **22-23**: Obtained an MA in International Studies, Leeds University, UK

- **23-25**: Obtained an MA in International Relations at Columbia University

- **25-27**:
  - Returned to Japan and worked for a commercial bank, Tokyo, Japan
  - Passed the JPO Exam

- **27-28**: *JPO (L-2)*, Department of Political Affairs, UN Headquarters, New York, USA

- **29-30**: *Special Assistant (L-2)* to the Special Representative to the Sudan, Sudan

- **30-31**:
  - *Head of UNOPS*, Tokyo Office, Tokyo, Japan
  - Passed the UN Competitive Exam

- **31-present**: *Political Affairs Officer (P-3)*, Department of Peace Keeping Operations, UN Secretariat, New York, New York, USA

Case F

Gender: Female
Age: 54 years old (at time of interview)
Birthplace: Madrid, Spain
Position: Assistant Administrator and Director (ASG), Bureau of Management, UNDP
Duty Station: New York, USA

Ms. F. was educated both in Japan and overseas due to her father's work. She graduated from Barnard College (Liberal Arts), Columbia University. She reflects that when she was at university and thought seriously of her future occupation, she thought that working in an international organization could be one of the alternatives. After graduating from university, she applied for the Associate Expert/JPO scheme managed by the Ministry of Foreign Affairs in Japan and passed it. She started her career in international organizations as Assistant to Deputy Regional Representative of UNDP in their Thailand Office. After about a year, she became Assistant to Coordinator of the United Nations Population Fund (UNFPA) in Bangkok, Thailand. During this period she was selected for the post of Programme Officer, Programme Support Division, Regional Bureau for Asia and the Pacific of UNDP headquarters, and became a regular staff member. She stayed in this post for about two years, and then she became Area Officer in the same Bureau in charge of China and the Philippines. While she was working in New York, she obtained an MA in Development Economics from the Graduate School of Arts and Science of New York University.

For the following four years she took special leave from the UNDP and worked in Japan. For the first two and a half years she worked at the Engineering Consulting Firms Association of Japan (ECFA) as a Project Research Officer, and for the following one and a half years, she worked as a freelance consultant in Japan. In 1988, she returned to UNDP as Assistant Regional Representative in its Thailand Office and worked for two and a half years, and then worked as Deputy Resident Representative in the Indonesia Office for three and a half years. After this assignment, she worked as Resident Representative in the UNDP Bhutan Office for four and a half years. During this period she was promoted from P-5 to D-1. She then again took special leave from UNDP and became Professor in the Global and Inter-Cultural Studies Department of Ferris University, Yokohama, Japan. She taught for three years both at undergraduate and postgraduate levels.

In 2002, she returned to UNDP and became Director in its Tokyo Office for four years. During this period she was promoted from D-1 to D-2. She has been in the present post at UNDP headquarters since September 2006, and she manages about 200 professional staff and 200 general service staff.

Since Ms. F. started working in the UNDP, she has worked in five countries and experienced nine posts within UNDP and three posts in Japan including while she was on leave, totaling 12 posts thus expanding her professional experience. Her current post is at a very senior level among Japanese staff who work in the United Nations Common System. This can be due to her capabilities as well as the result of frequent transfers based on her own initiative.

As for mentors, Ms. F. had never had one during her career within international organizations until now. However, in her first workplace she got along very well with two male colleagues, American and British (both in their thirties then), and they guided her about the way to work in an international organization.

Regarding networking within the UNDP, senior management meetings comprising of Bureau Directors are held at least once every month. She recognizes that communication with both Bureau Directors and Deputy Directors is indispensable for carrying out her present duties. She also answered that it is necessary to maintain good relationships with people in charge of related fields in other UN organizations such as UNICEF and UNFPA.

To the question about her level of satisfaction, she answered that it is important to keep a balance between job satisfaction and satisfaction in personal life. If one is overly emphasized, then the other may suffer; good work-life balance will not be attained.

She thinks her experience of working in Japan was useful. First, her knowledge acquired about Japan's ODA policies and procedures is considered useful when promoting collaboration between international organizations and Japan. Second, it is important to have a network of professionals in the development cooperation field in Japan. It would not be possible to build such a network with only short visits such as home leave.

Answering the question of whether the amount of income mattered when selecting her own job, she stated that she has never thought about the income when she had to choose her job. It would be a problem if it was too low, but a sufficient amount will do.

Finally, she said her sources of power are, first, a belief in herself, especially in times of difficulties. Second is the feeling that her life is privileged and her job is meaningful. Third, is the fact that her partner and her family are always supportive.

Case F Career Path

Age	Description
Childhood	• Educated up to high school both inside and outside Japan
18-22	• Studied and graduated from Barnard College, Columbia University • Passed the AE/JPO Exam
23-24	• *Assistant to Regional Representative (L-1)* Thailand Office, JPO UNDP, Bangkok, Thailand
24-25	• *Assistant to Coordinator (L-1)*, JPO UNFPA, Bangkok, Thailand
25-27	• *Programme Officer (P-2)*, Regional Bureau for Asia and the Pacific, UNDP Headquarters, New York, USA
27-30	• *Area Officer (P-3)*, Regional Bureau for Asia UNDP Headquarters, New York, USA • Obtained an MA in Development Economics from New York University
30-33	• *Project Research Officer*, Engineering Consulting Firms Association of Japan (ECFA), Tokyo, Japan
34-35	• *Freelance Consultant*, Tokyo, Japan
35-37	• Returned to UNDP as *Assistant Regional Representative (P-3)* of Thailand Office, Bangkok, Thailand
37-40	• *Deputy Resident Representative (P-4)* in the Indonesia Office, UNDP, Indonesia
40-45	• *Resident Representative of* UNDP Bhutan Office (P-5) • Promoted to (D-1)
45-48	• Special Leave • *Professor*, Global and Inter-cultural Studies Department, Ferris University, Yokohama, Japan
48-52	• *Director of UNDP Tokyo Office*, (D-1) to (D-2), Tokyo, Japan
52-present	• *Assistant Administrator and Director Bureau of Management* (ASG), UNDP, New York, USA

Case G

Gender:	Female
Age:	50 years old (at time of interview)
Birthplace:	Hyogo Prefecture
Position:	United Nations Secretariat, Social Affairs Officer, (P-4) Social Integration, Branch, Division for Social Policy and Development. Department of Economic and Social Affairs.
Duty Station:	New York, USA

Ms. G. was born and brought up in Japan. She had never been educated overseas until she studied in US at graduate school. Her undergraduate degree was in the Department of English Literature, Kansei Gakuin University. While she was at university, she participated in a study tour in Indonesia, sponsored by her university, and came to know the situation in Indonesia, through this experience. She subsequently became interested in the development projects of developing countries. However, it was only a vague idea to enter this field and she didn't expect that this dream-like idea would come true. After graduation, she was employed by a private company. She resigned after two and a half years thinking that there was no prospect for the future as long as she was a woman. She began to work as a staff member in the International Exchange Center of her alma mater. When she was transferred to the Chancellor's Office she took a leave of absence, and entered the Graduate School of Indiana University, USA, and obtained an MA in Higher Education and Public Policy. During this period, she came to know about the Associate Expert Examination conducted by the Ministry of Foreign Affairs, and thought seriously of working in an international organization. She applied for the exam, after returning to Japan, she went back to her former workplace but she couldn't make up her mind whether or not she should continue with her present career in Japan or choose a new career working in an international organization. She quit her position at the university and went back to graduate school at Indiana University. She passed the Associate Expert Exam while she was there and made up to become an international civil servant.

Ms. G. started working as a JPO at the UN Volunteer Programme Headquarters, which was under the UNDP in Geneva for two years. Towards the end of her first year as a JPO, she saw a vacancy announcement of a National Competitive Exam of the United Nations at P-3 level. She took the exam and passed it. She was posted to take charge of technical cooperation, especially poverty alleviation in the Department of Economic and Social Development (DESD), (later the Department for Development Support and Management Services (DDSMS), in the UN Secretariat Headquarters). After working in this post for a few years, she moved to the Women's Bureau under the Department of Economical and Social Affairs (DESA), which was newly created after the reorganization. There, she took charge of supporting the Commission on the Status of Women (CSW) and Committee on the Elimination of Discrimination Against Women (CEDAW). Specifically, she was in charge of supporting capacity building for the governments of developing countries, and supporting conflict prevention and peace building in countries in Africa, emphasizing how to put women's view-points across in the aforementioned processes. Since 2004, she has been in charge of linking social integration, conflict prevention, and building peace in the division of Social Policy and Development in the same department. As one can see from the above brief background, Ms.G. has continued to build a career in the field of socio-economic development. Although she is based in the headquarters, she visits developing countries carrying out poverty surveys in such least developed countries such as Myanmar or organizing workshops in various places in Africa. Thus, she visits the actual sites very frequently and sometimes for a long period.

When the author asked her if she could find any mentor in her first duty station in the UN Common System, she answered that the Deputy Director of the UN Volunteer Programme happened to be a Japanese, so she could ask this person for advice about her career path after being a JPO. Also, in the days when she started working in New York, a great senior of her university was the director of the same bureau where she worked, so she could get much advice from him. In New York she was once a vice president of the society of Japanese UN staff, so she could become acquainted with senior Japanese staff members in the UN and attachés from the Ministry of Foreign Affairs. As such, she could get both direct and indirect advice and support from them. To her regret after she had a baby, it became difficult to attend such study meetings and other such activities after working hours.

At present she has no mentor, but she has a network inside and outside of her office. More specifically, they are colleagues who work in other departments and bureaus that she became acquainted with through work, ex-colleagues she once worked with, people in NGOs and other international organizations and Japanese staff members. She has special networks with those members she was acquainted with through the management workshops she attended. These workshops were held for mid-level staff members, from different departments, to share similar problems. Advice from members of these workshops was helpful, as they have experienced similar kinds of problems. They are helpful in solving problems. Likewise the network of female staff is important in the UN.

Regarding the level of satisfaction, she answered that to her, job satisfaction is very important. If one's job is interesting, one will gain strength and can make one's private life satisfactory as well.

To the question of whether salary level matters in selecting a job, she answered it is good if the salary is high, but it is more important that the job gives you a sense of satisfaction.

She is conscious and thankful that she is privileged, because her life would have been completely different if she had been born in a poor agricultural village in a developing country. As such, she wishes her job; knowledge and experience should help those people in developing countries. In addition to her working life, she is also a mother of two children. She is very conscious that the life cycle of a woman is very different from that of a man.

Case G Career Path

18-22
- Graduated from the Department of English Literature from a Japanese University

22-25
- Office Administration in a private company, Japan

25-29
- International Exchange Center Staff and later the Chancellor's Office at her Alma Mater

29-32
- Studied at and graduated with an MA in Higher Education Public Policy, Indiana University, USA
- Passed the AE Exam

32-34
- *JPO (L-2)*, UN Volunteer Office Headquarters (UNDP), Geneva, Switzerland
- Passed the UN Competitive Exam

34-39
- *Programme Officer (P-3), Department of Economic and Social Development* (DESD), UN Secretariat, New York, USA

40-46
- *Programme Officer (P-3), Department of Economic and Social Affairs* (DESA), UN Secretariat, New York, USA

46-present
- *Social Affairs Officer (P-4)*, Worked in the Commission on the Status of Women (CSW) and Committee on the Elimination of Discrimination Against Women (CEDAW), DESA, UN Secretariat, New York, USA

Case H

Gender:	Male
Age:	41 years old (at time of interview)
Birthplace:	Osaka Prefecture
Position:	Program Specialist, UNDP (United Nations Development Programme) Crisis Prevention, in charge of Asia-Pacific Region, Reconstruction Assistance Bureau (P-4)
Duty Station:	New York, USA

Mr. H. was educated up to graduate level in Japan. He attended the Law Department of Kwansei Gakuin University. In one of his undergraduate classes, he studied international organizations and international civil servants from a professor of Osaka University. It was then that he became interested in this field. He was attracted to the work and influenced by this professor, so upon graduation he studied at the Graduate School of Law at Osaka University, where he received an MA in International Relations. During his graduate studies, he also studied at the graduate school of Hawaii University as an exchange student where he studied political science. On completion of his graduate studies at Osaka University, he moved to the Netherlands, studied at the Institute of Social Studies (ISS) and obtained his second MA in Development Studies.

While he was at the Graduate School in the Netherlands, he took the Japanese Foreign Ministry's Associate Expert Exam, which he passed. His first assignment as a JPO was at the UNDP office in Pakistan. After completing the initial two-year contract, he became a formal project staff member (L-3) and carried on working in Pakistan a further two more years. Mr. H. got married during graduate school, but he went to work in Pakistan by himself. While he was working in Pakistan, he began to think that family members should live together, so he went back to Japan to be with his family. He then worked in the Tokyo office of the UNOPS for a short time, and looked for a job in Osaka where his family lived. He then started working at the Osaka Branch of a major American consulting firm. Soon after he began working there, a UNDP recruitment mission visited Japan. He took the exam and

Appendix 1   The 23 Interviews from International Civil Servants and a Description of their Career Paths

passed. He was assigned to the UNDP Office in Tokyo. He worked as a Programme Manager (P-3) for three years, until he was transferred to the headquarters four years ago, where he has remained until now.

He is in charge of assisting in crisis prevention, developing strategic plans and giving support to field offices when they deal with natural disasters or peace building. He also takes charge of conflict prevention, strengthening reconstruction support work and coordination with other international organizations.

Mr. H. has worked for the UNDP for 11 years, though there was a break during that period. From when he started, until the present day he has worked in three countries; Pakistan, Japan and the USA (New York), and has experienced four different posts within the UNDP.   He says the foundation of his career is his work in Pakistan.

When asked if he had any mentor at his very first workplace within the UNDP, he said that at that time, the deputy representative of the Pakistan Office was a Japanese, and that his influence was enormous. The feeling that he was trusted in the office together with a British Resident Representative, made him feel confident at work, and gave him great encouragement. He does not have a mentor now.

At present, he said he enjoys his work while maintaining good team work and relations with relevant duty officers in New York, Geneva, and Bangkok. When he goes on field missions to developing countries, he works together as a team with other colleagues for about two weeks. As a result, they come to know each other closely. In addition, conferences with members in charge of the UN and other reconstruction and humanitarian assistance organizations, are held so frequently that even through daily work, a productive human network is spontaneously created.

Regarding the question of satisfaction, he used to seek job satisfaction when he was younger, but as he had a family, and as he became older, he became aware that overall satisfaction in one's private life is necessary, too. Mr. H. has worked in an international organization for a long time and this had required him to leave his family in his home country, Japan. He says that his partner has her own career in teaching in Japan and is interested in and understanding of Mr. H.'s life and work, that's why he could continue working in an international organization. At the of time of interview, his partner was on leave from her job and they were living together in New York with their children. He was married for 17 years but about half of this period they lived separately.

To the question of whether he wanted to work till the mandatory retirement age, he could not answer immediately, because he has to think of his family, his future prospects, and his work environment, which requires periodical transfers. Most UNDP organizations do not offer long-term contracts so the regular staff members have to find the next post or promotion by themselves. As a result, the number of Japanese men in their 40's working in the UNDP is not so high.

Answering the question of whether his experience of working in a Japanese organization proved useful to his present work, with the preamble that his company was a foreign capital company and it was only for a short period that he worked in a Japanese private company, he realized how hard it was to work as a consultant. The work procedures and value systems in private companies and in the public sector are widely different.

In answer to the question of whether the amount of income is important in choosing one's job, he answered that he had never thought of that when it came to choosing his own work. He expected that the United Nations would pay enough salary to live on.

Regarding the question of his career anchor, he stated that when he was very young he used to read a lot of books written by *Ryotaro Shiba*, a famous Japanese history writer.   Many of his books are about young patriots who contributed their lives to create a new Japan from the feudal Edo period to the Meiji period.   As such, he had long aspired to work like them, for example, he wanted to work for the people and for his country and international society. His present work is on the same lines as his aspirations.

Additional Notes: In the year following this interview, Mr. H. was transferred to Thailand as a Programme Specialist (P-4) in the UNDP, Bangkok. Two years later, he came back to New York, continuing with his current job.

Case H Career Path

Age	
18-22	• Graduated from the Department of Law from a Japanese University
22-25	• Obtained an MA in International Relations from a Japanese university and studied at the Graduate school, Hawaii University
26-28	• Studied and obtained an MA in Development Studies from ISS Netherlands
29-31	• *Programme Officer*, JPO (L-2), UNDP, Pakistan Office, Pakistan
31-33	• Programme Office (L-3), UNDP, Pakistan Office, Pakistan
33-34	• *Consultant*, Returned to Japan and worked for an American consulting firm • Passed the Recruitment Mission Exam
34-37	• *Programme Manager*, (P-3), UNDP, Tokyo Office, Tokyo, Japan
37-present	• *Programme Specialist*, (P-4), Reconstruction Assistance Bureau, UNDP, Headquarters, New York, USA

Case I

Gender: Female
Age: 60 years old (at time of interview)
Birthplace: Tokyo
Position: UN Secretariat, Chief of Information Processing & Collection Development, Dag Hammarskjold Library (P-5)
Duty Station: New York, USA

Ms. I. was educated in Japan until she graduated from a university. She majored in History at the School of Arts and Sciences, Tokyo Woman's Christian University. After graduation, she worked for a joint venture between Japanese and American companies for two years. Then, she got married. Soon she went to New York with her husband when he was transferred there for his work. In New York, she attended Long Island University and obtained an MS in Library Science from Palmer Graduate School of Library Science. She was recommended by her husband's friend (who was a staff member of the UN) to apply for a position at the UN Library. She sent her UN application form (P-11 form) to the UN Secretariat. She had a response from the Library, was interviewed and subsequently employed. On her appointment at the UN, her prior career in Japan was not considered as a professional career; therefore, she had to start her work at the UN from P-1 level, which is the lowest professional level (most young professional staff members start their career from P-2 level).

In the library, she was assigned in the area of UN documents indexing. She was promoted to P-2 level after two years. In the indexing area, the task of professional librarians of P-1, P-2, and P-3 levels was to conduct subject-analysis of UN documents for the library's bibliographic database. Only one of the P-3-level librarians was in charge of revising and editing the data that had been analyzed by other librarians. After one year from her P-2 promotion, Ms. I. was assigned to perform revising and editing functions over P-3 senior librarians. And three years after her P-2 promotion, she was promoted to P-3 level. She stayed in this P-3 position for 13 years as the editor and reviser. This position requires cooperation from subordinates, peers, supervisors, and staff of related departments. She stated that she had acquired managerial and negotiation skills through responsibilities of this position. When she was promoted to P-4, she had to manage 20 subordinates. When she became the chief of a section at P-5 level, she had 42 staff members under her supervision.

Ms. I. started to work for the UN Library not particularly because she wanted to work for the UN, but she simply wanted to work as a professional librarian with her degree in library science. Ms. I. herself was not thinking of working at the UN for such a long time. Her husband left his company when his transfer from New York to Tokyo was decided. He started his own business in New York. So she decided to continue working for the UN Library and stayed working until her retirement age. She has worked for the UN for 28 years. When she talked about her career, she said that her contributions and devotion in the area of the UN documentation database was highly appreciated. She could climb the ladder to the position deputizing for the Head of the Library.

Regarding the question about a mentor, she answered that she had had no mentor at all from the time she started her career at the UN until the present time. However, a librarian who was close to retirement age taught Ms. I. practical skills and knowledge in her first year at the UN.

As for networking, she mentioned four networks. The first one is the network of officers who attended a one-week training course for mid-managers. They belonged to different departments/offices and had no conflicts of interest; therefore they could share problems and give advice to each other very frankly. The second is the network of committees/panels within the Secretariat, particularly, in the Department of Public Information. They have various administrative purposes such as a promotion committee and a rebuttal panel. Members exchange frank views with each other, and they have come to know each other. The third network is within the UN Joint Appeals Board. The fourth is a close network of Japanese staff members working at the UN Headquarters in New York, regardless of their positions and fields.

As for networks outside the UN, there is an annual conference attended by librarians and library–related professionals from all over the world. She mentioned that the communications with them and contacts with professors in the area of library and information science are useful.

For professional development, she teaches at Japanese universities on UN organization and documentation, and international civil service. Since 2003 she has taught at Ritsumeikan University and since 2007 at the Graduate School of Waseda University. In addition, she gave special lectures at Mie University, Tokai University, and Tsurumi University. These lectures were treated as part of her official duties at the UN.

As for her levels of satisfaction, she answered that both job satisfaction and satisfaction in her personal life are necessary and important for her.

She doesn't know if her prior experience in Japan was useful. She had only worked for two years as general administrative staff and had no experience at managerial level. However, she said that work depended greatly on teamwork in Japan as well as at the UN Library, so she thought that her competency of teamwork acquired in Japan was very useful at the UN.

To the question of whether the amount of salary was a key factor for choosing a job, she answered that she had never thought of the amount of income. If one wants to get a high income, he or she would be better off not working for the UN, she said.

As for her attitude towards work, she answered, '*I always do my best at work!*'

Case I Career Path

Age	
18-22	• Studied and graduated from the School of Arts and Sciences, Tokyo Woman's Christian University, Japan
22-25	• *General Administration Staff*, Private Company, Tokyo, Japan
29-31	• Studied at and obtained an MS in Library Science at Long Island University, USA
31-34	• *Librarian (P-1)*, Dag Hammarskjold Library, UN Secretariat, New York, USA
34-37	• *Librarian (P-2)*, Dag Hammarskjold Library, UN Secretariat, New York, USA
37-50	• Librarian (P-3), Dag Hammarskjold Library, UN Secretariat, New York, USA
50-54	• *Section Chief (P-4) Information Processing and Collecting Documents*, Dag Hammarskjold Library, UN Secretariat, New York, USA
54-60	• *Chief (P-5) Information Processing and Collecting Documents*, Dag Hammarskjold Library, UN Secretariat, New York, USA
60	• Retired

Appendix 1 The 23 Interviews from International Civil Servants and a Description of their Career Paths

Case J

Gender:	Male
Age:	58 years old (at time of interview)
Birthplace:	Tokyo
Position:	Program Coordinator, Socio-economic Governance and Management Branch, Department of Economic and Social Affairs, the UN Secretariat (P-4).
Location:	New York (USA)

Mr. J. was educated to graduate level in Japan. After graduating from the College of Liberal Arts, International Christian University, he studied at graduate school and obtained an MA in Public Administration. He then went to the USA and entered Maxwell Graduate School, Syracuse University and obtained an MA in International Relations. He had been interested in the activities of the UN since his high school days, and when he was at university he was influenced by a professor of international law and began to think more seriously about working in the UN. Before completing graduate school, he attended three interviews for three international organizations as a way into working at the UN. He decided to work in the UN Secretariat because they contacted him first out of the three. He is still working there. He became a Programme Management Officer at the age of 28. As Mr. J. had had no professional experience before, he started his career at the lowest P-1 level.

When he was 35 years old, he began to question working in the UN so he took leave and went back to Japan. He started working at an association and a subsidiary organization of the government in Tokyo. There, he found that some staff members of an organization were excellent, but at the same time, some were not, and this is the case everywhere. So, he concluded that the UN was not such a bad organization to work for. After a year and a half, he went back to work at the UN.

In the UN he was in charge of technical corporation programmes for Vietnam and Laos, and later for China and other Asian countries. He then became an Assistant to the Director of Multi-national Corporation Programmes, and Acting

Director of Economic Policy and Social Policy. Since 2003, he has been working as a Programme Coordinator (P-4) in the Socio-economic Governance and Management Branch within the UN Department of Economic and Social Affairs. Mr. J. had been interested in development issues since high school, and he studied the subject at university. He came to work in the UN to pursue this interest, and he has worked in this field of technical cooperation throughout his career. Considering the length of time that he has worked for the UN and his age, his post level, P-4, is actually not so high. He told the author that this is due to issues relating to human relations and certain power relations among groups of people.

Regarding the question of a mentor, Mr. J. mentioned two Japanese who were in the development field in his early days at the UN, whom he met just after he started his career there. He says that his relationship with them is still continuing. Another mentor is a Chinese who was his superior. His relationship with this person is still close, but this very relationship later became the source of antagonism at his workplace and is believed to be the cause of his delayed promotion.

He mentioned two networks within the workplace. The first one was the network centering around the Chinese person mentioned above. The second was that of the Japanese who work in the technical corporation in the international organizations. These two networks were developed in the early days when Mr. J. started working in the UN Secretariat, and they still continue to exist.

As for networks outside the UN, he mentioned three that were significant. The first one is the network formed through Japanese Kendo. He is the deputy director of the Training Hall in New York and a director of the All-US Kendo Federation. This network is his contact point with American communities. The second is the network with those people who have something to do with Japan-related organizations. He says valuing the relationship with those Japanese whom he met or whom he came to know through his work will, in the long run, be reflected in his work in the UN. For example, he mentioned the success in organizing and implementing the World Conference of City Management. This was realized through a joint endeavor between the UN and Tokyo Metropolitan Government. It was held in 1993 with 50 cities participating. Apart from that, they have also succeeded in organizing an international conference with the cooperation of local governments such as Fukuoka City and Niigata Prefecture. The third is the network formed by volunteers who help the New York City Police.

Regarding self-development activities, although he could not get a degree due to his busy working life, he entered the Graduate School of New York University to study Public Administration. He said what he learned there including research methods, methods of analysis, programming, and management methods within the administrative management field, were very useful for his later work.

To the question about the level of satisfaction, he answered that the main satisfaction came from his work, but satisfaction of duty stations was important as well.

He says his experience of working in Japan was very useful. His experience of having worked in Japan supported his confidence that he could also survive working in Japan.

To the question of whether the amount of income is an important factor for choosing one's job, he answered that he is satisfied with what he earns. International organizations are non-profit, but they pay reasonably well compared with Japanese companies. He also mentioned that it is wrong to compare it with the very high income of certain Japanese companies.

When asked if he intends to work in the UN until the mandatory retirement age, he answered, "Yes, perhaps." However, he has many plans, so he might leave the UN some months before the due retirement time.

Lastly, as for a career anchor, he answered 'Work for people and be content with what you do.' It should be added that Mr. J. has gone through the training and has become a priest of the Shingon Sect of Buddhism.

Additional Note: Mr. J. was promoted to P-5 in the year following this interview.

Case J Career Path

- **19-23**: Graduated from the College of Liberal Arts, International Christian University, Tokyo, Japan

- **23-25**: Obtained an MA in Public Administration, Graduate School, International Christian University, Tokyo, Japan

- **26-28**: Obtained an MA in International Relations, Maxwell Graduate School, Syracuse University, USA

- **28-29**: *Programme Management Officer (P-1)*, Department of Development and Technical Cooperation, UN Secretariat, New York, USA

- **29-34**:
  - *Programme Management Officer (P-2)*, Department of Development and Technical Cooperation, UN Secretariat, New York, USA
  - *Leave of absence*

- **35-36**: *Staff Member*, subsidiary organization of a governmental organization, Tokyo, Japan

- **36**:
  - *Returned from leave*
  - *Programme Management Officer, (P-2)*, UN Secretariat, New York, USA

- **36-39**: *Programme Management Officer (P-3)*, UN Secretariat, New York, USA

- **39-59**: *Program Coordinator (P4)*, Socio-economic Governance and Management Branch, Department of Economic and Social Affairs, UN Secretariat, New York, USA

- **59-60**: *Program Coordinator (P-5)*, Socio-economic Governance and Management Branch, Department of Economic and Social Affairs, UN Secretariat, New York, USA

- **60**: Retired

Case K

Gender:	Female
Age:	53 years old (at time of interview)
Birthplace:	Gifu Prefecture
Position:	Deputy Director Division of Oversight Service, UNFPA (D-1)
Location:	New York (USA)

Ms. K. received her education up to undergraduate level in Japan. She first graduated from the Faculty of Sociology, Hitotsubashi University. After this, she reentered the university in the Faculty of Economics and gained a second undergraduate degree in Economics. Then, she went to the United States and entered the Graduate School of International Studies (GSIS) at the University of Denver, USA. She received an MA in International Studies. Upon graduation, she engaged in an Urban Planning Project for Iraq, implemented by a consulting firm, which took her to Iraq for about a year.

While she was working in Iraq, she was interviewed at the Bagdad Office of the UNDP, and was recommended for a JPO of the UNDP. Her first duty station was at the Eastern Caribbean Office in Barbados, where she worked for two and a half years as a JPO. After completing her contract as a JPO, she was employed as a formal staff member of the UNFPA and was assigned to the New York Headquarters. She worked there for four and a half years. During this period she was promoted from P-2 to P-3. After that she worked in the UNFPA China Office for two years, and during this period she was promoted to P-4. When her work in China was over, she went to Vienna to work in the then United Nations Office for Drug Control Programme (UNDCP) for about a year and a half. Following that she was transferred to the United Nations Office for Project Services (UNOPS) Headquarters in New York. She worked there for two years, before going back to the UNFPA Headquarters, where she stayed for six years. During those six years, she was promoted from P-4 to P-5. Following that, she became a representative of the UNFPA Laos Office (P-5) for three years. Two years ago she was selected for a D-1 post in the UNFPA Headquarters, where she still is now.

As seen from her brief background description, Ms. K. has experienced ten posts in four organizations over the course of her 24-year career in international organizations, and has worked in five countries (Barbados, the United States, China, Austria and Laos). Including Iraq where she worked after finishing graduate school, she has lived in six countries. After joining the international organization, in the first half of her career she expanded her occupational fields through job transfers and secondments, and as she was promoted, she has experienced many duty stations. In the Laos Office, she became the head of the country office and gained experience in managerial work, supervising the professional staff and General Service staff. Ms. K. was assigned to this managerial post because she has thorough knowledge of the UNFPA and her performance was well regarded. At present she has four professional subordinates, guides two General Service staff in New York, and coordinates 23 staff in all. Regarding the question about mentors, she was fortunate to have an excellent Representative to guide her during the JPO time, as some of the JPOs left the UN not feeling well supported or disappointed with the UN system.

To the question about networks in and out of the office, she had no network within her workplace in particular as the Division for Oversight Services, which is her present office, is expected to keep its independence. Networks outside the office don't really exist, except some that are related to her work.

As for self-development activities, she has attended language courses in French and Chinese that were organized by the UN. In addition, she has attended various other training courses and workshops in and outside the UN related to leadership, management, communication and areas such as evaluation, health reform, etc. To the question of whether she intended to work at the UN until her mandatory retirement age, she answered that she would.

Regarding the questions about her level of satisfaction, she answered that she had prioritized job satisfaction up to now, but in the future she wishes to increase the satisfaction of her personal life to some extent.

Ms. K. has never worked in Japan, so she could not answer the question of whether experience working in Japan was useful. With the exception of her time working as a representative in Laos, her work has had little to do with Japan. She said, only when she promoted family planning in developing countries, her knowledge of Japanese experience proved very helpful. As the Japanese ODA was very important in Laos, her contact with the Japanese Embassy helped facilitate her work.

To the question of whether the amount of income is important when choosing an occupation, she answered that if the salary is sufficient, job satisfaction is more important than the income. Regarding her attitude to work, she answered that even when things do not go well, she takes lessons from her experience and makes a fresh start each day. She feels dwelling on failures is not useful.

When interviewing her, she explained the selection process for the managerial posts above P-5 including representatives. First, the human resources department screens the candidates for the required qualifications and experience and a shortlist is made of three or four candidates. Next, interviews are conducted, involving three or four panelists. To judge their capacity and aptitude, those successful will go through reference checks and an external assessment by an independent company. The assessment includes presentation skills, analytical skills, verbal skills and simulations based on cases. After that, the successful candidate will be presented to the Contract Review Board for final approval by the Executive Director.

Ms. K. is one of the few Japanese women who are at the director level in international organizations in New York. When the author asked her about the competencies staff members are expected to possess at a managerial level, she answered that it is essential to have the competency to "guide and develop your staff successfully." In Ms. K.'s case, her experience of managing the Laos Office as its representative, enhanced her ability. She said that promotions in the UN Common System are influenced by talent, personal effort and by taking of opportunities when they arise. One can be promoted to the P-5 level through efforts and talent, but further promotion may be affected by luck and timing as the number of posts decrease. She also added that having good political ability becomes necessary at the senior level.

Additional Notes: Since the time of interview, Ms.K. has become a Director (D-2).

Case K Career Path

Age	
18-25	• Graduated from the Faculty of Sociology, Hitotsubashi University, Japan • Reentered the University in the Faculty of Economics gaining a second Undergraduate Degree in Economics.
25-27	• Obtained an MA in International Studies from the Graduate School of Denver University, USA
27-28	• *Staff*, Engineering Consulting Firm (ECFA), City Planning Project, Bagdad, Iraq • Passed JPO Exam
29-32	• *Programme Officer (L-2)*, JPO UNDP, Barbados
32-34	• *Programme Officer (P-2)*, UNFPA Headquarters, New York, USA
35-37	• *Special Assistant to the Assistant Executive Director (P-3)*, UNFPA Headquarters, New York, USA
37-39	• *Programme Officer (P-4)*, UNFPA, Beijing, China
39-40	• *Regional Adviser (P-4)*, Seconded to UNDCP, Vienna, Austria
40-42	• *Portfolio Manager (P-4)*, UNOPS Headquarters, New York, USA
43-47	• *Evaluation Adviser (P-5)*, UNFPA Headquarters, New York, USA
48-51	• *Representative (P-5)*, UNFPA Laos Office
51-present	• *Deputy Director (D-1), Division of Oversight Services*, UNFPA Headquarters, New York, USA

Case L

Gender:	Male
Age:	42 years old (at time of interview)
Birthplace:	Tokyo
Position:	UN Secretariat, Project Coordinator, Conventional Arms Branch, Office for Disarmament Affairs (L-3)
Location:	New York (USA)

Mr. L. was educated in Japan until he graduated from university. He studied in the Department of Law at Gakushuin University. After graduation, he went to the USA and studied at the Law School of The American University. He completed a Masters' program in international law (LL.M.). During this period, he took part in an internship program hosted by the Organization of American States (OAS). After finishing law school, he became engaged in research work on US-Japan trade friction, science and technology policy, environmental technology and industrial competitiveness in a think-tank attached to the US Congress in Washington D.C. for three years. He also worked in a law firm in the US. He then went back to Japan and established his own independent business, and through contracts, he conducted business with governmental agencies and law offices based in the US and Japan for five years.

During this period, he joined a project to identify Japanese descendants in the Philippines, which was jointly executed by the Japanese Ministry of Foreign Affairs and the Ministry of Justice. This survey aimed to help Philippine-Japanese get registered in Japan. He had the opportunity to hear from many Japanese descendants about their severe experiences during and after World War II.

Gradually, he became aware that his work experience could be useful in the field of international cooperation. So, at the age of 32, he entered a roster of UN Volunteers. Unable to squeeze time out of his work, he could not participate in PKO activities in Somalia and Rwanda, but he did manage to participate in a project to provide emergency humanitarian assistance against the winter (winterization support) for repatriated refugees in Kosovo, for three months from November 1999. Even after his planned period was over, he continued to support the activity in Kosovo, and participated in planning and implementing rehabilitation projects. After that, he participated in the planning of social recovery projects in the United Nations Interim Administration Mission in Kosovo (UNMIK), as well as in the United Nations Office for Project Services (UNOPS).

Mr. L.'s attitude to work at the UNMIK in Kosovo was highly evaluated by his boss, who, in 2002 recommended him to a temporary position at the UN Secretariat. As an Associate Political Affairs Officer (P-2), his portfolio included trust fund management and inter-agency coordination mechanism on small arms in the Department for Disarmament Affairs (currently, Office for Disarmament Affairs). He later became a project coordinator (L-3) on a fixed-term contract where he has remained until now.

As can be seen from his brief history, Mr. L. has advanced his career through his practical international legal and consulting work. At the same time, he participated in volunteer activities in the Philippines. The major turning point in his career was his UN volunteer work in Kosovo. The estimation of his contribution of those days led him to work in the UN Secretariat. He has worked in international organizations for eight and a half years altogether, including two and a half years as a UN Volunteer in Kosovo, and six years in the USA.

Mr. L. had been interested in the activities of the UN due to the influence of his professor at university in Tokyo, but he had never dreamed of working there himself. Regarding the question of a mentor, he answered that an experienced American woman, who was a General Service staff, taught him how work should be carried out (such as how the trust fund should be utilized, financial regulations, etc.). He answered that thanks to her help, he could perform his duties independently in a short time. Another person he mentioned is his Zimbabwean supervisor, whom he could talk to very frankly, even things off the job. He said he still maintains a good relationship with her.

As for intra-office networks, he mentioned two. One is a network of those participating in the inter-agency mechanism, which is comprised of 23 entities under the UN system. The other is the network of those ex-associates of Kosovo. Most of them are still working in international organizations and they keep in touch.

Regarding self-development efforts, he is engaged in making a database of conventional arms (especially small arms and light weapons). In that vein, he has participated in training programmes on online databases organized by the Information Technology Department of the UN. He also attended workshops on networking and presentation, organized by the UN Human Resources Office.

When asked about the level of satisfaction, Mr. L. answered that job-satisfaction has been the main goal so far, and the level is high. However, since he got married and will soon have a baby, overall life-satisfaction will be more important in the future.

To the question of whether he intends to continue working for the UN until the mandatory retirement age, he answered that he cannot foresee the future. He also mentioned that he is presently expecting to be involved in the organization of a major conference of which he has been engaged in since he started working in the UN. When that major conference is over, he would like to think and decide whether he will continue working in the international organization or go back to work in the private sector to utilize his specialist skills.

To the question about his experience of working in a private enterprise in Japan, he answered that work experience in Japan was of course useful, but his actual ability was enhanced through working in both Japan and the United States. When working in a team with Japanese professionals with legal and financial expertise, he felt that the level of shared sense of responsibility was very high among individuals. On the other hand, when he worked in the same situation with multinational staff, he found that even though some people were extremely intelligent, they were not as responsible as they could eloquently speak.

In order to increase the number of Japanese staff in international organizations, it is necessary to propagate and support, not only the UN National Competitive Exam, JPO and highly political appointments, but also other entry routes based on applicants' expertise and skills.   Those Japanese who are in their 30s and 40s who have international work experience, can have increased opportunities to switch to work in an international organization using their professional skills.

When answering the question of whether salary was important, he answered that when he was a consultant, or entrepreneur, his income was 1.5 times that of his present income.   If he had chosen his job solely because of income, he wouldn't still be working in the United Nations.

Lastly, he stated that his attitude to work was, 'Complete the work thoroughly once you have taken it on.' He said that some projects may take an unexpectedly long time, or significant efforts and patience.   He has had experience of clearing up the mess after some colleagues have given up, yet he believes this kind of experience and attitude to work is worthwhile.

Additional Note: Mr. L. was promoted to Political Affairs Officer (P-4) in December 2012.

Case L Career Path

Age	
18-22	• Graduated from the Department of Law, a Japanese University, Tokyo, Japan
23-24	• Obtained an MA in LLM from The American University, USA
25-28	• *Researcher*, Think-tank attached to the US Congress, Washington D.C., USA
29-33	• *Independent Consultant*, based in Tokyo, Japan
34-36	• *UN Volunteer*, UNMIK, UNOPS, Worked for Emergency Programme in Kosovo
36-38	• *Associate Political Affairs Officer (P-2)*, Office for Disarmament Affairs, UN Secretariat, New York, USA
39-present	• *Project Coordinator (L-3)*, Conventional Arms Branch, Office for Disarmament Affairs, UN Secretariat, New York, USA

Case M

Gender:	Female
Age:	53 years old (at time of interview)
Birthplace:	Hyogo Prefecture
Position:	Senior Advisor, United Nations Population Fund (UNFPA) (P-5)
Location:	New York (USA)

Ms. M. was born in Japan, but due to her father's job she was educated both in Japan and Taiwan. After graduating from the American High School in Taiwan, she entered Sophia University and graduated from the Faculty of Comparative Culture. After graduation, she entered the graduate school of New York State University, Buffalo Campus and received an M.A. in political science. Before completing graduate school she took a job interview at the Japanese Permanent Mission in New York, and she was recommended to work in an international organization. Until her duty station was decided, she worked in the New York branch of the Long-term Credit Bank of Japan, for half a year.

In those days, when Ms. M. was at university, the working environment for female graduates of university was not yet accommodating in Japan. Ms. M. didn't wish to serve tea to her colleagues or make copies of the documents in a Japanese company. That was the reason for her determination to go to the United States to study at graduate school. She chose New York State University Graduate School, Buffalo, which offered her a full scholarship.

Ms. M. was employed as a JPO of the UNFPA New York Headquarters at the age of 25. Her grade was L-1, the lowest professional level, because she had no prior work experience in the field concerned. (Please note, L/P-1 is no longer offered as a position). The following year, she was promoted to a formal staff member at P-1 level and two years after that she was transferred to Bangkok to work at the UNFPA at the P-2 level for a year. After Thailand, she was transferred to the China Office as a programme officer at P-3 level and worked there for four years. Following that, she was promoted to P-4 level and was assigned to the South-east Section of the Headquarters. In the evenings, during these four years working in the Headquarters, she studied economics at the graduate school of New York University. She decided to take leave for a year from 1990, and went to Oxford University Graduate School to study economics with a full scholarship from the Foundation for Advanced Studies on International Development (FASID). When she returned to work, she became a representative of the UNFPA office in Zimbabwe, where she worked for six years. During this period she was promoted to level P-5. When her term of office was complete, she became a UNFPA Interregional Training Advisor in the International Training Center of the Family Planning Bureau of the Indonesian Government. As soon as her term of office in Indonesia was over, she took a post in Phnom Penh as a Representative of the UNFPA, Cambodia. She worked there for four years. It was during this time that she discovered that her eldest son had a learning disability. She applied for a position in New York where the education system could provide more developed support for her son. However, she was not offered any post in the Headquarters by the UNFPA. So, she applied for a senior advisor position in the HIV/AIDS Section of the UNICEF New York Headquarters. She got the job and worked there for a year. After this, she worked as a section chief of the West Africa Branch, UNFPA Headquarters for two years, then as a Senior Advisor to the joint office of the development group for six months. Since 2007 she has been working as a Senior Advisor in the strategic planning section.

Ms. M. has a permanent contract with the UNFPA. She has submitted a proposal that when her son graduates from high school, she hopes to return to a position in a developing country. The present post as a senior advisor is not a formal post in the Headquarters, so in the worst case scenario, she may be dismissed if the headquarters goes through a reorganization. Currently, negotiations are being held with the UNFPA Headquarters concerning her future post.

Ms. M. has worked for international organizations for 27 years excluding one year leave. Twenty-five years of that period was spent working for the UNFPA promoting family planning. She has been stationed in six countries such as the USA, Thailand, China, Zimbabwe, Indonesia, and Cambodia. In total, she has worked in as many as 16 countries. In Zimbabwe and Cambodia she worked as a representative for a total of 10 years. Promotion came early, as she became P-5 level in the latter half of her thirties. However, she has remained at P-5. She has been working in the Headquarters for five years as her son needs special education. She said she was lucky to have a good opportunity to treat her son, but she has not been in an appropriate post to make good use of her skills and experience.

Regarding the question of a mentor, a Dutch female staff member at her first work place was her mentor. Through this supervisor's network she knew the then top management including a Pakistani Executive Director, thus Ms. M. has had various experience in different countries since the beginning of her career. However, when she came back to the Headquarters from Cambodia, those ex-supervisors who selected and promoted her had mostly retired. As succeeding top management had come from outside the organization, there were almost no senior officers who knew Ms. M.'s ability and job performance.

Ms. M. has no formal post within the organization upon return from the field, and as such, she has no network. As for networks outside the office, she stated two; the first one is a network of Japanese staff members, especially of female officers. The second is that of those who have worked in the UNFPA, both present and retired.

As for self-development activity, she mentioned the fact that she went to study economics at graduate school in New York and that after obtaining a scholarship from the FASID, and taking a leave of absence from her workplace, she studied economics at Oxford University Graduate School and deepened her knowledge of development issues.

Regarding the level of satisfaction, she was highly satisfied from when she started to work for the UNFPA until she became a representative in Cambodia, but her present level of satisfaction is low. Ms. M. said she can understand the present unhappy situation and accepts it as it is in the best interests of her child's education, but at heart, she is still not really happy.

She said she wants to work until her mandatory retirement age. If she had no obligation to support her two children, she might consider working in a different work place, but in reality Ms. M. has to support her family, and it is impossible to leave the present job as its educational support system is beneficial for her family.

Ms. M. has never worked in Japan, but from her experience of working in a Japanese company in New York, the way Japanese companies are run do not agree with her.

To the question of whether the amount of income is an important factor when choosing one's job, she answered that the work of the UN is of great significance, so it does not matter, as long as one can survive on that income.

Lastly, as for her attitude towards work she said a Chinese phrase, *'Don't move your crown under the pear tree.'* This means you should avoid to act suspiciously. In English, she keeps the following sentence in mind while working, *'You can bend the rules as far as you can, so long as you don't break them. You can interpret them as you like as long as it is for the good of the country & program and not for yourself.'*

Appendix 1   The 23 Interviews from International Civil Servants and a Description of their Career Paths

Case M Career Path

Age	Description
Childhood	• Educated both in Japan and Taiwan, Graduated from an American High School in Taiwan
20-23	• Graduated from the Faculty of Comparative Culture, Sophia University, Japan • Obtained an MA in Political Science, New York State University, Buffalo, USA • *Passed the AE Exam*
25	• General Administration work for a Japanese commercial bank in New York, USA
25-26	• *Program Officer (L-1) JPO*, UNFPA Headquarters, New York, USA
26-27	• *Program Officer (P-1)*, UNFPA Headquarters, New York, USA
27-28	• *Program Officer (P-2)*, UNFPA Thai Office, Bangkok, Thailand
28-32	• *Programme Officer (P-3)*, UNFPA China Office, Beijing, China
32-36	• *Programme Officer (P-4)*, UNFPA Headquarters, New York, USA
36-37	• *Leave of Absence* • Non-degree student of the Graduate School of Economics, Oxford University, UK
37-40	• Returned to UNFPA • *UNFPA Representative (P-4)* Harare, Zimbabwe
40-43	• *UNFPA Representative (P-5)* Harare, Zimbabwe
43-45	• *UNFPA Inter-Regional Advisor (as a Training Advisor) (P-5)*, Located in Indonesia Family Planning Ministry (BKKBN) Jakarta, Indonesia
45-49	• *UNFPA Representative (P-5)*, Phnom Penh, Cambodia
49-50	• *Senior Advisor, (P-5)*, HIV/AIDS Section, UNICEF Headquarters, New York, USA
50-52	• *Chief (P-5), West Africa Section* UNFPA Headquarters, New York, USA
52-53	• *Senior Advisor (P-5)*, Joint Office of Development Group UN Federation Office, UNFPA Headquarter, New York, USA
53-56	• *Senior Advisor (P-5)*, Strategic Planning Section, UNFPA Headquarters, New York, USA
56-present	• *Audit Monitoring Adviser (P-5)*, Office of the Executive Director, UNFPA Headquarters, New York, USA

Case N

Gender:	Male
Age:	45 years old (at time of interview)
Birthplace:	Chiba Prefecture
Position:	WFP Logistics Officer, Logistics Department (P-3)
Location:	Headquarters, Rome, Italy

Mr. N. was educated in Japan up to graduate level. He graduated from the American and English Literature Department of Gakushuin University and was employed by Japan Airlines. For four years he worked in the airport and the in-flight service section. During this period, he was in charge of Indo-China refugees when they are transiting an Airport in Tokyo for resettlement, so he gradually became concerned with global issues. He then changed companies and began work for Mitsui O.S.K. Lines. After three years, he applied for 'Camp Sadako,' in which participants experience living in a refugee camp in Kenya for a month. He was selected but as it was impossible to take an extended period of leave, Mr. N. resigned from the company and participated in the camp. After coming back to Japan, he entered an MA course in International Studies at Meiji Gakuin Graduate School. For the first two years he devoted himself exclusively to academic study, but from the third year (1997), he became a staff member of the National Federation of UNESCO Associations in Japan, he studied and wrote his master's thesis while working. He got his MA in 1999. During that year, the age limit for taking the AE Examination sponsored by Japanese Ministry of Foreign Affairs, was changed from 32 to 35. Mr. N. was 35 then, so he became eligible to apply. He took the exam and passed it.

He started working as a Logistics Officer (JPO, L-2) at the WFP Headquarters in 2000. After working in the Headquarters for a year, he was transferred to Nairobi, Kenya. In his fourth year, he became a formal staff member at the P-2 level. In the fifth year he was promoted to P-3 level. He worked in the Nairobi Office for four years, then, in 2005 he was transferred to Addis Ababa, Ethiopia. During this year, he became qualified as a permanent staff member. However, soon after

Appendix 1   The 23 Interviews from International Civil Servants and
a Description of their Career Paths

moving to Ethiopia, his partner fell sick, so he applied to work in the Headquarters where medical facilities were better equipped. He has been working in the Headquarters since 2006.

As seen from the description above, he started his career in an international organization quite late, at the age of 36. He has spent the eight years of his career within the WFP. He has worked in three countries (Italy, Kenya, Ethiopia), and experienced four posts. Though his participation in the international organization was late, his occupational experience and attitude to work were highly regarded by his superiors, and he is steadily accumulating professional experience.

Regarding the question of a mentor, he said that his direct supervisor in his first work place was a Ghanaian. He taught Mr. N. basic matters in carrying out his work. Furthermore, he provided various opportunities to increase Mr. N.'s experience. At present he cherishes a French ex-supervisor whom he respects as his role model, if not a mentor. He is retired but still works as a consultant for the WFP.

Mr. N. said that the Headquarters staff members should remain behind the scenes so that professional staff working in developing countries can perform their work more effectively. To the question of internal and external work networks he mentioned he had four. One is the network among actual site workers (the in-country office workers, and people in charge of logistics in the Regional Bureau, etc). The second one is the network of officers in charge of related departments within the Headquarters. Including those in the Headquarters, Regional Offices and Country Offices, there are about 300 professional staff members employed by the WFP in all duty stations, working in the field of logistics. They are said to have a strong sense of family. The third is related to ration distribution. It is a network of UNICEF and local NGOs that take charge of ration distribution. The fourth is a network with the private sector. He answered that in order to procure and ration food to those people of developing countries who suffer a shortage of food and starvation, partnerships and cooperation with transportation companies, the customers' agent, shipping companies, railways and air transport companies are indispensable. Regarding networks outside of work, he said there are none in particular.

When asked if he intends to continue working until his mandatory retirement age, he answered, 'Yes.' However, he will consider the health conditions of his parents who live in Japan and when necessary he will choose the best way at any given time.

To the question about the level of satisfaction, he answered that job-satisfaction is the most important.

Regarding the validity of his experience of working in Japan, he answered he found this experience 'very useful.' Firstly, his experience in a Japanese shipping company proved useful because the procedures of implementing work, reaching global standards and rules of the business, are the same. There is little difference. Secondly, he said he was trained as a competent Japanese businessperson. The level of staff education in Japanese private companies is said to be very high. He said the evaluation of Japanese at workplace and duty stations is, on the whole, high, like the high quality of Japanese products, and in this sense, the Japanese are lucky. As for his own assessment, he feels his working ability of the English language is not sufficient. He feels that Japanese staff have a high sense of responsibility and so they are trusted.

To the question about the amount of income he receives, Mr. N. answered that by continuing the work, financial satisfaction follows. One should not expect economical satisfaction from the initial stage. Generally, international organizations pay sufficiently.

At the end of the interview, Mr. N. said that the WFP looks after its staff well. When recruiting a new member, candidates within the organization are given the highest priority, and only when there is nobody suitable for the vacancy, they recruit from outside. So the retention rate of staff members within the WFP is high. However, the WFP is managed by voluntary contributions from the donor country, so its financial situation is greatly influenced. In 2007, early retirement and redundancy were encouraged and the recruitment of new members was frozen.

As for his attitude towards work he stated that, 'the heart should be hot, but the mind should be cool.'

Additional Notes: In August 2010, after the interview, Mr.N. was transferred as a Logistics Officer (P-3) to UNHRD (UN Humanitarian Response Depot) in Subang, Malaysia.

Case N Career Path

- **19-23**: Graduated from Department of American and English Literature, a Japanese University, Tokyo, Japan
- **23-27**: *Ground Staff*, Japan Airlines, Narita Japan
- **28-31**: Sales Staff, Mitsui OSK Lines, Tokyo, Japan
- **31**: *Volunteer*, Camp Sadako, UNHCR, Kakuma, Kenya
- **31-35**: Studied and obtained an MA in International Studies, Meiji Gakuin University, Tokyo, Japan
- **32-35**:
  - *Literary Education Support Staff*, National Federation UNESCO Associations in Japan, Tokyo, Japan
  - Passed AE Examination
- **36-37**: *Logistics Officer (L-2), JPO*, WFP, Rome, Italy
- **37-39**: *Logistics Officer (L-2), JPO*, WFP, Kenya Office, Nairobi, Kenya
- **39-40**: *Logistics Officer (P-2)*, WFP, Kenya Office, *Nairobi, Kenya*
- **41-42**: *Logistics Officer (P-3)*, WFP, Kenya Office, Nairobi, Kenya
- **42-43**: *Logistics Officer (P-3)*, WFP, Ethiopia Office, *Addis Ababa, Ethiopia*
- **43-present**: *Desk Officer (P-3)*, Logistics Department, WFP Headquarters, Rome, Italy

Case O

Gender:	Female
Age:	51 years old (at time of interview)
Birthplace:	Kanagawa Prefecture
Position:	Chief, Contributions and Project Accounting Branch, Finance Division, WFP (P-5)
Location:	Rome, Italy

Ms. O. attended a vocational college after graduating from high school. After graduation, she started working as a secretary in an American capital insurance company for five years. At the age of 28 she went to the US and entered a community college in Maryland. After studying there for two years, she was admitted to Maryland State University as a transfer student and obtained a BA in Management Administration. After graduation, she entered the graduate school of the same university and obtained an MBA. She was 34 years old. On the invitation of a friend, she took part in an internship at the World Bank during her summer vacation at graduate school.

After getting her degrees she went back to Japan and worked in another American corporation in Tokyo. At first she worked as an internal auditor in an American securities company for two years. Then, she changed to another American securities company as a Controller/Treasurer, and later she became the Vice President. After she had worked in this company for six years, she began to question her work and life. She thought about working somewhere that would contribute something to society, and began to think of working in an international organization. Soon after resigning from the security company, she worked for a small company, which she helped enter the market. At the same time, she registered herself on the personnel roster of the Ministry of Foreign Affairs. In 2003, a WFP recruitment mission came to Japan, so she was interviewed for a vacant post. The following year, she was interviewed at the Headquarters in Rome, and received an offer to work at the WFP. She has been working in the WFP Headquarters for four years.

Ms. O. considered working in an international organization when she was 45, and in the following year she was employed by the WFP. The timing of her search for a position coincided with the increase in the number of senior positions in the Finance division of the WFP.

To the question about her mentor, she stated that as she was employed as the branch chief, she didn't have a mentor.

Ms. O. said that the main work of the WFP was actually done in the field, in developing countries. As such, the finance and treasury division of the Headquarters is in charge of conducting adjustments and providing support to the work done in the field. Compared with the field of finance in private sector, she added the work of the finance and treasury division of the WFP is less advanced.

To the question regarding her networks, she mentioned those P-5, P-4 level officers in charge of finance in the Headquarters and networks with officers in charge of various programmes and logistics. Second, she said there were networks with officers in charge of finance in the Country offices and regional bureaus.

Regarding the network outside the workplace, she answered that she had none in particular, except ex-colleagues from the foreign capital securities company where she used to work, old friends and childhood playmates.

To the question of whether she intends to work in the international organization till the mandatory retirement age, she answered perhaps she will, because she would think it difficult to find a job of a similar level to her present job in Japan, when she is over 50 years old.

To the question regarding the level of satisfaction, she answered that the balance between job satisfaction and quality of life at duty station is important. She said that she lived a life centered only on work in a foreign-affiliated company in Japan. At that time, she came to think that job-satisfaction alone was not enough, but that satisfaction in overall life was necessary.

When the author questioned her about the benefits of work experience in Japan, experience of having worked in a foreign-affiliated company is more useful than the work experience in Japan. The reasons are; firstly she had no sense of difficulty using English at work. Secondly, the minimum knowledge necessary for the work in the WFP could be obtained in the foreign capital enterprise.

To the question of whether the amount of income is important when choosing a job, Ms. O. answered that, being single, a certain amount of income is necessary. A high level of income is not necessarily indispensable. Regarding the salary of international organizations, the written amount on the vacancy announcement appears low, but the additional allowance for education (for example, in the USA the education grant is a maximum of 32,000 US dollars per child, until age 25) and the amount of salary shown is one after tax. She thinks that salaries in international organizations are not low.

The WFP adopts a rotation policy, so the office staff members are usually work at the same duty station for four year, at the longest for six years. Then, they are transferred to another country. Ms. O. said that she had to decide the next position within one or two years.

Additional Note: Ms. O. was transferred to WFP Bangkok Office in the year following the interview, and now works as a Senior Regional Finance and Administration Officer (P-5).

Case O Career Path

Age	Event
23	• Graduated from Vocational College
23-28	• *Secretary*, American Capital Insurance Company, Tokyo, Japan
28-32	• Graduated from Faculty of Management Administration, Maryland State University, USA
32-34	• Obtained an MBA from Maryland State University USA
35-37	• *Internal Auditor*, American Securities Company, Tokyo, Japan
37-43	• *Controller, later Vice President*, American Investment Bank, Tokyo, Japan
43-47	• *Freelance Consultant for SME* Small Industry, Tokyo, Japan • Passed WFP Recruitment Mission exam
47	• *Chief (P-5) , Finance Division*, WFP Headquarters, Rome, Italy

Appendix 1 The 23 Interviews from International Civil Servants and a Description of their Career Paths

Case P

Gender:	Female
Age:	45 years old (at time of interview)
Birthplace:	Tokyo
Position:	Senior Human Resources Officer (P-4), Fundamental Principles and Rights or Work Department, (FPRW), ILO Headquarters
Location:	Geneva (Switzerland)

Ms. P. was first interested in the activities of the United Nations when as a high school girl, she watched television reports about starvation and refugees in Ethiopia. She thought English is indispensable for her to work in the UN, so she entered the English and American Literature Course, in the Faculty of Literature, Seikei University. After graduation, she specialized in International Relations and Administration Study at Delaware University Graduate School in the USA, and got an MA. While she was studying at graduate school, she took the AE Examination and passed it. She worked as a temporary support staff dispatched to a private Japanese company for one and a half years until she started her AE post.

In 1990 when she was 26 years old, she started her international career as a JPO at UNDP in Mauritius. After two years of working as a JPO she worked in the UN Volunteer Programme (UNV) in Geneva as an area officer. During this year she passed the ILO Recruitment Mission exam, UN Competitive Exam and WFP Recruitment Exam. ILO was the first to offer her a position as a formal staff member so she decided to work in the ILO.

In 1993 when MS. P. was 30 years old, she became a P-2 staff member in charge of personnel in the ILO. She was in this post for five years, and when she was 35 years old, she was promoted to P-3 level and became in charge of the selection panel of ILO staff members for two years. In 2000, she was promoted to P-4 level and became the head of recruitment and personnel relocation. She also controlled the performance evaluation center for the transfer of staff members as well as recruitment missions in member countries. In 2005, when she was 42 she became the person in charge of Fundamental Principals and Rights at Work Department for the International Programme on the Elimination of Child Labour (IPEC) and has been in that position until now.

Ms. P. started her career in the international organization when she was 26, and she is in her 19th year of service. When she was a JPO in the UNDP and the UNV, she worked as a programme officer. However, when she became a formal staff member of the ILO, she became a personnel officer and she has obtained promotions within this field. When she was working as a programme officer, JPO, for the first two years, she worked in developing countries, but since then she has worked in Geneva in Switzerland.

Regarding her mentor, she answered that in the very first station in Mauritius, a Belgian supervisor and the head of the program who was Mauritian, taught her how to work in an international organization, now she has none.

To the question about the network within the workplace, she mentioned five networks. The first one is the network of managerial level staff who are in charge in the Headquarters as well as in regional offices. These directors are engaged in IPEC-related work. The second is that of representatives of the ILO field offices. Her third network is the network with the personnel officers of the ILO Headquarters. The fourth network is with those who are in charge of personnel management and training managers employed in the UN Common System. Finally, the fifth network is with NGOs related to international organizations.

There are two networks outside the workplace. One is that of friends she has met in her private time, regardless of nationality. The second network includes people she has met through her children.

As for professional development activities after working in the UN, she stated that she has participated in language courses in French and Spanish. She also attended training sessions on management and leadership organized by the ILO. In addition, she participated in various seminars on human resource management sponsored by organizations outside of the UN.

When asked if she would work until her mandatory retirement age, she said she intends to work ten more years, but after that, she might retire early. Regarding the level of satisfaction, she replied that her private life and work life should be well balanced. She is trying to be with her family as much as possible. The present level of satisfaction is the highest she has had since she began working.

To the question of her prior work experience in Japan, she said it was useful. She could relate her work in the ILO to that of her work in Japan, and it helped her to understand the role of labour unions and health and safety concerns at the workplace. She said she used to feel uncomfortable in a Japanese working environment where one stays in the office even if one has no work to finish.

To the question of whether the amount of income matters in selecting a job, she answered that income did not matter. She had wanted to choose work that would serve people, so the present job is satisfactory. It is good for her as the results of her work can be seen clearly. Her attitude towards her work is *"Be idealistic, but be realistic."*

Case P Career Path

Age	
22	• Graduated from University, Tokyo, Japan
22-24	• MA in Public Administration and International Relations, American Delaware University, USA • Passed the AE Exam
24-26	• *Temporary Support Staff*, Two private companies, Market Research, Tokyo, Japan
26-28	• *Programme Officer (L-2)*, JPO UNDP, Port Louis, Mauritius
28-29	• *Programme Officer (L-2)*, JPO, UNV Headquarters, Geneva, Switzerland
29-35	• *Personnel Officer (P-3)*, Personnel Division, ILO Headquarters, Geneva, Switzerland
35-37	• *Section Head (P-3)*, Personnel Division, ILO Headquarters, Geneva, Switzerland
37-42	• *Chief Personnel Officer (P-4), Personnel Division*, ILO Headquarters, Geneva, Switzerland
42-present	• *Senior HR Officer (P-4), Fundamental Principles and Rights or Work Department (FPRW)* ILO Headquarters, Geneva, Switzerland

Case Q

Gender:	Female
Age:	45 years old (at the time of interview)
Birthplace:	Osaka
Position:	Global Influenza Programme, WHO Headquarters, Medical Officer (P-5)
Location:	Geneva, Switzerland

Ms. Q. spent one year in the United States as an exchange student when she was at high school. After graduation, she entered the Jikei University, School of Medicine, and while she was an undergraduate, she participated in a summer clinical training program in the USA. After graduation, she took a clinical training course in a hospital in the UK. After coming back to Japan, she obtained a PhD in the field of infectious disease from Jikei University, and began working there as part of the medical staff.

After obtaining her PhD, she began to work as a member of the medical research staff in the Infectious Disease Surveillance Center of the National Institute of Infectious Diseases. Two years later, in 1999 she became a Chief Researcher of the same Center. In 2002, when she was 39 years old, she was dispatched from the National Center to the WHO as a medical P-5 officer, and worked for the Infectious Disease Outbreak Measures Group.

She applied to the vacancy announcement of the WHO in 2004. The number of applicants was roughly 670. Six members were short-listed for the final screening and of those, two were female. From 2005, she worked as a member of the team to fight against dangerous disease agents including influenza and SARS. From 2006, she worked as a formal staff member at P-5 level in charge of the Global Influenza Programme. Ms. Q.'s task was to prevent the epidemic outbreak of such new types of diseases, as influenza, SARS, and avian flu. In the case that a mass epidemic breaks out, she is in charge of deciding how the treatment and management should be conducted, as well as taking charge of measures to block the infection. At the same time, she will take charge of the clinical management, treatment and infection control of pandemic influenza.

When Ms. Q. was a medical officer in charge of infectious disease surveillance at the National Institute of Infectious Disease of Japan (under the Ministry of Health and Labour), she was dispatched to the WHO as part of the technical cooperation programme. While working in the WHO, she experienced controlling SARS and avian influenza. At that time, she established her status as a bridge between Japan and the International Organization. This was the environment where she could utilize her specialist knowledge, so she chose a career as a professional at the WHO. She was vaguely expecting that she might be dispatched to WHO in the future. However, it was not her intention for it to happen in this way. She did not know about the secondment system to the WHO until much later, and she didn't begin working in the National Center with the specific aim of working in the WHO in the future.

To the question of whether she had a mentor she answered that when she became a formal staff member, she became assertive and tried to state her opinions clearly during meetings in order to make herself recognized. At the same time, she looked for a mentor, and asked two female professionals; a British female in a managerial position who already made herself distinguished among others and a French female who was a single mother with a distinguished talent and communication skills. Later, she had a conflict of interest with the British director. At present, her mentors are a Japanese-American male director who is the head of the Influenza programme and long standing co-researcher and the aforementioned French colleague.

To the question of her work networks, she mentioned four. The first network is with the researchers and professionals of influenza and dangerous bio-agents. The second is the network in the field of international public health. The third is in the clinical field, and the last one is the network within the field of controlling mass infections.

She says there are five networks outside of her work. The first one is the network of working mothers in the WHO. The second is the one of families whose children go to international school. The third is the network of her friends in the neighborhood, in the vicinity of Geneva. The fourth is with those friends who share the same interests such as skiing, climbing and walking in the mountains. The final network is with journalists, especially with newspaper reporters. Ms. Q. is a single mother supporting two children and is responsible for her family. Because of her work, she often goes on missions for up to three or four months at a time. She employs a live-in domestic help, but when she goes on these missions, she asks for the help of the aforementioned first, second and third networks.

When asked about professional development activities, she said that she initially attended language courses in French. In addition, she participated in courses or training sessions on Cultural Diversity, Conference Management, Presentation Skills, Conflict Management, Writing Skills, etc.

To the question of whether she wants to work for the international organization until her mandatory retirement age, she answered she did not know. She said she will consider the possibilities in the future.

Regarding the question of her level of satisfaction, she answered that her work is the most important thing to her. Her present level of satisfaction is the highest she has had since she began working.

To the question of whether her experience of working in Japan was useful, she answered that she worked as a medical doctor in the technical field. However, this experience in Japan was not useful for working in the WHO or surviving in the WHO. The Japanese hierarchical system within an organization is not valid, the art of getting along with people and personal connections are more important than qualifications and career. One has to fight against others' obstructions, power games, and the negative comments against Japan by China and South Korea.

Regarding whether the amount of income is important in choosing one's occupation, she said that a high income is important as a reward to one's work. She says that her present employer, the WHO, pays her well.

Regarding her attitude to work, Ms. Q. instantly answered, "*Don't look at the ailment, but look at the patient.*" and stated that, "*work based on the actual needs of the site*" is important.

Case Q Career Path

High School
- Exchange Student in USA for one year during high school

18-24
- Graduated from Jikei University School of Medicine, Tokyo, Japan
- Clinical Study in USA

24-25
- Clinical Medicine Study in U.K., St. Thomas Hospital, London, UK

25-34
- *Medical Staff*, Jikei University School of Medicine, PhD on Infectious Diseases

34-36
- *Researcher*, Information Center, National Institute of Infectious Diseases, Tokyo, Japan

36-39
- *Chief Research Officer*, Information Center, National Institute of Infectious Diseases Tokyo, Japan

39-41
- *Secondment from the Japanese Government to the WHO*
- *Medical Officer (P-5)*, Infectious Disease Outbreak Measures Group, WHO Headquarters, Geneva, Switzerland

42-present
- Resigned from the Japanese Government
- *Medical Officer (P-5)*, Dangerous Pathogenic Organism Team, World Influenza Program, WHO Headquarters, Geneva, Switzerland

Case R

Gender:	Female
Age:	41 years old (at the time of interview)
Birthplace:	Chiba
Position:	Budget Coordination, Division of Budget and Resource Coordination, WHO Headquarters, (P-4)
Location:	Geneva, Switzerland

Ms. R. was educated in Japan and studied in the English Department, of the Faculty of Education, Ochanomizu University. When she graduated from the university, it was just after the Law for Equal Employment Opportunity for Men and Women came into force and the comprehensive work system was introduced in Japan. She was then employed by a private company, as one of their comprehensive-track (*sogoshoku*) staff members. Three years afterwards she was selected as a scholarship student and entered Walton School, a business management graduate school within Pennsylvania University, USA. She obtained an MBA. After returning to Japan, she worked three more years in the field of Personnel and Event Planning for the same company. However, working conditions for women were still difficult, and she came to the conclusion that it would be impossible to continue working in this company. As such, she decided that she wanted to work in the field of international cooperation and at the age of thirty she resigned, and looked for a position in that field.

After resigning from the company, she worked in the UNDP, Tokyo Office for six months as a part-time staff, then she was employed by an NPO called Plan Japan, and worked there for a year. She collected public information about donors and planning. During this period she took the AE Exam and ILO Recruitment Mission Exam and passed them both. ILO offered her a P-2 level formal staff member post as an Internal Auditor, so she decided to work in the ILO Headquarters. She was 32 years old.

After working in the Internal Audit Office for two years, she was transferred to the Division of Program Management, and was promoted to P-3 level. She worked there for four years.

When she was 38 years old she applied to the post of P-4 level Budget and Finance Officer, which was being advertised at WHO and she was selected. In the WHO she was in charge of financial work for three years. At present, due to the changes within the organization, she had been transferred to the post which is responsible for preparing budget plans for the WHO.

Ms. R. had not particularly wished to work in an international organization, but knowing about the UN PKO activities in Cambodia made her think about the possibility of working in the field of international cooperation. It is conceivable that the fact that women are not well utilized in Japanese private enterprises made Ms. R decide to work in the field of international cooperation.

Ms. R. has worked in organizations within the UN Common System for nine years, and during this period she has experienced four posts in two organizations; the ILO and WHO. At present, she answered she was contemplating what to do in the latter half of her life.

To the question regarding her mentor in her first job, she answered that she could not meet any supervisor or colleague who influenced her, including her mentor in the first office in ILO. She said she can call her present Danish supervisor her mentor. This person is very able and competent and is the first person whom she can respect.

As for networks in her present position, Ms. R. mentioned two. One is the network with program officers and directors of the technical sector and with general service staff depending on their subjects. The second network is with those in charge of coordinating with other relevant departments within the WHO Secretariat and Finance Division. She has no network in particular outside her workplace.

To the question of professional development activities she answered that she received courses in French and other training sessions organized by the organization.

When asked if she intends to work until the mandatory retirement age, she said she didn't know. The future is open, and she is not opposed to working in an international organization.

Regarding the level of satisfaction, she stated that one's job is important and that one should face it sincerely. Yet, the balance with work and life is important. Life is not work alone. (NB: during the interview, the author had the impression that Ms. R. spends fairly long hours for her work.)

To the question of whether her experience of working in a Japanese company was useful, she said that the experience of having a hard time under the strict conditions of a Japanese company made her thrive in the face of adversity. Regarding the aspect of professional skills in the workplace, she doesn't particularly believe that her experience in a Japanese company was useful. In order to work in an international organization, one should be a professional, and one needs to have actual work experience either in Japan or outside Japan.

To the question of whether the amount of income was an important factor when choosing a job, she said she did not mind if the income decreased, and that actually, she had made that choice. She is now content with her income as well as the content of her work.

Regarding her attitude toward her work and career, she answered, "Think deeply until you are entirely convinced."

Additional notes: From age 30-31 Ms. R. worked for the Foster Plan Association, Japan. This organization is now called Plan Japan.

Appendix 1 The 23 Interviews from International Civil Servants and a Description of their Career Paths

Case R Career Path

Age	
18-22	• Graduated from Ochanomizu University, English Department, Tokyo, Japan
22-25	• *Career Track Staff*, Private Company, Tokyo, Japan
25-27	• MBA Walton School, Pennsylvania University, USA
28-30	• On return to Japan, In charge of Personnel and Event Planning Private Company, Tokyo, Japan, Tokyo, Japan
30	• *Part Time Staff*, UNDP, Tokyo, Japan
31-31	• *PR for Donators*, Foster Plan Association, Tokyo, Japan • Passed ILO Recruitment Mission exam and also passed AE Exam
32-34	• *Internal Auditor (P-2)*, ILO Headquarters, Geneva, Switzerland
34-38	• *Budget Officer (P-3)*, Division of Program Management, ILO Headquarters, Geneva, Switzerland
38-42	• *Budget and Finance Officer (P-4)*, WHO Headquarters
42-present	• *Budget and Resource Coordination Officer (P-4)*, WHO Headquarters

Case S

Gender:	Female
Age:	54 years old at the time of interview
Birthplace	Tokyo
Position:	Chief Internal Auditor, Office of Internal Audit and Oversight (IAO), (D-1), ILO Headquarters
Location:	Geneva, Switzerland

Ms. S. says that she was brought up in a rather poor family. Due to her parents' conventional way of thinking that girls didn't need a higher education, she was not allowed to go to university. Instead she went to a vocational college for two years. After graduating from the vocational college she was employed by a subsidiary organization of the government affiliated to the Science and Technology Agency, and worked there for two years. However, she was uncomfortable with the atmosphere of the office, so she left. Her alma mater introduced her to Lloyds Bank International, Tokyo Branch where she worked for six years. She was promoted to a section chief, which was very rare at that time in Japan. She attended translation training school in the evening, and obtained the highest-level qualification in translation (hon-yakushi, ikkyu).

In her late twenties she had a strong desire to study at university, but she was not sure if she could study with students who were ten years younger than her. At that time, a friend of hers recommended her to take part in a short-term study abroad program in the U.S. She enrolled herself on a course at the University of North Carolina. She intended to stay for a short time in the U.S., but she found herself interested in accounting. As the university recognized her credits acquired at the vocational college in Japan, she decided to pursue an undergraduate course. Two years later she obtained a bachelor's degree (BSc) in Accounting.

After graduating from university, she was employed by KPMG Peat Marwick, a public accounting firm, as an entry-level Auditor in New York. She worked there for three years. During this period she was promoted to a Senior Supervising

Auditor and became qualified as a CPA (Certified Public Accountant).

Her time working in the public accounting firm in New York was at the height of the world-wide bubble economy. Ms. S. was responsible for many client portfolios. She was overwhelmed with work related to Japanese enterprises that were expanding into the American market. She began to question her way of life as she was working day and night, and also on Saturdays and Sundays. As she had married a non-Japanese, non-American national, she needed a green card to carry on working in the U.S. It was then that an acquaintance of hers suggested the possibility of working in the UN, and introduced her to a Japanese official who was working in the UNDP.

When a Japanese staff member passed around Ms. S.'s CV at a section chiefs' meeting, her work experience at the accounting firm and her qualification as a U.S. CPA attracted attention. Interviews were immediately held by section heads, department managers and the director of the department. After the interviews, Ms. S. was directly employed to a vacant post as an Accountant at P-3 level, within the Travel Services Section. She held this post for two and half years, after which she was promoted to Chief of the same section at P-4 level. Two years later, she was appointed to a Unit Chief post (P-5) within the Accounts Section. She was responsible for the financial accounting and reporting of the UNDP and all other funds and programmes administered by the UNDP as well as deputizing for the Section Chief (D-1). She was then asked to head a newly created Finance Policy Unit as a Senior Finance Policy Adviser to the Director of Finance until the spring of 1998.

In 1997, Ms. S. began discussing with her husband their wish to work in a city other than New York, taking advantage of being in the UN Common System. She found that a post of Chief Accountant (P-5) was advertised in the ILO Headquarters. She applied for the post and got the job. She was 45 years old.

Two years later, her boss, the Chief of Treasury and Accounts Branch (D-1) took early retirement. Ms. S. became the officer in charge. The following year, 2001, she was appointed to be the Chief of Treasury and Accounts Branch, at D-1 level. Ms. S.

remained in this position for seven years. In 2007, she applied for the position of the Chief Internal Auditor at a D-1 level. She was selected, and remained in this post until 31 December 2010.

As seen from the above biography, Ms. S. has never aspired to work in an international organization. She had even thought that working in an international organization was a distant dream for her. The Travel Services Section and Accounts Section of the UNDP, and the Treasury and Accounts Branch of the ILO had problems both technically and in terms of staff management within the office. She exerted herself very hard to reform the work processes in her section, enhance its functions and build teamwork among her colleagues. Ms. S.'s efforts and attitude towards work can be said to have led to her rather quick promotion.

Ms. S. has worked for 19 years in two international organizations: the UNDP and the ILO. Both of her duty stations were at their Headquarters.

Regarding her mentor, she said she did not have any mentors in the UNDP. However, a Canadian female supervisor who was the Chief of Treasury and Accounts Branch at ILO, when Ms. S. started to work there, became her mentor. She has remained her mentor since then.

She mentioned four networks within her workplace as the Chief Internal Auditor. The first one is that of senior officers who are considered higher than directors in the Headquarters and representatives and deputy representatives of Country Offices. The second one is with directors or peers of other international organizations. The third is the network with directors and senior officials dealing with international organizations in the private sectors, such as banks and consulting firms. The fourth network is the network of former colleagues whom she met through various committees until she was assigned to the work of an internal auditor.

She has two networks outside her workplace. The first one is with parents whose children attend international school and sports clubs. Many of them work in International Organizations and diplomatic corps. The second network is with friends she made in her former UNDP office and the accounting firm in New York.

To the question of self-development after starting work in the UN, she answered that she tried to develop her skills and competencies through her actual work. In addition to her main duties, she served various decision-making committees where she could confer with officers and peers of other sectors and institutions, which contributed to her understanding of the management of the organization as a whole, creating networks, training and education of subordinates, and so on.

When asked if she intends to work in the international organization until the mandatory retirement age, she answered that she would. She also mentioned that she wanted to work in a developing country before she retired.

To the question about the level of satisfaction, she answered that Geneva is a good place to keep a balance of work and private life. Now that she has less of a burden of raising two children, her life centers on her work, and therefore the degree of satisfaction at present is very high.

When asked if her work experience in the past in Japan and the U.S was useful, it was gathered that her variety of experience in Japan including part-time jobs even as a high school student, developed her understanding of human psychology in the workplace. In addition, while she was working in a bank, she often had to deal with auditors and this experience helped her with the work as a public auditor at KPMG Peat Marwick and as Chief Internal Auditor at the ILO.

To the question of whether the amount of income was crucial when choosing one's job, she answered she would never decide important things by the amount of money it would bring. She said it is important that people appreciate her work and that it serves both the organization and society as a whole. To the question about her attitude towards work, she answered, 'only this way makes my life worth living, therefore I shall go on this way.'

Case S Career Path

- **20**: Associate Degree in Business Administration, Tsuda School of Business, Tokyo, Japan
- **20-22**: *Administrative Staff*, International Section, Union of Japanese Scientists and Engineers, Tokyo, Japan
- **22-28**: *Section Chief*, Lloyds Bank International Ltd., Tokyo
- **28-30**: BS in Accounting, University of North Carolina, Charlotte, USA
- **31-34**: Obtained CPA, *Auditor, later Senior Supervising Auditor*, KPMG, Peat Marwick, New York, USA
- **34-38**: *Travel Accountant (P-3)*, Travel Services Section, UNDP, Headquarters, New York, USA
- **38-40**: *Section Chief (P-4)*, Travel Services Section, UNDP Headquarters, New York, USA
- **40-44**: *Senior Finance and Accounting Officer* (P-5), UNDP Headquarters, New York, USA
- **44-46**: *Accounting Senior Section Chief*, (P-5) Treasury and Accounting Branch, ILO Headquarters, Geneva, Switzerland
- **46-53**: *Finance and Accounting Director* (D-1), Treasury and Accounting Branch, ILO Headquarters, Geneva, Switzerland
- **53-present**: Chief Internal Auditor (D-1), Office of Internal Audit and Oversight, ILO Headquarters, Geneva, Switzerland

Appendix 1 The 23 Interviews from International Civil Servants and a Description of their Career Paths

Case U

Gender:	Male
Age:	50 years old at the time of interview
Birthplace:	Hokkaido Prefecture
Position:	Former Industrial Development Officer (L-4), UNIDO
Location:	Tokyo, Japan

Mr. U. was educated in Hokkaido. He studied at the Faculty of Economics, Hokkaido University. When he was in the fourth year he won a government scholarship and studied at Massachusetts University in the USA for one year. He was then employed by Nippon Steel Corporation (presently Nippon Steel and Sumitomo Metal), thinking that this company would have much business overseas. After working in Japan for some years he was dispatched to work in the actual production site in Songkhla Province, Thailand for a year in 1984. In 1988, he was assigned to the Steel Plant in the Yawata Area Development Project in Kitakyushu city. Meanwhile the company's overseas business grew stagnant. Mr. U. had wanted to work overseas in the future, so he took the Associate Expert Examination sponsored by the Japanese Ministry of Foreign Affairs and he passed.

Mr. U. left for his new position in the UNIDO Nairobi Office in Kenya as an Associate Expert (present JPO) when he was 31 years old. He worked as a Project Coordination Officer of Leather Waste Water Treatment for two years, then worked another year as a short-term contract Project Officer. During this period he applied to the vacancy advertisement for an L-3 level Industrial Development Officer in Tokyo. He was selected and became a formal staff member. Mr. U. worked for eight years as a UNIDO Industrial Development Officer in charge of the transfer of technology. Later in 2003, he was promoted to L-4 Senior Industrial Development Officer in the same UNIDO Tokyo Office, and further to Deputy Director of the UNIDO Tokyo Office. Besides his routine work, Mr. U. attended a vocational college to acquire the qualification to become a registered management consultant of Japan. In 2007 he passed the exam. In 2008, he resigned from the UNIDO and established his own independent business as a small-medium enterprise

Management Consultant (*chushokigyo shindanshi*). He still works in this business and receives some short-term consulting orders from UNIDO Headquarters as well as from European Bank for Reconstruction and Development (EBRD).

Mr. U. had applied to P-5 or L-5 posts which have budgetary control in the organization. However, he was not accepted. One of the reasons might be the fact that he had no Master's degree. In those days when Mr. U. took the Exam, the Master's degree was not required. However, it is now necessary to apply for the JPO Exam. So it is considered that Mr. U. was at a disadvantage when he was screened for promotion. He had a hard time trying to decide which qualification he should get, an academic MA or a vocational qualification as a Registered Management Consultant. Eventually he decided to choose the consultancy qualification.

Mr. U. is thinking of helping Japanese local industries to acquire more industrial power. he wants to help them to transfer their industrial power and technology to developing countries by means of utilizing his knowledge and experience he gained in his days working in the UNIDO.

To the question of whether he had a mentor in the first office of the international organization, he answered he had two mentors when he was working in the UNIDO Nairobi Office. One was a German supervisor of L-5 level in the Nairobi Office. He used to go on missions with him. Another mentor was the Finnish Section Chief in the Headquarters in Vienna. He used to make telephone calls to the Japanese JPO who worked on the actual sites of developing countries to ask how things were going. They were very kind and considerate. He said he still respects this ex-supervisor. He also mentioned that when he was working in the UNIDO Tokyo Office, he didn't meet anyone who he could call his mentor.

To the question of the networks in his work place, he mentioned there were three networks in the Tokyo Office. The first one was with staff in charge of private industries, JETRO (the Japan External Trade Organization), Japan Chamber of Commerce and Industry, Local and Central Government Public Corporation to Promote Industry, and various types of other business communities.

The second network was the channel with those people concerned with the transfer of technology to developing countries, that is, universities concerned in developed and developing countries, research institutes including NEDO (New Energy and Industrial Technology Development Organization) and AIST (National Institute of Advanced Industrial Science and Technology).

The third network was with those in charge of Personnel, Finance Processing, and Financial Affairs Divisions who work in the Field Administrative Department in the UNIDO Headquarters. He said that the relationship with those in the third channel increased after his post was promoted to L-4.

As for a network outside his workplace, he connected with people through academic activities and members of such organizations as the Japan Society for International Development, various study groups and APIC (Association for Promotion of International Cooperation).

Mr. U. worked in an international organization for 16 years, then became an independent consultant before he reached the mandatory retirement age. The main reason why he resigned from the international organization was because he judged that further promotion to a level higher than L-5 level would be difficult.

Regarding his job-satisfaction, he thinks that both job satisfaction and life satisfaction are important. To the question of whether his work experience in a Japanese private company was useful, he answered that what he had learned at Nippon Steel Corporation about procedures and preparation planning were useful for his consulting work.

To the question of whether the amount of income mattered in choosing a job, he said in his case whenever he chose a new job, his income decreased. When he changed from Nippon Steel to the Nairobi Office of UNIDO, his income decreased by 20%, but it did not matter too much as the living standard in Nairobi was also low, and he didn't have to spend much money to live. When he resigned from UNIDO and became independent, his income in the first year dropped greatly, but in the following year (when this interview was held) he had a prospect of more income so that decrease of income did not influence him after all.

His guiding principle is *shikoseien* (Chinese Proverb), which means that one's ambition should be high, pure and reach far. He puts these characters on the alcove of his home and always tries to make sure that he keeps these ideals in mind.

Appendix 1 The 23 Interviews from International Civil Servants and a Description of their Career Paths

Case U Career Path

Age	
23	• Graduated from the Faculty of Economics, Hokkaido University, Japan • One year scholarship at Massachusetts University USA
23-25	• *Staff*, Nippon Steel Corp., Tokyo, Japan
25-26	• Dispatched to Nippon Steel Corp. Songkhla Province, Thailand
26-31	• *Regional Development Staff*, Nippon Steel Corp., Yawata, Japan
31-33	• AE (L-2), UNIDO, Nairobi, Kenya
33-34	• *Short-term Contract Staff (L-2)*, UNIDO, Nairobi, Kenya
34-42	• *Industrial Development Officer, (L-3)*, UNIDO, Tokyo, Japan
42-48	• *Senior Industrial Development Officer (L-4)*, UNIDO, Tokyo, Japan
48-present	• *Independent Consultant*, for small and medium enterprises, Chiba, Japan

Case V

Gender:	Male
Age:	50 at the time of interview
Birthplace:	Kanagawa Prefecture
Position:	Director and Treasurer, Office of the Treasurer, Finance and Administration Department (IFAD) (D-1)
Location:	Rome, Italy

Mr. V.'s. interest in working in an international field began at high school. He studied International Relations at university and became an exchange student in the USA, studying International Politics for one year.

After coming back to university Japan, he took recruitment examinations for only companies that would offer opportunities to work overseas. He was employed by a leading Japanese company.

Since his employment in 1982, he worked mainly in the international field. Between 1987 and 1989 he was sponsored by his company and studied at Harvard Business School in the USA. After he came back to Japan, he continued working in Tokyo head office. During this period he enrolled in the Faculty of Law, Keio University and obtained a BA in Law while working full-time.

Between 1996 and 2000, he worked in Washington D.C. in the USA, and took charge of the corporate social responsibility program, whereby he gained a new perspective on business and society. Through his contacts with people in the World Bank, the Inter-American Development Bank, and those involved in various think-tanks in Washington D.C., Mr. V. became more interested in working for an international organization. At that time, he made up his mind to become qualified as a Certified Public Accountant (CPA). He took the examination in 2001, passed it and acquired the license.

When he was 44 years old in 2003, Mr. V. applied for a vacancy at IFAD. He was selected for the post of Director and Treasurer at D-1 level. In the following year he took up the position in Rome, IFAD headquarters, and has remained in that post. Mr. V. had worked in a Japanese private company for more than 20 years before becoming employed by the IFAD, and he had had no experience of changing jobs until that time.

To the question of whether he had a mentor, he mentioned a Japanese senior staff member working for the ILO. Mr. V. met her when he was considering whether he should apply for a position with ILO, and he was given very helpful advice. This experience led him to seek employment with the IFAD. He said that even now, though he works for a different organization, Mr. V. regards her as his mentor since their professional field is the same. When Mr. V. has something he doesn't understand, he contacts and consults with the attaché at the UN mission in New York. He answered that there are few people he can trust and be completely frank with in his present workplace at the IFAD.

To the question regarding his networks in the workplace, he mentioned two networks. The first one is that of division managers of related divisions. The second is the network with those directors of such committees as Auditing, Investment, and Management, who attend cross-sectional conferences. Those members are the same level as Mr. V.

As for a network outside his workplace, he mentioned a channel with those in charge of finance in the UN Common System and those in finance offices in the World Bank and other Development Banks. With those people he tries to share and strengthen the issues common among the organizations and among them.

To the author's question of his future, he answered he wishes to continue working on solving global issues from a financial standpoint within an international organization and would not only like to expand his own skills and knowledge but would also like to create more opportunities and routes for Japanese members to play active roles in the organization.

To the question of his level of satisfaction, he rated his satisfaction as four out of five. In order to lead a team comprising of people from different countries, much energy is needed, he feels tremendous strain from such work. The stress from his work is so great that it may give a burden on his family. For that reason, the balance of work and life is the biggest task for him to achieve a satisfactory working life.

He answered that the experience of working in a private company proved very useful. In the international organization the result is achieving a goal. One must show the results in the most effective and efficient way. In this sense, the experience in the private company is useful. Mr. V.'s various careers in private companies, especially his experience of working for the corporate social responsibility program in Washington D.C. was very unique, and thus created an opportunity for him to change careers to his present job in the IFAD. On the other hand, the largest difference between a private company and international organization is the HR policy. Decision-making processes in a private company are, generally speaking, from the top to the bottom, whereas decision-making processes are more democratic in the UN Common System. Annual performance evaluation includes an evaluation by supervisors, colleagues and subordinates, what is termed a '360 degree feed-back evaluation' and team leaders are constantly requested to evaluate whether an employment contract should be renewed or not.

Is the amount of income important when choosing a job? To this question Mr. V. answered that he did not care so much about that when he was choosing a job. However, housing cost is more expensive and medical facilities are different in Rome compared with those in Japan. For his family members, a great amount of effort and ingenuity is necessary to live in Rome.

His philosophy is to "*Go back to the basis.*" Mr. V. said that when he is in a situation where he cannot solve a problem, he would always go back to the basics. Lastly, he expressed his hopes that he should be able to have some sort of impact on the organization and society to which he belongs. He also wishes to provide such opportunities for as many Japanese professionals as possible to play active roles in international organizations.

Additional Notes: After serving in IFAD for 8 years, Mr. V. decided to seek a new challenge. In August 2012, he was appointed Chief Financial Officer of the Global Green Growth Institute (GGGI) which became a treaty-based inter-governmental organization in October 2012. As a member of the executive management team, he has been responsible for strengthening financial and administrative management for a greater level of transparency.

Case V Career Path

22
- Graduated from university in Japan, majored in International Politics, Exchange student in USA for one year

22-28
- Employed by a leading Japanese company, Assigned to international business cooperation division, Tokyo, Japan

29-31
- Studied abroad sponsored by company
- Business School in the USA
- Obtained MBA

31-37
- Returned to Japan and his company
- Re-enrolled in university and obtained a BA in Law

37-41
- Remained with the same company
- Seconded to a Corporate Office in Washington, D.C., USA

41-44
- Returned to Tokyo, Japan and assigned to launch the Corporate Venture Capital Division of the same company
- Obtained a qualification as a CPA

45-present
- *Director and Treasurer (D-1)*, IFAD Headquarters, Rome, Italy

Case W

Gender:	Male
Age:	48 years old at the time of interview
Birthplace:	Fukuoka
Position:	Coordinator, TB, AIDS and Malaria, Division of Communicable Disease Control (P-6), WHO
Location:	Cairo, Egypt

Mr. W. was educated in Japan. When he was a student at the Medical school of Kochi University, he read a book, *Ninngen no Daichi* (The Great Earth of Human Beings) written by Michiko Inukai who is a famous Japanese writer. The book influenced him to work overseas for the people of developing countries. In order to realize his objective, Mr.W. planned to achieve two aims. One was to study English and gain experience in different areas of clinical medicine. The second aim was then to accumulate professional experience in the field of public health. There was only one place where he could fulfill both objectives of his first aim, Yokosuka Hospital of American Military Forces in Japan. He worked there as an intern in the American military hospital for one year in the fields of internal medicine, surgery, pediatric and gynecology. During this period he met many people and listened to their advice about his future plans. Regarding his second aim, he sent more than 50 public health related organizations letters to ask if there were any vacancies. The Research Institute of Tuberculosis (TB), Japan Anti-Tuberculosis Association offered him a post, so when he finished his intern period he commenced his job in their office.

Three years later he was seconded by the Institute to Yemen, TB Project of JICA, and worked in Yemen for three years. He went back to Japan to work a further two years. He was then employed as a Medical Officer P-4 level, on a short contract by the WHO Eastern Mediterranean Office in Egypt, and was engaged in work on TB control. For the following two years he worked in the same office and continued his work as a seconded member of personnel from the JICA. When that contract expired, he was formally employed as a medical officer of the WHO P-4 level. Two years later, in the year 2000, he was promoted to P-5 level Regional Advisor in the same office. For one year between 2003 and 2004 he took study leave and engaged in research on international health and TB at the School of Public Health, Harvard University as a Takemi International Health Research Fellow. He returned to his workplace in 2004 and continued disseminating knowledge about TB prevention in the Middle East and Africa. In 2009, he was promoted to P-6 Coordinator. (There is only a P-6 level in the WHO but the rate of pay is the same as D-1 level). He is now in charge of measures against malaria as well as TB. (Then in 2011, he was promoted to D2 level director: see diagram below).

As it is clear from the above history, Mr. W. has been working in developing countries as a specialist in measures against infectious diseases. The opportunity to work within the WHO came about when the Japanese director of the WHO at that time, recognized his talents and recommended him for the position. He was 34 years old when he first started working as a medical officer, then he was employed as a formal member of the WHO at the age of 37. He worked for the WHO for 13 years, experienced three positions in the field of measures against infectious diseases, and within the same organization he was promoted from P-4 to P-6. The area under his charge covers 22 countries in the East Mediterranean Sea area. He said that he often has to go on missions.

To the question of whether he had mentors in his first workplace, he mentioned two. One was the previously mentioned Japanese Director of TB who worked in the WHO Headquarters. The other one was his direct Director in the WHO (of Syrian nationality). The first mentor gave him indirect advice, while the second mentor taught Mr. W. how to conduct his work properly within the organization. He said that the Syrian chief was a very capable person. At present he has no mentor but he has good superiors and colleagues he can talk to freely and frankly.

To the question regarding his networks within his workplace, he mentioned that in the Eastern Mediterranean Office there are about 200 staff members above professional level and 500 general service staff, there are four Technical Divisions and Administration Division that would take charge of personnel and general affairs, etc. Mr. W. belongs to the TB, AIDS, Malaria Group and engages with professionals within these fields. He firstly mentioned the network of professionals within the group and related administration people. Secondly, a network of staff in the WHO Headquarters, their partners in the 22 governments of the countries concerned, and all other people concerned with working in research institutes of Europe and America and organizations of contributing countries. He said that his work is highly specialized, so that the network outside his specialized field is often limited.

As for his efforts for professional development, he mentioned a paid leave of absence he took for a year which he spent as a research fellow at the graduate school of Harvard University.

To the question of whether he intends to stay in the international organization until the mandatory retirement age, he answered he can't tell at the moment. At present, he enjoys his work so he has no current plan of resigning from the WHO.

Regarding the question of satisfaction, he said he would rank his level of satisfaction at the top of the scale. He also said that his source of satisfaction is his job.

To the question of whether his experience working in a Japanese organization proved useful, he answered that the skills and the ways of thinking which he learned in the Japan Anti-Tuberculosis Association have proved to be useful in his present job.

To the question of whether the amount of income is an important factor when choosing one's job, he answered that if he could live an ordinary life he should be content. If his skill is useful, he wishes to use it to serve others. (In the country where Mr. W. takes charge, the monthly salary of civil servants in Africa who deal with tuberculosis is almost equivalent to Mr. W.'s daily income. As such, observing them working so hard, he feels one could not complain).

To the question of his attitude towards his work and career, he says, 'Use the correct techniques in your work so the results are reflected in the actual work conducted by the WHO and member governments. Think of the essence of the matter, simplify it and achieve results.'

Additional Notes: In 2001, Mr. W. was awarded the *Karel Styblo* Public Health Award for disseminating DOTS (Directly Observed Treatment Short-course) by the International Union Against Tuberculosis. He is the first and the only Japanese recipient of this award. In 2010, he was selected as the Director of the Health Program at United Nations Relief and Works Agency (UNRWA) and Special Representative at WHO D-2 level.

Appendix 1 The 23 Interviews from International Civil Servants and a Description of their Career Paths   241

Case W Career Path

18-25
- Graduated from Medical School, Kochi University, Japan

25-26
- *Intern* (Clinical Medicine) Yokosuka Hospital of American Military Forces in Japan, Yokosuka, Japan

26-29
- *Medical Specialist Staff*, The Research Institute of Tuberculosis Japan Anti-Tuberculosis Association in Japan, Tokyo, Japan

29-31
- *In charge of TB Team*, Seconded to JICA, Sana City, Yemen

31-33
- *Medical Professional*, International Department, The Research Institute of Tuberculosis Japan Anti-Tuberculosis Association, Tokyo, Japan

34-36
- *Contra-TB Medical Professional (Dispatched by JICA) (P-4)*, WHO, Eastern Mediterranean Headquarters, Cairo, Egypt

36-38
- *Contra-TB Medical Professional (P-4)*, WHO, Eastern Mediterranean Headquarters, Cairo, Egypt

38-40
- *Contra-TB Regional Advisor (P-5)*, WHO, Eastern Mediterranean Headquarters, Cairo, Egypt

40-41
- *Research Fellow*, Institute of Public Hygiene Research
- Temporary Leave of Office (paid)
- Harvard University, Boston, USA

41-46
- *Reinstated*
- *Contra-TB Regional Advisor, (P-5)*, WHO, East Mediterranean Headquarters, Cairo, Egypt

46-present
- Chief Coordinator, (P-6) (D-1 equivalent), WHO, East Mediterranean Headquarters, Cairo, Egypt

Case X

Gender:	Male
Age:	51 at the time of interview
Birthplace:	Finland
Position:	Senior Evaluation Advisor, Evaluation Office, UNDP
Location:	New York, USA

Mr. X. was educated in his native country, Finland, until he finished his Master's Course in Helsinki University majoring in Geography. Then he continued to take a Doctorate Course at Lund University, Sweden. When he was in the doctoral course, the Government of Finland put out a newspaper advertisement to recruit an Associate Expert to be seconded to the IFAD (International Fund for Agricultural Development). He applied and was accepted.

In the IFAD Headquarters he was engaged in agricultural development in Asia and the Middle East for three years, specializing in monitoring and evaluation (M&E). After that Mr. X. became a researcher at the Scandinavian Institute of African Studies (now Nordic Africa Institute). During that time he devoted himself to completing his doctoral dissertation. After obtaining a PhD in Social and Economic Geography from Lund University in Sweden in 1989, in order to strengthen his practical skills in international development, he began to work as a development consultant. He was in charge of feasibility studies and ex-post evaluations of ODA projects by Finnish and Swedish governments and also did two short-term consultancies for IFAD. During this period he applied for a post at P-3 level, in the UNESCO Division of Ecological Sciences. He was instead approached by the United Nations University (UNU) Headquarters in Japan, and was offered a P-3 level post as an Academic Officer working in the environment research and training program. Mr. X. accepted it and started his new job in the UNU. He was 33 years old.

His work at the UNU consisted of a combination of work within the fields of international development and environment. Five years after he started his career

Appendix 1   The 23 Interviews from International Civil Servants and
a Description of their Career Paths

at the UNU, he was promoted to P-4 level. Two years later he was further promoted to P-5 level as Senior Academic Officer. Mr. X. established his status as a specialist in the field of the environment during his nine years working at the UNU. Following this he applied for a post at the World Bank as an M&E Specialist in the Global Environment Facility (GEF) which was at an equivalent level to P-5. After working for the World Bank for three years, he applied to and was selected for an L-5 (equivalent to a P-5 but funded from an extra-budgetary source, i.e. GEF) post in the UNDP Headquarters.

In his first four years in the UNDP he was in charge of evaluating projects in the environment area, participating in international conferences, and developing policies and strategies in the field of environmental M&E and results-based management for the whole UNDP. He was then selected for a regular P-5 post in the UNDP Evaluation Office where, for the past two years, he has been managing programmatic evaluations at the country and regional levels. He also supervises staff as a team leader, including four professional officers and one general service staff.

Mr. X. started his career in international organizations at the age of 27, and has worked in four different organizations in three different countries. At present, he is in charge of program evaluations in Asia and the Pacific, Europe and CIS, and Arab States. He is frequently on mission, but his duty stations have all been in UN Headquarters locations. Before joining the UN, he aimed to become a specialist of international development. He then became a specialist in the field of the environment and has been working as a specialist in sustainable development, combining international development and the environment.

To the question of whether he had a mentor in his first workplace, he answered that a Norwegian supervisor in IFAD and a senior Italian advisor taught him the importance of keeping one's beliefs at heart and how to work in an international organization. Additionally, two months after he started his job, he followed a senior Japanese male staff member on mission to Pakistan, which was a good hands-on learning experience. Similar missions with senior staff followed. When he was working at the UNU, an American vice-rector introduced him to extensive academic networks in international development and the environment. In his present workplace, a D-1 supervisor from Bangladesh who had worked for the UNDP for 32 years, pointed out the difficulty of carrying out managerial work at the same time as being a specialist. They are now talking about next steps for the future.

To the question of his networks in and out of his workplace, he mentioned three channels. The first channel is the set of friends he made while working as an Associate Expert in Rome. Some of these friends are still so close that he has a feeling of solidarity with them. Their specialties and workplaces are different, yet most of them are playing a central role either in international organizations or ODA programs in their governments. The second channel is of specialists within the environmental field. The network expands in a cross-sectoral manner all over the world including international organizations and university institutes. The third channel is a network of Japanese staff members he came to know while he was working at the UNU. Among the various organizations within which he has worked, he spent the longest time, nine years, at the UNU. As such, he still maintains relations with the Japanese he met at that time. Some of them are now working in an international organization or at universities in New York.

To the question of whether he would work in an international organization until the mandatory retirement age, he answered that it would depend on future opportunities. Mr. X. is interested in working in the field of his specializations, both in academic and practical terms, but not so much in management. In the future he may have a chance for promotion but he is not so keen to move up to a higher position. He would rather be in a position that is related to his specialized field. If such a position should be offered outside of the UN, he would give it much consideration.

Regarding the question of level of satisfaction he answered that the combination of job-satisfaction and overall satisfaction is important and are closely interlinked. As he has a family, he cannot only follow his own career path.

To the question of whether his experience in Japan was useful, he answered that he learned discipline, thoughtfulness and politeness while working in Japan.

To the question of whether the amount of income is important when choosing a job, he answered it is important, but it is not the most important factor. He would consider a job offer based on how interesting the job was, even if it paid 20% less than his current salary.

As for his attitude to work, he would like to continue to have meaningful work in an international context. When he was in high school, Mr. X. became interested in global issues through his encounters with a geography teacher. As such, he decided to specialize in geography at university, and subsequently to select this international career. He reflected that en route to the present position he has benefited from the advice given to him by his more senior colleagues. Now he said he is trying to give such advice to young professionals who are establishing their careers in the field of the environment and international development.

Additional Notes: In the year following the interview, Mr. X. applied for and was selected as a Deputy Director at the UNDP Evaluation Office, (D-1). Mr. X. also expressed a wish not to hide his identity, as such, Case. X is revealed as Juha I. Uitto, PhD.

Case X Career Path

- **24**: Graduated with a BSc from Helsinki University, Finland
- **25**: Gained an MSc Geography from Helsinki University, Finland
- **25-27**:
  - Lund University, Doctoral Course, Sweden
  - Passed AE Exam
- **27-30**: *Agricultural Development Program Officer (L-2) AE*, IFAD Headquarters, Rome, Italy
- **30-32**:
  - *Research Fellow*, Uppsala, Sweden
  - Obtained a PhD in Social and Economic Geography from Lund University
- **32-33**: *Development Consultant*, Helsinki, Finland
- **33-38**: *Academic Officer (Environment) (P-3)*, UN University, Tokyo, Japan
- **38-40**: *Academic Officer (Environment) (P-4)*, UN University, Tokyo, Japan
- **40-42**: *Senior Academic Officer (Environment) (P-5)*, UN University, Tokyo, Japan
- **42-45**: *GEF Monitoring and Evaluation Specialist, (P-5)*, World Bank, Washington, D.C., USA
- **45-48**: *GEF Senior Monitoring and Evaluation Coordinator, (L-5)*, Project Evaluation Division, UNDP, New York, USA
- **48-present**: *Senior Evaluation Advisor (P-5)* Project Evaluation Division, UNDP, New York, USA

Appendix 2

Results of the First Survey Conducted on Japanese Formal Staff Members Employed in the UN Common System

(Cross Tabulation of Formal Staff members by Sex (n.170) Conducted in June 2003)

		Male	Female	Total
Q1. Have you ever worked in Japan?				
A	Yes	67	67	134
B	No	12	18	30
	Total	79	85	164
Q2. If your answer is "a" in Q1, where did you work? (Multiple answers accepted)				
A	Private company/companies	41	44	85
B	Research institution/institutions	13	11	24
C	Government	19	9	28
D	NGO/NGOs	4	7	11
E	Self-employed	1	0	1
F	UN Agency/Agencies located in Japan	3	7	10
G	Others	3	4	7
	Total	84	82	166
Q3. If your answer is "a" in Q1, how many years did you work in Japan?		9.3	4.1	6.7
Q4. How many different jobs have you had before you started working for the UN Common System?				
A	None	18	15	33
B	One	31	29	60
C	Two	11	23	34
D	Three	13	8	21
E	Four	2	5	7
F	Five	0	3	3
G	More than 5	2	2	4
	Total	77	85	162
Q5. How often did you change your job in Japan?				
A	Never	46	35	81

	B	One	7	20	27
	C	Two	8	8	16
	D	Three	6	5	11
	E	Four	0	1	1
	F	Five	0	0	0
	G	More than 5	2	1	3
		Total	69	70	139

Q6. Were you satisfied with your job/work prior to working for the UN Common System)

	A	Yes	51	46	97
	B	No	18	27	45
		Total	69	73	142

Q7. When did you start preparations for working in the UN Common System?

	A	Below 18 (High school student)	4	4	8
	B	University student/Graduate student	19	39	58
	C	After graduation〜29	26	25	51
	D	30〜34	11	14	25
	E	35〜39	3	2	5
	F	40〜44	7	2	9
	G	45〜49	5	0	5
	H	More than 50	1	0	1
		Total	76	86	162

Q8. At what age did you first get a regular funded post?

	A	20〜24	1	6	7
	B	25〜29	17	36	53
	C	30〜34	33	33	66
	D	35〜39	9	7	16
	E	40〜44	10	5	15
	F	45〜49	5	0	5
	G	More than 50	3	0	3
		Total	78	87	165

Q9. How did you get a position within the UN Common System?

	A	Applying for a vacant post	24	13	37
	B	Through AE/JPO/APO scheme	21	37	58
	C	Secondment	4	1	5
	D	Recruitment mission	7	8	15
	E	YPP	5	6	11
	F	Others (Please specify)	12	12	24
		Total	73	77	150

Q10. What was your motive for applying for a UN Common System post?
(Multiple answers accepted, maximum of 3)

Appendix 2 Results of the First Survey Conducted on
Japanese Formal Staff members Employed in the UN Common System

A	To contribute to the peace of the world	26	30	56
B	To help people of the developing countries/refugees	50	50	100
C	To utilize my specialty/specialties	54	43	97
D	To live overseas	22	17	39
E	To work with people of different backgrounds in culture, religion, etc	33	44	77
F	Other motive(s) (please specify)	7	10	17
	Total	192	194	386

Q11. Among the following, which elements do you think are the most important for working in the UN Common System?
(Multiple answers accepted maxium of 3)

A	Adaptability/Flexibility	41	63	104
B	Specialty/Specialties	48	30	78
C	Ability for negotiation	22	17	39
D	Language ability	47	50	97
E	Positive attitude	21	28	49
F	Leadership	13	8	21
G	Work experience of the relevant field of the UN activities	9	12	21
H	Experience of having lived overseas	3	5	8
I	Coordination skill with local staff/people	10	10	20
J	Understanding/knowledge of the programs implemented at the UN	4	5	9
K	Others (Please specify)	9	14	23
	Total	227	242	469

Q12. Are you satisfied with your work in the UN?

A	Very satisfied	30	27	57
B	Satisfied	33	46	79
C	Average	12	10	22
D	A little unsatisfied	2	2	4
E	Very unsatisfied	2	2	4
	Total	79	87	166

Q13. What is the reason for your answer in Q12
(Multiple answers accepted, maximum of 3)?

A	Substance of the job	55	56	111
B	Work environment	26	30	56
C	Work hours	7	10	17
D	Equal work for both sexes	2	22	24
E	Development of specialty/specialties	12	22	34
F	Room for discretion	7	6	13
G	Feeling of accomplishment	38	23	61
H	Contribution to the society	28	30	58
I	Utilization of my abilities	24	30	54
J	Others (Please specify)	6	10	16
	Total	205	239	444

Q14. The work hours in the UN, as compared to those in Japan, are

A	About twice as long or longer	1	0	1
B	50% longer	2	7	9
C	20~30% longer	5	10	15
D	About the same	28	24	52
E	20~30% shorter	22	19	41
F	About half as long	1	1	2
G	Less than half as long	1	0	1
	Total	60	61	121

Q15. Generally speaking, do you think that the salary at the UN Common System is?

A	Very high	0	6	6
B	Somewhat high	22	43	65
C	Average	39	29	68
D	Somewhat low	16	8	24
E	Very low	1	1	2
	Total	78	87	165

Q16. Compared with the salary you would be receiving if you had been working in Japan, the salary you are now receiving is:

A	Very high	2	9	11
B	Somewhat high	15	18	33
C	Average	29	25	54
D	Somewhat low	19	19	38
E	Very low	7	3	10
	Total	72	74	146

Q17. Compared with the salary you were receiving in Japan, the present salary at the UN Common System is

A	More than double	7	10	17
B	About double	0	3	3
C	20 to 50% more	13	12	25
D	About the same	13	11	24
E	20 to 50% less	16	9	25
F	About half	7	0	7
G	Less than half	0	2	2
	Total	56	47	103

Q18. Do you think the fringe benefits given at the UN Common System are:

A	Very high	4	21	25
B	Somewhat high	40	42	82
C	Average	25	19	44

Appendix 2 Results of the First Survey Conducted on
Japanese Formal Staff members Employed in the UN Common System

D	Somewhat low		6	4	10
E	Very low		2	1	3
	Total		77	87	164

Q19. Your degree of satisfaction in regard to your living is:

A	Very high	7	21	28
B	Somewhat high	42	40	82
C	Average	26	23	49
D	Somewhat low	3	3	6
E	Very low	1	0	1
	Total	79	87	166

Q20. What is your overall satisfaction in working for the UN Common System?

A	Very high	23	27	50
B	Somewhat high	45	45	90
C	Average	9	12	21
D	Somewhat low	1	2	3
E	Very low	1	1	2
	Total	79	87	166

Q21. What is the reason for your answer in Q20? (Multiple answers accepted, maximum of 3)

A	Substance of the job	57	60	117
B	Work environment	26	29	55
C	Remuneration	9	14	23
D	Work hours	11	5	16
E	Fringe benefits (pension, annual leave, etc.)	11	14	25
F	Equal work for both sexes	1	23	24
G	Development of specialty/specialties	11	12	23
H	Room for discretion	6	6	12
I	Feeling of accomplishment	29	26	55
J	Contribution to the society	27	27	54
K	Utilization of abilities	12	14	26
L	Work environment where political decisions often take place	6	6	12
M	Too many transfers among duty stations	0	0	0
N	Unfair treatment at the workplace	3	2	5
O	Low remuneration	0	2	2
P	Poor utilization of specialty/specialties	2	1	3
Q	Others (Please specify)	6	8	14
	Total	217	249	466

Q22. Many women are working at the senior level in the UN Common System. What do you think is the reason for that?

A	Commitment of top management	34	41	75
B	Trend of the society	16	14	30

C	Women have higher aptitude than men	6	0	6
D	Women have higher flexibility than men	2	3	5
E	No specific reasons	7	5	12
F	Others (Please specify)	10	20	30
	Total	75	83	158

Q23. Do you think it is possible to introduce the affirmative action implemented at the UN Common System to Japan?

A	Yes, it is possible	18	30	48
B	Yes, but to some extent	25	22	47
C	I do not know	14	10	24
D	No, I do not think so	14	21	35
E	Definitely no	3	1	4
	Total	74	84	158

Q24. If you answered "d" or "e" in Q23, what is your reason for that? (Multiple answers accepted, maximum of 3)

A	Top management of Japanese companies has not sufficiently valued women's contributions	13	18	31
B	There is no appropriate environment for women both to fulfill work professionally and to carry out family responsibilities	14	18	32
C	Work hours are long in Japan	5	8	13
D	Women are not willing to work on a full-time basis, especially after having a baby	1	8	9
E	I do not know			
F	Others (Please specify)	5	6	11
	Total	38	58	96

Q25. Do you think the number of Japanese formal staff will be increased in the future, say, in 10 to 15 years?

A	Yes, of course it will	19	16	35
B	Yes, but to some extent	36	43	79
C	I do not know	10	17	27
D	I doubt it	12	11	23
E	I definitely do not think so	1	0	1
	Total	78	87	165

Q26. If you answered "a" or "b" in Q25, what is your reason for that? (Multiple answers accepted, maximum of 3)

A	The language proficiency of Japanese has increased	35	31	66
B	It is easier to find an appropriate job in Japan, after working for the UN Common			

Appendix 2 Results of the First Survey Conducted on
Japanese Formal Staff members Employed in the UN Common System

	System for a considerable number of years	3	3	6
C	More young Japanese have shown an interest in working for the UN Common System	43	45	88
D	Others (Please specify)	11	17	28
	Total	92	96	188

Q27. If you answered "c" or "d" in Q25, what is your reason for that? (Multiple answers accepted, maximum of 3)

A	The qualifications/requirements are very high	4	9	13
B	The remuneration is rather low at the UN Common System	6	6	12
C	The Japanese Government does not have strong political power internationally	8	9	17
D	It is exhausting to work overseas for so many years	1	2	3
E	Employment practices in Japan are quite different from those at the UN Common System	13	15	28
F	Others (Please specify)	5	7	12
	Total	37	48	85

Q28. If you have an effective plan to increase the number of Japanese formal staff, please write your plan below:

Q29. Which factor do you think is the most difficult to adjust yourself to when you are assigned to a new duty station?

A	Substance of work	13	11	24
B	Relationship with local staff	8	16	24
C	General matters, not directly relating to work such as security, access to reliable medical facilities, food, etc.	31	28	59
D	The language used at the duty station	8	5	13
E	Others (Please specify)	11	19	30
	Total	71	79	150

Q30. Have you taken any pre-departure training prior to working for the UN Common System?

A	Yes	10	14	24
B	No	66	71	137
	Total	76	85	161

Q31. To improve the benefits of the training, which do you think is more useful?

A	Pre-departure training itself	14	5	19
B	Post-assignment training (such as mentoring service from senior Japanese staff)	15	15	30
C	Both are important	22	42	64
D	Neither of them is important	17	7	24
E	Others (Please specify)	6	4	10
	Total	74	73	147

Q32. Do you wish to work for the UN Common System until you reach your mandatory retirement age?

A	Yes	50	57	107
B	No	22	24	46
	Total	72	81	153

Q33. If you answered "a" in Q32, what is your reason for that? (Multiple answers accepted, maximum of 3)

A	I can utilize my expertise	25	37	62
B	I can utilize my specialization	19	24	43
C	Work environment is very comfortable	15	18	33
D	I can expect promotion	7	3	10
E	I can do my work with discretion	4	8	12
F	Remuneration at the UN Common System is higher than in Japan	4	3	7
G	Workload is less at the UN Common System than in the private sector in Japan	4	2	6
H	It is difficult to find an appropriate job outside the UN Common System	11	18	29
I	Others (Please specify)	7	14	21
	Total	96	127	223

Q34. If you answered "b" in Q32, what is your reason for that? (Multiple answers accepted, maximum of 3)

A	I am not satisfied with work	5	2	7
B	I would like to utilize my expertise better outside the UN Common System	14	21	35
C	Work at the UN Common System is different from what I originally expected	3	6	9
D	Working in the international environment does not suit me	1	0	1
E	My capacity does not reach the requirements of working in the UN Common System	0	1	1
F	Others (Please specify)	10	9	19
	Total	33	39	72

Appendix 2 Results of the First Survey Conducted on
Japanese Formal Staff members Employed in the UN Common System

Q35.Have you ever seriously thought of resigning from the UN Common System and of finding a job in Japan?					
	A	Yes	26	14	40
	B	No	53	72	125
		Total	79	86	165
Q36.If you answered "a" in Q35, what is your reason for that? (Multiple answers accepted, maximum of 3)					
	A	I am not satisfied with the present work at the UN Common System	6	3	9
	B	I do not agree with my boss	5	6	11
	C	I can not utilize my abilities	6	2	8
	D	I am concerned about the education of my children	6	1	7
	E	I need to take care of old parents	7	7	14
	F	I am exhausted from working and living overseas	2	1	3
	G	Others (Please specify)	11	5	16
		Total	43	25	68
Q37.If you answered "a" in Q35, then tell us why you actually did not resign from the UN Common System? (Multiple answers accepted, maximum of 3)					
	A	I could not find an appropriate job in Japan	9	4	13
	B	I found a job in Japan, but the overall entitlements including remunerations were lower than those at the UN	2	1	3
	C	Family members did not want to return to Japan	2	2	4
	D	I could not make the final decision to return to Japan as the work environment in Japan is so different from that at the UN	3	5	8
	E	Others (Please specify)	10	8	18
		Total	26	20	46
Q38.Which of the following are your most pressing concerns at present? (Multiple answers accepted, maximum of 3)					
	A	Renewal of contract	8	5	13
	B	Promotion	26	39	65
	C	Education of children	28	11	39
	D	Care of parents	24	22	46
	E	Life after retirement	18	10	28
	F	Getting a job in Japan	4	4	8
	G	I do not have any pressing concerns	19	22	41

H	Others (Please specify)		11	24	35
	Total		138	137	275

Q39. If you have any comments/advice you wish to convey to us relating to this questionnaire or employment at the UN Common System, please write them below. For example, tell us your prior experience or work experience at the UN Common System please write them below. For example, tell us your prior experience or work experience which is useful for carrying out duties at the UN Common System.

Q40. Do you wish to receive a summary of this questionnaire?

A	Yes		64	70	134
B	No		13	11	24
	Total		77	81	158

Q41. At which organization are you employed now (IBRD and WTO are included for comparison)?

A	UN Headquarters		8	22	30
B	UN Subsidiary Organizations		22	26	48
C	Specialized Agencies		31	25	56
D	World Bank Group		12	12	24
E	World Trade Organization and others		4	0	4
F	N.A.		77	85	162
	Total				

Q42. What is your current grade (staff grade)?

A	ADG and above		1	0	1
B	D-2		2	0	2
C	D-1		9	4	13
D	P-5		19	8	27
E	P-4		23	26	49
F	P-3		13	30	43
G	P-2		4	11	15
H	P-1		0	2	2
I	Other		2	2	4
	Total		73	83	156

Q43. What is the type of your contract?

A	Continuing/Indefinite		46	57	103
B	Fixed Term		31	28	59
C	Other		2	2	4
	Total		79	87	166

Appendix 2 Results of the First Survey Conducted on
Japanese Formal Staff members Employed in the UN Common System

Q44.What is your status? (Multiple answers accepted)					
	A	Regular post staff	79	87	166
	B	Secondment	0	0	0
	C	AE/JPO/APO	0	0	0
	D	YPP	0	0	0
	E	Others (Please specify)	0	0	0
		Total	79	87	166
Q45.How many organizations have you worked for within the UN Common System?					
	A	One	61	57	118
	B	Two	11	18	29
	C	Three	3	8	11
	D	Four	2	1	3
	E	Five	0	0	0
	F	More than 5	1	3	4
		Total	78	87	165
Q46.How many different posts and countries have you had through promotion(s)/transfer(s) after you started working in the UN Common System?					
	A	No. of posts	3.50	3.13	3.31
	B	No. of countries	2.47	2.32	2.39
Q47.How many years have you been employed at the present agency?					
	A	Less than 2 years	5	6	11
	B	2 to less than 5 years	18	22	40
	C	5 to less than 10 years	19	30	49
	D	10 to less than 15 years	19	13	32
	E	Longer than 15 years	18	16	34
		Total	79	87	166
Q48.How many years have you been employed within the UN Common System?					
	A	Less than 2 years	3	1	4
	B	2 to 5 years	17	18	35
	C	6 to 9 years	18	30	48
	D	10 to 15 years	16	18	34
	E	Longer than 15 years	25	19	44
		Total	79	86	165
Q49.What is your field of specialization? (Multiple answers accepted, maximum of 2)					
	A	Politics	7	13	20
	B	Economic/Social Development	33	30	63
	C	Humanitarian Assistance	6	7	13
	D	Human Rights	2	2	4
	E	Environment	4	1	5

F	Project /Program Management	23	16	39
G	Information Technology (IT)	5	7	12
H	Administration/Personnel	4	7	11
I	Legal Affairs	4	3	7
J	Public Information	1	6	7
K	Finance	14	10	24
L	Public Health	3	8	11
M	Education	1	8	9
N	Engineering	10	2	12
O	Others (Please specify)	14	11	25
	Total	131	131	262

Q50. What is your current field of work? (Multiple choice accepted, maximum of 2)

A	Politics	3	9	12
B	Economic/Social Development	26	22	48
C	Humanitarian Assistance	12	12	24
D	Human Rights	3	2	5
E	Environment	5	2	7
F	Project /Program Management	28	22	50
G	Information Technology (IT)	4	7	11
H	Administration/Personnel	3	8	11
I	Legal Affairs	3	4	7
J	Public Information	2	3	5
K	Finance	10	10	20
L	Public Health	3	9	12
M	Education	1	6	7
N	Engineering	5	1	6
O	Others (Please specify)	11	9	20
	Total	119	126	245

Q51. Have you changed your field of specialty or type of work after you were employed in the UN Common System?

A	Yes	24	39	63
B	No	53	47	100
	Total	77	86	163

Q52. If you answered "a" in Q51, how many times have you changed your field of specialty or type of work?

	2.58	1.68	2.03

Q53. What is your gender?

A	Male	79	0	79
B	Female	0	87	87
	Total	79	87	166

Q54. If you do not mind, please tell us your age (Average age shown)

46.47	39.37	42.85

Appendix 2 Results of the First Survey Conducted on
Japanese Formal Staff members Employed in the UN Common System

Q55.If you do not mind, what is your marital status?					
A	Married		66	44	110
B	Single		9	35	44
C	Others (Please specify)		1	3	4
	Total		76	82	158
Q56.What is your highest academic level?					
A	BA or BS		11	5	16
B	MA or MS		40	58	98
C	PhD candidate		5	9	14
D	PhD holder		17	9	26
E	Others (Please specify)		2	3	5
	Total		75	84	159
Q57.What is your field of specialization in your latest academic degree?					
A	Law		6	3	9
B	Economics		12	6	18
C	Commerce		19	13	32
D	Literature		1	2	3
E	International Relations		9	20	29
F	Development Studies		5	12	17
G	Science		6	2	8
H	Engineering		7	2	9
I	Medicine		4	5	9
J	Education		1	5	6
K	Others (Please specify)		6	16	22
	Total		76	86	162

Appendix 3

Results of the Second Survey Conducted on Japanese and Non-Japanese Staff Members Employed in the UN Common System

(Survey conducted in May 2007 (n.90))

Questions	Japanese	Non-Japanese	Total
1.1 What is your gender?			
1.Male	28	18	46
2.Female	31	11	42
No Answer	2	0	2
Total	61	29	90
1.2 What is your marital status?			
1.Married	37	20	57
2.Single	19	5	24
3.Do not want to disclose	0	0	0
4.Other	4	3	7
No Answer	1	1	2
Total	61	29	90
1.3 What is your age?			
Average	44	41	43
1.4 Please select the code number of your country of 1st nationality from the Country Code Sheet.			
Belgium	0	3	3
Canada	0	1	1
Denmark	0	3	3
Egypt	0	1	1
France	0	7	7
Germany	0	2	2
India	0	1	1
Iran, Islamic Republic of	0	1	1
Italy	0	3	3
Japan	61	0	61
Luxembourg	0	1	1
Netherlands	0	1	1
Norway	0	1	1

Sweden	0	1	1
United States of America	0	2	2
Incomplete Answer	0	1	1
Total	61	29	90
1.5 In which country are you currently stationed?			
Afghanistan	2	0	2
Austria	1	1	2
Azerbaijan	0	2	2
Bosnia and Herzegovina	2	0	2
Cambodia	2	0	2
Canada	1	1	2
China	1	0	1
Cyprus	1	0	1
Denmark	0	3	3
Djibouti	0	1	1
Egypt	1	0	1
France	3	0	3
Honduras	0	1	1
Iran, Islamic Republic of	1	0	1
Italy	8	0	8
Japan	1	0	1
Jordan	0	1	1
Lao People's Democratic Republic	0	2	2
Lebanon	0	1	1
Madagascar	0	1	1
Malaysia	1	0	1
Papua New Guinea	0	1	1
Philippines	2	0	2
Poland	1	0	1
Somalia	0	1	1
Swaziland	1	0	1
Switzerland	10	4	14
Tajikistan	1	0	1
Thailand	4	0	4
United States of America	17	3	20
Yemen	0	3	3
Incomplete Answer	0	3	3
Total	61	29	90
1.6 How many UN Agencies have you worked for?			
Average	1.7	2.0	1.8
1.7 How many countries have you been posted to since you entered the UN Common System?			
Average	2.1	3.3	2.5

Appendix 3 Results of the Second Survey Conducted on Japanese and Non-Japanese Staff Members Employed in the UN Common System

1.8 How many years have you worked in the UN Common System?			
Average	12	11	12
1.9 What is your highest academic level?			
1. BA or BS	7	1	8
2. MA or MS	43	20	63
3. PhD candidate	2	3	5
4. PhD holder	4	4	8
5. Other	2	0	2
No Answer	3	1	4
Total	61	29	90
1.10 What is your field of specialization in your latest academic degree?			
1. Law	6	1	7
2. Economics	4	7	11
3. Commerce/Management	1	0	1
4. Business Administration	4	4	8
5. Public Administration	5	0	5
6. Literature	1	0	1
7. International Relations	14	5	19
8. Development Studies	4	3	7
9. Science:	6	2	8
10. Engineering	3	0	3
11. Medicine/Public Health	4	3	7
12. Education	2	0	2
13. Other	2	1	3
No Answer	5	3	8
Total	61	29	90
1.11 By which organization are you currently employed?			
FAO	6	0	6
IAEA	2	0	2
IFAD	1	0	1
ILO	7	2	9
ITU	1	0	1
Other	0	2	2
UN	19	1	20
UNAIDS	0	1	1
UNDP	2	15	17
UNESCO	5	0	5
UNFPA	1	2	3
UNHCR	5	0	5
UNICEF	4	0	4
UNIDO	1	2	3
WFP	3	0	3
WHO	3	2	5
WIPO	1	0	1

Incomplete answer	0	2	2
Total	61	29	90
1.12 What is your status?			
1.Regular post staff, including project staff	58	23	81
2.Regular post staff seconded to the UN system, maintaining the status in another organization	1	1	2
3.Others (Staff whose contract is less than one year), etc.	1	1	2
No Answer	0	3	3
Incomplete answer	1	0	1
Total	61	29	90
1.13 What is your current grade (staff grade) ?			
1.ADG and above	1	0	1
2.D-2	1	2	3
3.D-1	6	5	11
4.P/L-5	12	7	19
5.P/L-4	16	5	21
6.P/L-3	18	4	22
7.P/L-2	6	2	8
8.P/L-1	0	0	0
9.Other	0	1	1
Incomplete	1	3	4
Total	61	29	90
1.13 The average annual gross base salary calculated from grade and step (US$):			
Gross average	100,931	106,898	102,686
1.14 How many professional staff members are you overseeing at work?			
Average	7	6	7
1.14 How many General Service staff members are you overseeing at work?			
Average	8	10	8
1.15 What type of contract are you on?			
1.Continuing/Indefinite	33	8	41
2.FT (Fixed Term)	28	19	47
3.Other, including long term consultancy	0	1	1
No Answer	0	1	1
Total	61	29	90
1.16 What is your current field of work?			
1.Political Affairs	4	3	7
2.Economic/Social Development	10	11	21
3.Humanitarian Assistance	5	0	5
4.Human Rights	1	0	1

Appendix 3 Results of the Second Survey Conducted on
Japanese and Non-Japanese Staff Members Employed in the UN Common System

5. Environment	1	0	1
6. Project/Program Management	6	6	12
7. Information Technology (IT)/Statistics	3	1	4
8. Administration/Personnel	7	0	7
9. Legal Affairs	3	1	4
10. Public Information	3	1	4
11. Finance	3	0	3
12. Medicine/Public Health	4	3	7
13. Education	2	0	2
16. Other	6	0	6
No Answer	3	2	5
Incomplete answer	0	1	1
Total	61	29	90

2.1 In your career, have you ever left the UN Common System and later returned?

1. Yes, I have. This is not my first job with the UN system.	12	7	19
2. No, I have not. This is my first job in the UN system.	48	22	70
No Answer	1	0	1
Total	61	29	90

2.2 Before you most recently joined the UN Common System, in which organization(s) had you worked?

1. Academic or research institution/ institutions	12	5	17
2. Government/Government related organization	14	13	27
3. NGOs/ Non Profit Organizations	7	4	11
4. UN/UN related organization	4	0	4
5. Private company/companies	19	3	22
6. Self employed such as consultant	0	1	1
7. Other	2	0	2
No Answer	3	2	5
Incomplete answer	0	1	1
Total	61	29	90

2.3 How long did you work in total before you most recently joined the UN Common System?

Average (years)	6.0	4.1	5.4

2.4 How many different full-time, professional jobs did you have before you entered the UN Common System?

Average	1.6	1.7	1.6

2.5 To what degree were you satisfied with your work/job prior to work for the UN Common System?			
1. Very satisfied	10	11	21
2. Somewhat satisfied	30	12	42
3. Average	9	3	12
4. Somewhat unsatisfied	6	2	8
5. Very unsatisfied	3	0	3
No Answer	3	1	4
Total	61	29	90
2.6 How old were you when you most recently became a formal staff member funded by the UN Common System?			
Average	32	31	32
2.7 How did you get a position within the UN Common System?			
1. Applying for a vacant post	11	8	19
2. Through AE/JPO/APO scheme	23	18	41
3. Through UN Competitive Exam	13	1	14
4. Seconded to the UN system, maintaining the status in another organization	4	0	4
5. Recruitment Mission	4	0	4
6. Young Professional Program	2	0	2
7. Through network/personal connections	2	1	3
8. Other	1	1	2
No Answer	1	0	1
Total	61	29	90
2.8 What was your motivation for applying for a UN Common System post?			
1. To contribute to world peace	27	8	35
2. To help people of developing countries/refugees	45	25	70
3. To utilize your specialty/specialties	43	19	62
4. To live in country/-ies outside your home country	11	15	26
5. To work with people of different backgrounds in culture, religion, etc	27	11	38
6. It is difficult to find an appropriate job in your home country.	1	3	4
7. To represent your country in an international context	3	1	4
8. To receive better salary/entitlements compared to those in your home country	1	2	3
9. Equal opportunities/pay among males and females	12	1	13
10. Other	1	0	1

Appendix 3 Results of the Second Survey Conducted on
Japanese and Non-Japanese Staff Members Employed in the UN Common System

2.9 Did you do any of the following to get a job in the UN Common System?			
1. Studied abroad	6	5	11
2. Mastered English or UN working language(s)	2	1	3
3. Took a graduate or post-graduate degree	15	0	15
4. Had the relevant work experience	5	8	13
5. Took part in an internship program	3	3	6
6. Did not do any particular preparations	14	7	21
7. Other	6	0	6
No Answer	2	1	3
Incomplete answers	8	4	12
Total	61	29	90
3.1 To what degree/extent can you utilize your professional skill by working in the UN system?			
1. Very high	22	9	31
2. Somewhat high	24	11	35
3. Average	10	6	16
4. Somewhat low	2	3	5
5. Very low	2	0	2
No Answer	1	0	1
Total	61	29	90
3.2 To what degree can you develop / have you developed additional professional skills by working in the UN Common System?			
1. Very high	17	12	29
2. Somewhat high	27	7	34
3. Average	11	7	18
4. Somewhat low	5	1	6
5. Very low	1	2	3
Total	61	29	90
3.3 Have you done any of the following for your career development after you entered the UN Common System?			
1. Studied at a graduate school and got additional degree(s)	4	2	6
2. Took relevant courses at a graduate school or technical school	8	3	11
3. Studied additional language and got a certificate	13	4	17
4. Taken in-service or external training in your field of specialization	18	8	26
5. Other	5	1	6
No Answer	9	7	16
Incomplete answer	4	4	8
Total	61	29	90

3.5 What is your degree of satisfaction in regard to your working hours in the UN Common System?			
1. Very satisfied	24	6	30
2. Somewhat satisfied	18	11	29
3. Average	12	8	20
4. Somewhat unsatisfied	2	3	5
5. Very unsatisfied	4	1	5
No Answer	1	0	1
Total	61	29	90
3.6 Are you satisfied with the salary in the UN Common System?			
1. Very satisfied	16	13	29
2. Somewhat satisfied	24	11	35
3. Average	16	2	18
4. Somewhat unsatisfied	4	3	7
5. Very unsatisfied	1	0	1
Total	61	29	90
3.7 Are you satisfied with the fringe benefits in the UN Common System?			
1. Very satisfied	20	7	27
2. Somewhat satisfied	26	15	41
3. Average	9	5	14
4. Somewhat unsatisfied	5	2	7
5. Very unsatisfied	1	0	1
Total	61	29	90
3.8 What is your degree of satisfaction in regard to life at your current duty station?			
1. Very satisfied	20	10	30
2. Somewhat satisfied	23	12	35
3. Average	14	4	18
4. Somewhat unsatisfied	3	2	5
5. Very unsatisfied	1	0	1
No Answer	0	1	1
Total	61	29	90
3.9 What is your overall satisfaction in regard to your work and life at your current duty station?			
1. Very satisfied	22	12	34
2. Somewhat satisfied	29	13	42
3. Average	7	3	10
4. Somewhat unsatisfied	2	1	3
5. Very unsatisfied	1	0	1
Total	61	29	90

Appendix 3   Results of the Second Survey Conducted on Japanese and Non-Japanese Staff Members Employed in the UN Common System

3.10 Among the following, which elements do you think are the most important for working in the UN Common System?			
1. Adaptability/Flexibility	31	18	49
2. Specialty/Specialties	29	6	35
3. Education	2	2	4
4. Negotiation skills	8	1	9
5. Interpersonal skills	38	17	55
6. Language skills	25	4	29
7. Positive commitment to the organization	18	10	28
8. Leadership	4	9	13
9. Ability to work as a member of a team	14	8	22
10. Work experience in the relevant field of the UN activities	9	4	13
11. Experience of having lived abroad	2	2	4
12. Coordination skill with local staff at duty station	0	4	4
13. Knowledge of the programs implemented by the UN	1	1	2
14. Other	2	0	2
3.11 Which factor do you think is the most difficult to adjust yourself to when you are assigned to a new duty station?			
1. Substance of work	8	2	10
2. Relationship with local staff	1	2	3
3. Relationship with boss/ supervisor(s)	6	5	11
4. Relationship with colleagues	9	0	9
5. General matters, not directly relating to work such as security, access to reliable medical facilities, food, etc.	22	9	31
6. Local language	1	3	4
7. Cultural difference	4	5	9
8. Other	5	1	6
No Answer	4	1	5
Incomplete answer	1	1	2
Total	61	29	90
3.12 Which of the following is your most pressing job-related concern at present?			
1. Renewal of contract	4	8	12
2. Promotion	15	8	23
3. Getting a job outside the UN Common System	3	1	4
4. I do not have any pressing concerns	25	7	32
5. Other	11	3	14
No Answer	3	2	5
Total	61	29	90

3.13 Which of the following is your most pressing concern in your non-professional life?			
1.Education of children	11	8	19
2.Care of parents, aging parents	19	0	19
3.The country to live after retirement	2	0	2
4.Activities after retirement	3	0	3
5.Separation from close family members who live in a different country	5	10	15
6.Current living condition	3	3	6
7.Personal health	1	0	1
8.I do not have any pressing concerns	12	5	17
9.Other	3	3	6
No Answer	2	0	2
Total	61	29	90
3.14 Do you wish to work for the UN Common System until you reach the mandatory retirement age?			
1.Yes, of course I do.	17	13	30
2.Yes, to some extent.	23	8	31
3.I do not know.	12	3	15
4.I doubt it.	3	3	6
5.I definitely do not think so.	5	2	7
No Answer	1	0	1
Total	61	29	90
3.15 Have you ever seriously thought of resigning and of finding a job outside the UN Common System?			
1.Yes, of course I have.	22	11	33
2.Yes, but not seriously.	21	10	31
3.I do not know	2	0	2
4.I doubt it.	3	3	6
5.No, I have definitely not.	13	5	18
Total	61	29	90

Recommended Links

1. This is a link to the official UN website.
   - United Nations (www.un.org)

2. This PDF file provides a useful guide to writing styles and strategies in the UN Common System. It contains advice about formal writing styles, use of language and UN terminology and the formal rules to following when drafting UN-related official documents.
   - A Guide to Writing for the United Nations (http://www.un.org/depts/OHRM/sds/lcp/English/docs/a_guide_to_writing_for_the_united_nations.pdf)

3. These are official links to information about official Human Resource Management procedures in the UN Common System. They provide advice about professional development and career opportunities.
   - UN HRM Website (https://jobs.un.org/elearn/production/home.html)
   - Human Resources Handbook (http://www.un.org/hr_handbook/English/)
   - UN Staff Development Website (http://www.unejn.org/documents/CareerDevelopment/CareerDevelopmentWebsites.htm)

4. This link is the official website of the General Assembly
   - General Assembly (http://www.un.org/ga/)

5. This links is the official website of the UN Forum.
   - UN Forum (www.unforum.org)

6. This link provides a comprehensive guide to UN Country Teams.
   - UN Country Teams (http://www.undg.org/index.cfm?P=217)

7. This is the official homepage of the Model UN, an organization for young people aspiring to careers in the UN Common System. The organization has

a worldwide network of students who meet and model UN conventions and procedures
- Model UN (http://www.un.org/cyberschoolbus/modelun/index.asp)

8. This is a link to the official journal of the UN, the UN Chronicle. It provides up to date information on current projects and work of the UN.
   - UN Chronicle (http://www.un.org/Pubs/chronicle/)

9. This is a link to the official publications of the UN. Here you can find reports, white papers and articles about UN operations.
   - UN Publications (https://unp.un.org/)

10. This is a link to the official website locator for UN system organizations.
    - Official website locator for United Nations system organizations (http://www.unsystem.org/)

11. This website provides the most up-to-date list of current UN officials.
    - Directory of United Nations system senior officials (http://doso.unsystem.org/)

12. This website provides up-to-date data on all aspects of the UN.
    - Chief Executives Board (CEB) for Coordination (http://ceb.unsystem.org/)

13. This website is the official website of the UN Dag Hammarskjold Library.
    - UN Dag Hammarskjold Library (http://unbisnet.un.org)

14. Further details regarding the surveys in this book can be found in English and Japanese on the author's homepage (http://www.ba.tyg.jp//~yokoyama/)

Postscript

This book is based on the *Career Design* of International Civil Servants, which was written in Japanese and published by *Hakuto Publishers*, Japan in 2011. This English version has been redesigned and updated with digital content to provide a more comprehensive guide to working as an international civil servant.

Translations provided by:
Chapter 1: Pranvera Zhaka & Kazuko Yokoyama
Chapter 2: Kazuko Yokoyama
Chapter 3: Motoko Tsuchiya & Kazuko Yokoyama
Chapter 4: Pranvera Zhaka & Kazuko Yokoyama
Chapter 5: Motoko Tsuchiya & Kazuko Yokoyama
Chapter 6: Motoko Tsuchiya & Kazuko Yokoyama
Chapter 7: Kazuko Yokoyama
Appendix 1: (including all interview records): Motoko Tsuchiya (translations were also edited and verified by the collaborators themselves)
Appendix 2: Kazuko Yokoyama
Appendix 3: Kazuko Yokoyama

Translator Bios
Motoko Tsuchiya
Former Professor, Faculty of Business Administration, Toyo Gakuen University, Tokyo, Japan.

Pranvera Zhaka PhD
Currently working for Nikon in the Global HRM Department.
PhD in Economics, Waseda University, Tokyo, Japan.
Former Research Associate, the School of International Liberal Studies, Waseda University, Tokyo, Japan.

Editor
Sarah Louisa Birchley EdD
Associate Professor, Faculty of Business Administration, Toyo Gakuen University, Tokyo, Japan.
Adjunct Lecturer, University of Tokyo, Tokyo, Japan.
Sarah Louisa has a doctorate in Education Management from the University of Bath, UK. Sarah's research focuses on Sensemaking, trust in the workplace and HE management.

Bibliography

Asakura, M. (1999). *Kintoho no shin sekei*. [New world of equality law]. Yuuhikaku sennsho.

Arimura, S. (2007). *Daibershiti. Management no kenkyu*. [Study of diversity management]. Bunnshinndou.

Bartlet, C. and Goshal, D. (1998) (Translated by K. Enatsu). *Shoshikiri ron to takokuseki kigyou*. [Organizational theory and multi-national corporations]. Bunshin-do.

Beilin, L. (2001). translated by Miyoshi, Katsuyo. career innovation - *shigoto seikatsu no toinaoshi ga tsukuru kosei soncho no shoshiki bunka*. [Career innovation–Organizational culture to respect individuality is created as a result of requestioning the ways of working]. Hakuto-shobo.

Beltran, M. (1991). (Trans. by Y. Yokota) *Kokurensei sei no scenario* [Refaire L'ONU! Un programme pour la paix]. Kokusai Shoin.

Black, J.S., Gregerson, H.B., Mendenhall, M.E. and Stroh, L.K.translated by Shiraki, M. (2001). kaigai hakken to global business - *i bunka management senriyaku* [Working overseas and global business - Strategy of inter-cultural management]. Hakutou Shobo.

Drucker, P.F. (1991). (Trans. A. Ueda & M.Tashiro.) *Hi eiri soshiki no keiei*. [Management of non-profit organizations]. Diamond-sha.

Enomoto, S. (2004). *kaigai kogaisha kenkyu josetsu*. [Introduction to study affiliated companies overseas]. Ochanomizu Shobou,

Freedman, T. (2001). (Trans. by I. Fushimi). *flat to ka suru seikai*. [The World is Flat]. Nihon Keizai Newspaper Publisher, Inc.

Gabman, E.L., translated by Hata, Y. (1999). *jinzai sen riyaku.* [Manpower strategy]. Toyo Keizai Shiposha.

Hayashi, Y. (1994). *Ebunka interface.* [Cross-cultural interface management]. Nihon Keizai Newspaper Publisher, Inc.

Hirasawa, K., Moriya, T., Mishima, R. Nakamura, T., Yamamoto, T., Fujihara, T., Akari, M., Shinohara, K., Nakagawa, K., Morita, S., Makino, Y. (2001), *kokusai jinji kanri no kompon mondai* [Fundamental issues in international personnel management]. Yachiyo Shuppan.

Hirano. M. (2013). Human resource departments of Japanese corporations: Have their roles changed? *Japan Labor Review.* Vol. 10. No.1.

Hirano. M. (2011). Diversification of employment categories in Japanese firms and its functionality: A study based on the human resource portfolio system. In Bebenroth, R. & Kanai, T. (eds.) *Challenges of Human Resource Management in Japan.* pp.188-209. Routledge.

Hirano. M. (2006). *Nihon gata jinji kanri – shinkagata no hasei purposesu to kinosei* [Japanese-type personnel management system]. Chuo Keizai sha.

Iguchi Y. (1997). *Kokusaitekina hito no ido to rodo shijyo.* [International human movement and labor market]. Japan Institute for Labour Policy and Training.

Ishida, H. (1985). *Nihon kigyo no kokusai jinji kanri.* [International personnel management Japanese enterprises]. Japan Institute for Labour Policy and Training.

Inoki, T. (1995). *nihon no hoyo system to rodo shijyo.* [Japanese employment system and labour market], Nihon Keizai Newspaper Publisher, Inc.

Japan ILO Association. (2003). *Obe no komuinn seido to nihon no komin seido.* [Public servant system in America and Europe vs. Public Servant System in Japan]. Japan

ILO Association.

Japan ILO Association. (2005). *Obe no shakai rodo jijyou.* [Socio-Labour situations in America and Europe]. Japan ILO Association.

Japan Association for the United Nations Studies. (2002). *Global actor to shite no kokuren jomu koku - kokuren kenkyu dai san go.* [UN Secretariat as a global actor]. UN Studies, Vol. 3. Koukusai Shoinn.

Japan Institute for Labour Policy and Training. (2001). *dai yon kai kaigai hoken gimusha no shoku gyou no to seikatsu ni kan suru chosa kekka.* [The 4th survey results on occupation and life of Japanese expatriates seconded to work overseas]. The Japan Institute for Labour Policy and Training.

Japan Institute for Labour Policy and Training. (2001). *Nihon kigyou no kaigai hakken sha shokugyou to seikatsu no jitai.* [Japanese expatriates dispatched by Japanese companies: Their actuals situations of work and life]. The Japan Institute for Labour Policy and Training.

Jones, B. (1984). *Post, service shakai.* [Post-Service society]. Jiji Tsushin-sha.

Kanai, A. (2000). *Career, stress ni kan suru kenkyu.* [Study on career stress]. Kazamashobo, Co., Ltd.

Kram, K.E. (2003). (Translated by N. Watanabe & T. Ito.) *Mentoring* [Mentoring at Work - Developmental relationships in organizational life]. Hakuto-shobo.

Kurokawa, K. & Ishikura Y. (2006). *Seikai kyu career no tsukurikata.* [How to develop a world-class career]. Toyokeizai-shimpo-sha.

Koike, K. (1996). *shokuba no rodo kumiai to sanka.* [Labor Unions within the workplace and participation]. Tokyo Keizai Shinpo-sha.

Koike, K. (1996). Shigoto no keizai gaku [Economics of work]. Toyokeizai-shimpo-sha.

Koike, K. (2006). *Professional no jinzai kaihatsu* [Professional human resources development]. Nakanishiya Publishing Co. Ltd.

Koike, K. (2008). *Kaigi nihon kigyo no jinzai keisei* [Human resources formation of Japanese companies overseas.] Tokyo Keizai Shinpo-sha.

Koike, K. & Inoki, T. (1987). *Jinzai keisei no kokusai hikaku - to nan asia to nihon* [International comparison of Human Resources formation-Southeast Asia and Japan]. Tokyo Keizai Shimpo-sha.

Marsden, D (2007). (Trans. M. Miyamoto, M. & Kubo , K). *Koyo system no riron shakai teki no taiyosei hikaku seido bunseki* [Theory of employment system - Comparative institutional analysis of social diversities]. NTT Press.

Maslow, A.H. (1987). (Translated by Oguchi, T.). *Ningansei no shin ri gaku kaitei shinpan*. [Psychology of Humanity]. Revised Edition. Sangyou Noritsu University Press.

Mercer Japan, Ltd. (2008). *Koikasu daiversity senriyaku* [Diversity strategy to make the most of individuals]. First Press.

Ministry of Foreign Affairs International Recruitment Centre (2005). *Kokusai koumin enomichi – kiso hen*. [The road to an international civil servant], Basic Edition Retrieved from: http://www.nifa-irc.go.jp/shiryo/kisohen090205pdf. Retrieved in October 2009.

Ministry of Health, Labour & Welfare, Equal Employment, Children and Families Bureau (2004). *Koso ro do sho heisei 15 nen do ban josei rodo hakusho* [The 2003 white paper of women's labour]. Japan Institute of Workers Evolution.

Ministry of Health, Labour & Welfare, Equal Employment, Children and Families Bureau. (2009). *Josei rodo no bunseki 2008 nen* [Analysis of Women's Labour 2008].

Japan Institute of Workers Evolution.

Nagai, H. (2002). *Nihon jin kaigai hakensha no ibunka tekiyo no sokushin youinn - gojyu san kakoku. chiki o taishou toshita teki o dankai.* [Factors that promote Japanese expatriates to adapt different cultures Japanese. Levels of adaptation in 53 countries and areas]. Japan Journal of Human Resource Management, Vol. 4 No.2.

Nakatani, I. (1987). *Borderless economy.* [Borderless Economy]. Nihon Keizai Newspapers Publishers.

Ohta, H. (1999). *Shigoto jin to soshiki.* [Working man and organization]. Yuhikaku Publishing Co. Ltd.

Otoshi, T. (2002). *Kigyono kokusaika (Yasahi keizaigaku keiei nyumon.)* [Internationalization of enterprises, easy economics, business management]. Nippon Keizai Shinbun.

Rickert, R. (1964). (translated by J.P. Misumi). *Keiei no kodo kagaku* [Behavioral science in management.] Diamond-sha.

Sano, Y. and Kawakita, T. (1993). *White collar no career kanri* [Career management of white collar workers]. Chuo Keizai-sha.

Sato, H. (2011). *Work-life balance to hatarakikata kaikaku* [Work Life Balance: Reforming the way of working to achieve work-life balance]. Keiso shobo.

Shein, E.H translated by Nimura, T. & Miyoshi, K. (1991). *Career dynamics* [Career dynamics]. Hakuto Shobo.

Shiraki, M. (1995). *Nihon kigyou no kokusai jinteki shigen kanri* [International human resource management of Japanese companies]. Japan Institute for Labor Policy and Training.

Shiraki, M. (2006). *Kokusai jinteki shigen kanri no hikaku bunseki* [Analytical comparison of international human resource management]. Yuhikaku.

Sasajima, Y. (2002). *Gendai no rodo mondai dai san pan.* [Current labour issues] third edition, Chuo Keizai-sha.

Sato, H. (2004). *Kawaru hatarakikata to career design* [Changing ways of working and career design]. Keisho Shobo.

Suda, T. (2004). *Nihon gata chingin seido no yukue.* [Future of Japanese-type wage system]. Keio University Press.

Takeda, K. (1993). *Shogai career hatatsu.* [Lifetime career development]. Nippon Roudou Kikou.

Umezawa, T. (2001). *Shokugyo to career- jinsei no jutaka to ha.* [Occupation and Career - What qualifies as richness in life?]. Gakubunsha.

Wakisaka, A. (2008). *Keiei senriyaku to shite no work-life balance* [Work-life Balance as a Management Strategy]. Dai ichi houki.

Watanabe, T. (2001). *Kokusai kaihatsu gaku nyumon* [Introduction to the international development studies]. Kobundo Press.

Watanabe, M. (2003). *Career no shinrigaku* [Psychology in career development.] Nakanishiya Press.

Yamamoto, C. (2006). *Global jinzai management ron* [Global human resources management theory]. Toyo Keizai Shimpo-sha.

Yashiro, A. (2013). Selection and promotion of managers in Japanese companies: Present and future perspectives. *Japan Labor Review*, Vol. 10 No.1.

Yashiro, A. (2011). *Kanrishoku e no senbatsu. Ikusei kara mita nihonteki koyo seido.* [Japanese employment system: From the view of selection and staff development to managerial positions]. *The Japanese Journal of Labor Studies.* Vol. 606.

Yashiro, N. (1997). *Nihon teki koyo kan ko no keizaigaku.* [Employment practices in Japan]. Nihon Keizai Newspaper Publisher, Inc.

Yoshimori, K. (1996). *Nihon no keiei. obe no kei ei - hikaku kei ei eno shotai* [Business management in Japan and management in the USA and European countries - Invitation for to comparative management]. The society of the promotion of the Open University of Japan Press.

Yokoto, Y. (2001). *Shinpan kokusai kikoron.* [Theory of international institution]. New Edition. Kokusai Shoin.

Yokoyama, K. (1994). *Kokusai kikan no jinji seido in keizai gaku kenkyu.* [Personnel system of international organizations]. Keizaigaku Kenkyu, Hokkaido University, Vol.44 No. 3.

Yokoyama K. (1998). *Kokusai kikan okeru josei ko yo sokushin seisaku. nihon romu gakkai 28 kai zenkoku taikai kenkyu hokoku ronshu.* [Affirmative action programs in international organizations]. Japan Society of Human Resource Management: Collection of Research Papers of 28th National Convention of Japan Society of Human Resources Management.

Yokoyama, K. (2009). *Kokusai komu in naru ni ha.* [How to become an international civil servant]. Pelican Press.

Yokoyama, K. & Nakamura, J. (2005). *Kokusai teki career kakuju no tame no kento kadai - nihon jin kokuren kikan shoku inn anketto chosa kara.* [The present situations and issues of Japanese UN formal staff members -A career survey from the diversity management point of view]. Bulletin of Toyo Gakuen University, No.13.

Yokoyama, K. & Nakamura, J. (2005). *Nihon romu gakkai dai 35 kai zenkoku taikei kenkyuhoukoku ronshu.* [Career analysis of Japanese international civil servants based on a career survey using email]. Society of Human Resource Management:

Collection of Research Papers of the 35h National Convention of Japan Society of Human Resources Management.

Yokoyama. K. & Nakamura, J. (2006). *Nihonjin kokuren shoukin no genjyou to kadai - daiversity . management no shiten kara no career chosa.* [Career analysis of Japanese formal staff members employed in the UN Common System results from the survey using email]. Japan Society of Human Resource Management: Collection of Research Papers of the 36h National Convention of Japan Society of Human Resources Management.

Yorimitsu, M. (2003). *Kokusaika suru nihon no rodo shijyo.* [Internationalizing the Japanese labour market]. Toyo Keizai Shimpo-sha.

Yoshihara, H. (1992). *Nihon kigyo no kokusai keiei.* [International management of Japanese companies]. Doubunkan Press.

Further details regarding the surveys in this book can be found in English and Japanese on the author's homepage: http://www.ba.tyg.jp//~yokoyama/

Index

ABD, *43, 45, 90, 101*
ability to negotiate, *53*
academic degree, *259, 263*
academic qualifications, *45, 90*
adaptability/flexibility, *53*
administration, *118*
Administration and HR Group, *118, 120*
AE, x, *15*
affirmative action, *28, 37, 252*
age, *50, 69, 89, 143, 266*
age of recruitment, *69*
allowances, *19*
annual paid leave, *22, 37, 57*
appointment of staff members, *12*
assignment of staff members, *32*
Assistance to Developing Countries Group, *118, 121, 123, 131*
Associate Experts, *15*
Attitude for work, *144*
average age, *43, 44, 65, 88, 110*
average grade, *43, 63, 88, 110*

Bartlett and Ghoshal, *3*
basic salary, *19*
Black, *64*
bucho, *27*
business administration, *103*

care of parents, *63*
career anchor, *6, 125, 127, 136, 144*
Career Design of International Civil Servants, ii
career development, *137, 142, 267*
career development in the UN Common System, *7*

career development programs, *103*
Career Dynamics, *125*
career paths, *100*
career satisfaction, *78*
career-satisfied, *74, 75, 76, 80, 81, 83, 108, 116, 133, 134, 137*
career-satisfied group, *130*
Case A, *145*
Case B, *149*
Case C, *153*
Case D, *157*
Case E, *160*
Case F, *164*
Case G, *168*
Case H, *172*
Case I, *177*
Case J, *181*
Case K, *185*
Case L, *190*
Case M, *195*
Case N, *200*
Case O, *205*
Case P, *209*
Case Q, *213*
Case R, *218*
Case S, *222*
Case U, *227*
Case V, *232*
Case W, *237*
Case X, *242*
CEB, x, *25, 272*
change of specialized field, *122, 124*
change specialized field, *127*
Chief Executive Board for Coordination, *25, 272*

Index

commerce, *90*
comparative analysis, *85*
concerns, *62, 97, 255, 269, 270*
Convention on the Elimination of All Forms of Discrimination against Women, 24
correlations, *75*
cost-of-living of a duty station, *20*
country of duty station, *89*
CPA, *117*
cumulative variance, *74*

D, *x*
data collection, *41, 85, 87*
day-care centers, *25*
descriptive statistics, *72*
developed countries, *16, 89, 100, 103*
developing countries, *16, 103*
development studies, *64, 130*
difficulties at duty stations, *60, 97*
discretion of staff members, *36*
dissatisfaction, *78*
dissatisfied, 74, 75, 76, 80, 108, 133, 134
dissatisfied group, *130*
diversity, *11, 135*
diversity management, *3, 23*
duty stations, *17, 89, 268*

early-career entry methods, *31, 38, 53, 63, 111, 119, 130*
economic/social development, *92*
economics, *90, 101, 103*
education, *44*
education grants, *19, 57, 83*
education of children, *63, 98*
educational background, *45*
employment security, *36, 79, 83*
entry method, *52*
entry routes, *93*
Equal Employment Opportunity Law, 3, 27, 132, 140

equal opportunities, *48*
equal work for both sexes, *55*
equitably represented, 29, 30
Ethnocentric, 4
evaluation of salary, *69*

factor analysis, *73, 76, 136*
field of specialization, *92*
field of work, *258, 264*
field service category, *15, 20*
Finance Specialist group, *118, 119, 121, 123*
financial contributions, *29*
finding a job in Japan, *62*
First Survey, *41, 69, 87*
flextime, *22*
foreign-affiliated companies, *113, 132*
formal Japanese staff members, *107*
formal staff members, *14, 42, 93*
former UN competitive exam, *52*
founding nations, *16*
fringe benefits, *21, 57, 69, 73, 76, 77, 84, 96, 250, 268*

G/S, *x*
gender, *44, 45, 76, 88, 258*
General Assembly, *25, 271*
generalist fields, *46*
Geocentric, 4
Geographic Distribution, 16, 30
global candidates, *140*
global management, *11*
globalization, *1, 142*
government, *93, 100*
grade, *15, 44, 69, 91, 256, 264*
grade distribution, *15*
grievance committee, *23*

health insurance, *22*
Hertzberg, *82*

Hitachi, *1*
hitogara, *32*
home leave, *23*
housing allowance, *19*
HR, *92*
HR department, *29*
HR practices in Japan, *142*
HRM practices in the UN Common System, *11*
humanitarian assistance, *92*
humanitarian assistance organizations, *18, 130*
hygiene factor, *82*

IBM, *3*
ICSC, *x, 19*
IFAD, 232
ILO, *13, 209, 222*
intercultural communication skills, *104*
International Civil Servants, *14*
International Civil Service Commission, *19*
international development, *131*
International Management, *3*
International Organizations, *2, 11*
international relations, *64, 90, 101, 130*
interview records, *137*
interview, *139*
Ishida, 4

Japan Business Federation, 7
Japanese, *102, 106*
Japanese formal staff members, *69, 85, 88, 131*
Japanese International Civil Servants, *59*
Japanese staff members, *136*
jinji-bu, *29*
job classification, *12*
job mobility, *104*
job satisfaction, *54, 73, 76, 77, 79, 83,* *105, 118, 130, 131, 133, 248*
job security, *130, 135*
JPO, *x, 14, 35, 42*
JPO Scheme, *31, 52, 93, 111, 138*
Junior Professional Officer, *14*

kakaricho, *27*
Koike, 4

L, *x*
L level staff, *15*
language ability, *53*
language course, *95*
language skills, *104*
languages, *18*
leadership, *53, 142*
League of Nations, *16*
legal affairs, *90*
level of education, *44*
Levine's test, *69*
Life-role Theory, 6
living conditions, *17*

management, *92*
managerial staff members, *15*
mandatory retirement age, *61, 73, 77, 79, 99, 270*
maternity leave, *22, 25, 66*
matters not directly related to work, *64*
maximum likelihood estimation, *73*
MBA, *x, 46, 90, 117*
medicine, *90*
mentor, *114, 115, 127, 144*
mentoring, *142*
mid-career employment market, *139*
mid-career entry method, *31, 32, 38, 53, 63, 73, 80, 112, 117, 119, 120, 121, 130*
Ministry of Foreign Affairs, *18*
Ministry of Health, Labour and Welfare,

27, 32, 140
Mitsui, 2
Model UN, 272
motivation, 49, 83, 94, 102, 266
motivation factor, 82
motivation-hygiene theory, 82
MPA, 46, 64, 90, 130
multiple regression analysis, 78, 130
multiplier points of post adjustment, 20

Nagai, 64
nationality, 16, 89, 261
net base salary, 19
networks, 144
NGO, 2, 51, 93, 136
Nikkei-ren, 7
Noblemaire Principle, 19
non-Japanese, 102
non-Japanese formal staff members, 131
Non-Japanese staff members, 85, 88, 140
non represented, 29, 30
NPO, 51, 93, 136

occupational field, 46, 92, 105, 118, 131, 133
occupational group, 124
ODA, x, 51, 93, 100, 101, 113, 131
Ota, 6
over represented, 29, 30
overall satisfaction, 57, 73, 76, 77, 96, 251, 268

P, x, 15
Panasonic, 1
Parsons, 5
pension, 21, 37, 57, 83
performance-based HRM practices, 132
performance-oriented HRM, 129
Perlmutter, 3, 129
PhD, 45, 90, 101, 103

political power, 59
Polycentric, 4
positive attitude, 53
post adjustment, 19, 20
preliminary survey, 41
preparation, 48, 63, 94, 140, 248
prior work experience, 51
private companies, 51, 93, 113
private enterprises, 100
Private Information Protection Law, 86
professional development, 14, 33, 95, 131, 132, 144
professional skills, 95, 267
Program Management Coordination group, 118, 120, 123
Programme Management Coordination, 131
project management, 92
Promax rotation, 74, 76
promotion, 32, 38, 63, 98

Rakuten, 2
recruitment mission, 52
recruitment policies, 28
Recruitment Policy of Specialized Organizations, 35
recruitment policy, 34, 130
Recruitment Policy of Humanitarian Assistance Organizations, 35
Recruitment Policy of the UN Secretariat, 34
Recruitment Policy of the UNDP, 35
regression analysis, 136
relationship agreements, 14
relocation, 38
renewal of contract, 63, 98
representation, 24
research institute, 93
rotation policy, 124

salary, *12, 19, 56, 64, 73, 76, 77, 88, 91, 100, 116, 144, 250, 264, 268*
salary scale, *20*
satisfaction, *110, 144, 251, 266, 268*
satisfaction at duty station, *57, 64, 69, 73, 76, 77, 133*
satisfaction at prior organization, *73, 76, 77*
Sato, *6*
Schein, *6*
Schlossberg, *6*
science, *90*
Second Survey, *85, 87, 136*
Secretariat of the United Nations, *13*
separation from close family members, *98*
SG, *x*
shigoto-jin, *6*
Shiraki, *4*
snowball sampling, *107*
specialist, *49, 83, 138, 139*
Specialist Group, *118, 119, 123*
specialization, *257, 259, 263*
specialized field of study at the last degree held, *45, 64, 90*
specialized fields of study, *65*
Specialized Organizations, *12, 13*
staff assessment, *19*
staff exemption, *19*
statistical analysis, *69*
step, *x, 20*
study abroad experience, *116*
subordinates, *92*
Subsidiary Organizations of the United Nations, *13*
substance of job, *55*
substance of work, *64*
Super, *5*

teamwork, *142*

tennkin, *33*
Theory of Characteristic Parameter, *6*
Theory of Life Stages, *6*
Three-Step Process, *5*
TN-M, *4*
training programs, *95*
trait/factor theory, *5*
transfer to other occupational fields, *127*
transfers, *36*
transnational management, *4*
treatment satisfaction, *78*
treatment-satisfied, *74, 75, 76, 80, 81, 108, 133, 134*
treatment-satisfied group, *130*
t-test, *69, 80, 136*

UN, *x*
UN Charter, *16*
UN Chronicle, *272*
UN Common System, *5, 7, 13, 86, 263, 265, 266, 267*
UN Forum, *107, 271*
UNFPA, *185, 195*
UNIDO, *227*
UN HRM Website, *271*
UN Publications, *272*
UN Secretariat, *34, 157, 160, 168, 177, 181, 190*
UN system organizations, *272*
UN website, *271*
under-represented, *29, 30*
UNDP, *x, 12, 35, 145, 153, 164, 172, 242*
UNDP JPO Service Centre, *87*
UNESCO, *13*
UNHCR, *xi, 12, 17*
UNICEF, *12, 17, 35*
UNIQLO, *1*
United Nations Common System, *12*
United Nations Joint Staff Pension

Funds, *21*
University, *93*
UNJSPF, *xi, 12, 21, 149, 150*

vacancy announcement, *29, 93*
vacant posts, *33, 34, 52*
Varimax rotation, *74*

Wakisaka, *6*
WFP, xi, *12, 17, 35, 200, 205*
WHO, *213, 218, 237*
Williamson, *6*
work, *64*
work experience, *53, 94*
work experience in the relevant field, *102*

work experiences in Japan, *8, 43, 106, 107, 113, 114, 131, 132, 143, 247*
working conditions, *12*
work environment, *55, 64, 114*
working hours, *22, 37, 55, 64, 66, 73, 76, 77, 96*
working language, *16, 18, 64, 97*
work-life balance, *37, 66, 141*
workshops, *95*
World Bank, *13, 86*
World Trade Organization, *13, 86*

years of service, *45, 88, 90, 110, 144*
YPP, *xi*
YPP exam, *31, 32, 34, 52, 93, 111, 138*
YPP programs, *32*

About the Author

Kazuko Yokoyama

Currently, Kazuko Yokoyama is a Professor in the Department of Business Administration and the Graduate School of Business Administration, Toyo Gakuen University, Tokyo, Japan specializing in HRM (Human Resource Management) and Career Development. She also an adjunct lecturer at GSID (Graduate School of International Development), Nagoya University, Nagoya, Japan, teaching International Career Development.

After graduating from the Department of Economics, Hokkaido University, Japan, she studied in the USA and obtained an MBA, from Indiana State University. She received a Ph.D. in Economics from Kyoto University, Kyoto, Japan in 2012.

She worked for the ILO and UNHCR in Geneva from 1980 to 1985. She worked for the FAO in Rome for five years from 1985 to 1990.

Upon returning to Japan in 1990, she has been teaching in the field of HRM at university. In 1993, Kazuko took three months sabbatical leave to participate in the UN peacekeeping operations as a UN Volunteer in Cambodia. In 2007, she took a five-month sabbatical to conduct this research and was based in the Graduate Center, CUNY (City University of New York), New York, USA.

Kazuko has over twenty years of consulting experience advising business people wishing to become International Civil Servants in Japan.

Her publications include: *For Those Who Wish To Become a UN Volunteer* (in Japanese, Iwanami Shoten, Publishers), *How To Become An International Civil Servant* (in Japanese, Pelican Publishing Co.), *Career Design of International Civil Servants* (in Japanese, Hakuto-Shobo Publishing Co.), *How to Become a Japan Overseas Cooperation Volunteer (in Japanese*, Pelican Publishing Co.).

http://www.ba.tyg.jp/~yokoyama/index_Eng.html

■Human Resource Management in the UN
 : A Japanese Perspective　　　　　　〈検印省略〉

■発行日──2014年3月6日　初版発行

■著　者──横山　和子
　　　　　　よこやま　かずこ

■発行者──大矢栄一郎

■発行所──株式会社　白桃書房
　　　　　　　　　　　はくとうしょぼう
　　　〒101-0021　東京都千代田区外神田5-1-15
　　　☎03-3836-4781　📠03-3836-9370　振替00100-4-20192
　　　http://www.hakutou.co.jp/

■印刷・製本──藤原印刷
　© Kazuko Yokoyama 2014　Printed in Japan　ISBN 978-4-561-25627-4 C3034

JCOPY　〈(社)出版者著作権管理機構　委託出版物〉
本書の無断複写は著作権法上での例外を除き禁じられています。複写される場合は，
そのつど事前に，(社)出版者著作権管理機構（電話03-3513-6969，FAX03-3513-6979，
e-mail : info@jcopy.or.jp）の許諾を得てください。
落丁本・乱丁本はおとりかえいたします。